מסורה

ArtScroll Mesorah Series

THE PESACH HAGGADAH

הגדת גדולי תנועת המוסר

Haggadah

WITH A COMMENTARY CULLED FROM THE CLASSIC BAALEI MUSSAR

by
Rabbi Shalom Meir Wallach

The Pesach

Published by
Mesorah Publications, ltd
in conjunction with
ArtScroll / ארטסקרול/ירושלים בע"מ
Jerusalem, ltd.
A TVUNAH PUBLICATION

FIRST EDITION
First Impression . . . March 1989
Second Impression . . . January 1992

Published and Distributed by
MESORAH PUBLICATIONS, Ltd.
Brooklyn, New York 11232
in conjunction with
TVUNAH / *Jerusalem*

Distributed in Israel by
MESORAH MAFITZIM / J. GROSSMAN
Rechov Harav Uziel 117
Jerusalem, Israel

Distributed in Australia & New Zealand by
GOLD'S BOOK & GIFT CO.
36 William Street
Balaclava 3183, Vic., Australia

Distributed in Europe by
J. LEHMANN HEBREW BOOKSELLERS
20 Cambridge Terrace
Gateshead, Tyne and Wear
England NE8 1RP

Distributed in South Africa by
KOLLEL BOOKSHOP
22 Muller Street
Yeoville 2198
Johannesburg, South Africa

THE ARTSCROLL MESORAH SERIES®

Typography by CompuScribe at ArtScroll Studios, Ltd.
4401 Second Avenue / Brooklyn, N.Y. 11232 / (718) 921-9000

Printed in the United States of America by Moriah Offset
Bound by Sefercraft Quality Bookbinders Ltd. Brooklyn, N.Y.

Publisher's Preface

The masters of *mussar* [ethical thoughts] have made a major contribution to Torah life in the last hundred and fifty years. Entirely apart from their influence on *yeshivah* education and the efforts of countless people to perfect themselves, they have provided new kinds of insight into the interpretation of the Scriptures and teachings of the Sages. It is this last facet of their activity that is the basis of this book.

One of the primary themes of their analysis has always been the Exodus and the events and lessons surrounding it. As the commentators note, the Exodus was God's public proclamation that He is all-powerful, that nature is His tool, and that exile has a purpose and a duration. Since the *Haggadah* is the sacred narrative that serves as the bond between generations in passing one these teachings, it was only natural that the *mussar* thinkers would treat it and the passages on which it is based as major sources of insight.

Consequently, when an anthology of their teachings on the *Haggadah* appeared in Hebrew, it was snatched up with alacrity, and it fulfilled every expectation. Drawn from dozens of books, it offered a wealth of teachings, perspectives, and interpretations. The English-reading public is fortunate that the anthologizer of the Hebrew edition has culled the finest of the finest for translation into the English. The result is this excellent volume, one that we are sure will be a cherished companion to the *Haggadah* and will serve as a source of inspiration all year round.

We are grateful to the anthologizer, Rabbi Shalom Meir Wallach, the translator, Yaakov Petroff, and the editor, Shlomo Fox-Ashrei. And to Shmuel Blitz, director of ArtScroll/Jerusalem, who has once again distinguished himself in shepherding this volume to completion. May the readers find in it a vindication of all the work and hopes of those who produced it.

הגדת גדולי
תנועת המוסר

בדיקת חמץ

The *chametz* search is initiated with the recitation of the following blessing:

בָּרוּךְ אַתָּה יהוה אֱלֹהֵינוּ מֶלֶךְ הָעוֹלָם, אֲשֶׁר קִדְּשָׁנוּ בְּמִצְוֹתָיו, וְצִוָּנוּ עַל בִּעוּר חָמֵץ.

Upon completion of the *chametz* search, the *chametz* is wrapped well and set aside to be burned the next morning and the following declaration is made. The declaration must be understood in order to take effect; one who does not understand the Aramaic text may recite it in English, Yiddish or any other language. Any *chametz* that will be used for that evening's supper or the next day's breakfast or for any other purpose prior to the final removal of *chametz* the next morning is not included in this declaration.

כָּל חֲמִירָא וַחֲמִיעָא דְּאִכָּא בִּרְשׁוּתִי, דְּלָא חֲמִתֵּהּ וּדְלָא בִעַרְתֵּהּ וּדְלָא יְדַעְנָא לֵהּ, לִבָּטֵל וְלֶהֱוֵי הֶפְקֵר כְּעַפְרָא דְאַרְעָא.

ביעור חמץ

The following declaration, which includes all *chametz* without exception, is to be made after the burning of leftover *chametz*. It should be recited in a language which one understands. When *Pesach* begins on *Motzaei Shabbos,* this declaration is made on *Sh*abbos morning. Any chametz remaining from the *Shabbos* morning meal, is flushed down the drain before the declaration is made.

כָּל חֲמִירָא וַחֲמִיעָא דְּאִכָּא בִּרְשׁוּתִי, דַּחֲזִתֵּהּ וּדְלָא חֲזִתֵּהּ, דַּחֲמִתֵּהּ וּדְלָא חֲמִתֵּהּ, דְּבִעַרְתֵּהּ וּדְלָא בִעַרְתֵּהּ, לִבָּטֵל וְלֶהֱוֵי הֶפְקֵר כְּעַפְרָא דְאַרְעָא.

בְּדִיקַת חָמֵץ

The search for leaven

R' Yerucham of Mir

The early commentators have noted that the Torah is exceptionally harsh on the subject of *chametz*, or leaven, in regard to both the prohibition and the punishment. Not only is it not to be eaten or used, it may not even be seen or found in a man's possession — בַּל יֵרָאֶה וּבַל יִמָּצֵא (*Shemos* 12:20) and whoever violates the prohibition is to be rooted out and destroyed (כָּרֵת).

Leaven symbolizes the evil nature (יֵצֶר הָרָע) of man (*Berachos* 17). Just as leaven causes the dough to rise willy-nilly, without reason, so too does the evil nature work its way. It does not persuade by means of wisdom, but by the force of its strength. As the Sages have said: When the evil nature holds sway, one does not pay attention to the arguments of the good nature — יֵצֶר טוֹב (*Nedarim* 32). The evil nature, when it first insinuates itself into man's

SEARCH FOR CHAMETZ

The *chametz* search is initiated with the recitation of the following blessing:

Blessed are You, HASHEM, our God, King of the universe, Who has sanctified us by His commandments, and commanded us concerning the removal of chametz.

Upon completion of the *chametz* search, the *chametz* is wrapped well and set aside to be burned the next morning and the following declaration is made. The declaration must be understood in order to take effect; one who does not understand the Aramaic text may recite it in English, Yiddish or any other language. Any *chametz* that will be used for that evening's supper or the next day's breakfast or for any other purpose prior to the final removal of chametz the next morning is not included in this declaration.

Any chametz which is in my possession which I did not see, and remove, nor know about, shall be nullified and become ownerless, like the dust of the earth.

BURNING THE CHAMETZ

The following declaration, which includes all *chametz* without exception, is to be made after the burning of leftover *chametz*. It should be recited in a language which one understands. When *Pesach* begins on *Motzaei Shabbos*, this declaration is made on *Shabbos* morning. Any chametz remaining from the *Shabbos* morning meal, is flushed down the drain before the declaration is made.

Any chametz which is in my possession which I did or did not see, which I did or did not remove, shall be nullified and become ownerless, like the dust of the earth.

---

consciousness. is as fragile as a cobweb and, in the end, it is like a tightly woven ship's canvas (*Bereishis Rabbah* 22:1). There is no taking precautions against it other than to guard the dough, so to speak, against even a smidgin of this leaven.

With this in mind, let us examine the laws of the "search for leaven" (בְּדִקַת חָמֵץ). "Do not make the search by the light of the sun but at night by candle light" (*Pesachim* 7) — at night, when darkness covers the earth; with a single candle (נֵר) which spreads its glow in a limited circle in which all of its light is concentrated. And the manner of search bears thinking about. One takes the small light from room to room, from corner to corner, inspecting every crack and cranny for any crumb of leaven. He descends into pits and cellars until all the forbidden material is cleared from his property. An amazing procedure, this *mitzvah*!

The *gemara* cites a verse with reference to the search: "The soul of man is HASHEM's light (נֵר); it searches all the chambers of his belly" (*Mishlei* 20:27). The soul is an only light in the body. This image conveys to us how thick the

עירוב תבשילין

It is forbidden to prepare on *Yom Tov* for the next day even if that day is the Sabbath. If, however, Sabbath preparations were started before *Yom Tov* began, they may be continued on *Yom Tov. Eruv tavshilin* constitutes this preparation. A *matzah and* any cooked food (such as fish, meat or an egg) are set aside on the day before *Yom Tov* to be used on the Sabbath and the blessing is recited followed by the declaration [made in a language understood by the one making the *eruv*]. If the first days *of Pesach* fall on Thursday and Friday, an *eruv tavshilin* must be made on Wednesday. [In *Eretz Yisrael,* where only one day *Yom Tov* is in effect, the *eruv* is omitted.]

בָּרוּךְ אַתָּה יהוה אֱלֹהֵינוּ מֶלֶךְ הָעוֹלָם, אֲשֶׁר קִדְּשָׁנוּ בְּמִצְוֹתָיו, וְצִוָּנוּ עַל מִצְוַת עֵרוּב.

בְּהָדֵין עֵרוּבָא יְהֵא שָׁרֵא לָנָא לַאֲפוּיֵי וּלְבַשּׁוּלֵי וּלְאַצְלוּיֵי וּלְאַטְמוּנֵי וּלְאַדְלוּקֵי שְׁרָגָא וּלְתַקָּנָא וּלְמֶעְבַּד כָּל צָרְכָּנָא, מִיּוֹמָא טָבָא לְשַׁבְּתָא לָנָא וּלְכָל יִשְׂרָאֵל הַדָּרִים בָּעִיר הַזֹּאת.

הדלקת נרות

The candles are lit and the following blessings are recited.
When *Yom Tov* falls on *Shabbos,* the words in parentheses are added.

בָּרוּךְ אַתָּה יהוה אֱלֹהֵינוּ מֶלֶךְ הָעוֹלָם, אֲשֶׁר קִדְּשָׁנוּ בְּמִצְוֹתָיו, וְצִוָּנוּ לְהַדְלִיק נֵר שֶׁל [שַׁבָּת וְשֶׁל] יוֹם טוֹב.

בָּרוּךְ אַתָּה יהוה אֱלֹהֵינוּ מֶלֶךְ הָעוֹלָם, שֶׁהֶחֱיָנוּ וְקִיְּמָנוּ וְהִגִּיעָנוּ לַזְּמַן הַזֶּה.

---

darkness is within us, how many unlit recesses there are. The task of the light of the soul is to search these dark corners, and "the light of a candle is effective for the search." How similar the laws of the search for leaven — the slightest forbidden particle (אִסּוּר מַשֶּׁהוּ) "shall not be seen or found;" search all the secret places of the home to ensure that not a crumb remains. Who can touch the holiness of the Jew searching out the *chametz*?

And so, too, with the baking of *matzos*. How great the reverence and the care lest the dough rise, even in the slightest! What a heavy responsibility! It is, indeed, told of one great man that he was unable to stand by and supervise the baking of *matzos*, because he was beset by constant doubts and worry. Care must be taken to the nth degree. Yet man, being man, cannot but hope to completely avoid the leavening process; the Torah was not given to angels (*Berachos* 25).

ERUV TAVSHILIN

It is forbidden to prepare on *Yom Tov* for the next day even if that day is the Sabbath. If, however, Sabbath preparations were started before *Yom Tov* began, they may be continued on *Yom Tov*. *Eruv tavshilin* constitutes this preparation. A *matzah* and any cooked food (such as fish, meat or an egg) are set aside on the day before *Yom Tov* to be used on the Sabbath and the blessing is recited followed by the declaration [made in a language understood by the one making the *eruv*]. If the first days *of Pesach* fall on Thursday and Friday, an *eruv tavshilin* must be made on Wednesday.
[In *Eretz Yisrael*, where only one day *Yom Tov* is in effect, the *eruv* is omitted.]

Blessed are You, HASHEM, our God, King of the universe, Who sanctified us by His commandments and commanded us concerning the commandment of eruv.

Through this eruv may we be permitted to bake, cook fry, insulate, kindle flame, prepare for, and do anything necessary on the festival for the sake of the Sabbath — for ourselves and for all Jews who live in this city.

LIGHTING THE CANDLES

The candles are lit and the following blessings are recited.
When *Yom Tov* falls on *Shabbos*, the words in parentheses are added.

Blessed are You, HASHEM, our God, King of the universe, Who has sanctified us through HIs commandments, and commanded us to kindle the flame of the (Sabbath and the) festival.

Blessed are You HASHEM, our God, King of the universe, Who has kept us alive, sustained us, and brought us to this season.

Here again the task corresponds to the task of the spirit. We must take the highest of care and be most diligent, lest the evil nature cause damage and leavening. This correspondence has given rise to the rabbinic dictum: "Should a *mitzvah* come to hand, don't let it lie about and become *chametz*" — i.e., do it immediately. This is based on a conscious play on the word *matzos*, מַצּוֹת, as against the word *mitzvos*, מִצְוֹת (*Rashi* to *Shemos* 12:17).

Contemplation of the actions of the *mitzvos* on the eve of *Pesach* (עֶרֶב פֶּסַח) — the search for leaven and the baking of *matzos* — makes one realize that he cannot fully grasp the level of purification achieved by the Jew with these actions. An angel is not fit to stand in the shoes of the eve-of-*Pesach* Jew. And who can really understand the inestimable value of the *mitzvos* of the night of the *Seder* itself? Fortunate are you, O Israel!

ᵉ⁄§ Preparing for the Seder

The Seder preparations should be made in time for the Seder to begin as soon as the synagogue services are finished. It should not begin before nightfall, however. Matzah, bitter herbs and several other items of symbolic significance are placed on the Seder plate in the arrangement shown below.

ג' מצות
3 MATZOS

Matzah — Three whole matzos are placed one atop the other, separated by a cloth or napkin. Matzah must be eaten three times during the Seder, by itself, with maror, and as the afikoman. Each time, the minimum portion of matzah for each person should have a volume equivalent to half an egg. Where many people are present, enough matzos should be available to enable each participant to receive a proper portion.

Maror and **Chazeres** — Bitter herbs are eaten twice during the Seder, once by themselves and a second time with matzah. Each time a minimum portion, equal to the volume of half an egg, should be eaten.

The Talmud lists several vegetables that qualify as Maror, two of which are put on the Seder plate in the places marked Chazeres and Maror. Most people use romaine lettuce (whole leaves or stalks) for Chazeres, and horseradish (whole or grated) for Maror, although either may be used for the mitzvah of eating Maror later in the Seder.

Charoses — The bitter herbs are dipped into charoses (a mixture of grated apples, nuts, other fruit, cinnamon and other spices, mixed with red wine). The charoses has the appearance of mortar to symbolize the lot of the Hebrew slaves, whose lives were embittered by hard labor with brick and mortar.

Z'roa [Roasted bone] and **Beitzah** [Roasted egg] — On the eve of Passover in the Holy Temple in Jerusalem, two sacrifices were offered and their meat roasted and eaten at the Seder feast. To commemorate these two sacrifices we place a roasted bone (with some meat on it) and a roasted hard-boiled egg on the Seder plate.

The egg, a symbol of mourning, is used in place of a second piece of meat as a reminder of our mourning at the destruction of the Temple — may it be rebuilt speedily in our day.

Karpas — A vegetable (celery, parsley, boiled potato) other than bitter herbs completes the Seder plate. It will be dipped in salt water and eaten. (The salt water is not put on the Seder plate, but it, too, should be prepared beforehand, and placed near the Seder plate).

קדש

Kiddush should be recited and the Seder begun as soon after synagogue services as possible — however, not before nightfall. Each participant's cup should be poured by someone else to symbolize the majesty of the evening, as though each participant had a servant.

On Friday night begin here:

(וַיְהִי עֶרֶב וַיְהִי בֹקֶר)

יוֹם הַשִּׁשִּׁי: וַיְכֻלּוּ הַשָּׁמַיִם וְהָאָרֶץ וְכָל צְבָאָם. וַיְכַל אֱלֹהִים בַּיּוֹם הַשְּׁבִיעִי מְלַאכְתּוֹ אֲשֶׁר עָשָׂה, וַיִּשְׁבֹּת בַּיּוֹם הַשְּׁבִיעִי מִכָּל מְלַאכְתּוֹ אֲשֶׁר עָשָׂה. וַיְבָרֶךְ אֱלֹהִים אֶת יוֹם הַשְּׁבִיעִי וַיְקַדֵּשׁ אֹתוֹ, כִּי בוֹ שָׁבַת מִכָּל מְלַאכְתּוֹ אֲשֶׁר בָּרָא אֱלֹהִים לַעֲשׂוֹת.[1]

יוֹם הַשִּׁשִּׁי / *The sixth day*

The Alter of Kelm

A man who has reached heights in the realm of the spirit wishes to bequeath his spiritual gains. He does not want to leave behind an estate of the physical only. And there is evidence that such is the proper attitude.

When the Torah says: "And there was evening and there was morning, *the* sixth day" (יוֹם הַשִּׁשִּׁי), it is a reference to a particular sixth day, the sixth of *Sivan,* the day on which the Torah was given at Sinai. The Creator set a condition. The continued existence of all that He had made would depend on Israel. If, two thousand years in the future, the people of Israel would accept the Torah, well and good. Should Israel refuse, God would reduce Creation to primeval chaos (*Shabbos* 88a).

A strange condition! After all, the Creator had brought the world into existence for the benefit of His creatures. Even if Israel would not accept the Torah and the dimension of the spiritual would be lacking, why should He wish to destroy the world? He could continue to bestow physical bounty on all the creatures who were happy with their lot.

This tells us that physical good is not a sufficient reason for the creation of the world. It has no true value in and of itself.

וַיִּשְׁבֹּת / *And He abstained*

The Alter of Kelm

The world is extensive and all-encompassing. It was created in the six days, but was not, as yet perfect. "What was the world lacking? Rest! When *Shabbos* came, rest came to the world" (*Rashi* to *Bereishis* 2:2). Rest is the sign of harmony and perfection.

In a like manner, man's personality is made up of a multitude of traits and emotions, but it is with the tranquility of the soul that he gains his perfect state. Man looks to the World-to-Come as the goal of all his efforts — "that

KADDESH

Kiddush should be recited and the Seder begun as soon after synagogue services as possible — however, not before nightfall. Each participant's cup should be poured by someone else to symbolize the majesty of the evening, as though each participant had a servant.

On Friday night begin here:

(And there was evening and there was morning)

The sixth day. Thus the heaven and the earth were finished, and all their array. On the seventh day God completed His work which He had done, and He abstained on the seventh day from all His work which He had done. God blessed the seventh day and hallowed it, because on it He abstained from all His work which God created to make.[1]

---

1. *Bereishis* 1:31-2:3.

---

day which is entirely *Shabbos* and rest" (*Tamid* 32), the world of harmony and perfection. That is why our prayers, which contain so many requests, each as necessary as the other, end with "Grant us peace" (שִׂים שָׁלוֹם) — tranquility and perfection.

And, on the other hand, the Sages say: "Peace is great, because it was not granted to the wicked" (*Bamidbar Rabbah*). Just as the righteous reach a harmony and a perfect state of character, so the wicked are cursed with turmoil of the soul, a lack of tranquility. They move from misfortune to misfortune, from delight to burning desire, from honor to shame. They do not allow themselves the possibility of calm. They constantly envy others; those who possess hundreds seek thousands; those who have thousands strive for millions. "Lack of Peace" is the curse of the wicked.

Chazal comment in the *Yerushalmi* (The Jerusalem Talmud) that they wished to permit the performance of work on *Chol HaMoed* (the Intermediary Days of the Festivals). For work had been forbidden then, only in order to allow the people the opportunity to occupy themselves with learning Torah. But rather than do that, people ate and drank and acted frivolously. *Chazal* thought that a mere eight days without a sense of responsibility would bring man to such a state of instability that it seemed appropriate to allow work on *Chol HaMoed*. What hope, then, is there for those who spend days on end in a constant state of instability?

וַיְבָרֶךְ אֱלֹהִים אֶת יוֹם הַשְּׁבִיעִי וַיְקַדֵּשׁ אֹתוֹ
God blessed the seventh day and hallowed it

R' Eliahu Lopian

The *halachah* is that a man who enters the Temple (*Beis HaMikdash*) in a state of impurity (טָמֵא) is subject to the death penalty. This is so because the builders erected the Temple to

On all nights other than Friday, begin here;
on Friday night include all passages in parentheses.

סַבְרִי מָרָנָן וְרַבָּנָן וְרַבּוֹתַי:

בָּרוּךְ אַתָּה יהוה אֱלֹהֵינוּ מֶלֶךְ הָעוֹלָם, בּוֹרֵא פְּרִי הַגָּפֶן:

בָּרוּךְ אַתָּה יהוה אֱלֹהֵינוּ מֶלֶךְ הָעוֹלָם, אֲשֶׁר בָּחַר בָּנוּ מִכָּל עָם, וְרוֹמְמָנוּ מִכָּל לָשׁוֹן, וְקִדְּשָׁנוּ בְּמִצְוֹתָיו. וַתִּתֶּן לָנוּ יהוה אֱלֹהֵינוּ בְּאַהֲבָה [שַׁבָּתוֹת לִמְנוּחָה וּ]מוֹעֲדִים לְשִׂמְחָה, חַגִּים וּזְמַנִּים לְשָׂשׂוֹן, אֶת יוֹם [הַשַּׁבָּת הַזֶּה וְאֶת יוֹם] חַג הַמַּצּוֹת הַזֶּה, זְמַן חֵרוּתֵנוּ [בְּאַהֲבָה] מִקְרָא קֹדֶשׁ, זֵכֶר לִיצִיאַת מִצְרָיִם, כִּי בָנוּ בָחַרְתָּ וְאוֹתָנוּ קִדַּשְׁתָּ מִכָּל הָעַמִּים, [וְשַׁבָּת] וּמוֹעֲדֵי קָדְשֶׁךָ [בְּאַהֲבָה וּבְרָצוֹן] בְּשִׂמְחָה וּבְשָׂשׂוֹן הִנְחַלְתָּנוּ. בָּרוּךְ אַתָּה יהוה, מְקַדֵּשׁ [הַשַּׁבָּת וְ]יִשְׂרָאֵל וְהַזְּמַנִּים.

---

be sacred to God. How much more so must we take care to enter the Sabbath in a proper state of purity (טָהֳרָה). For the Sabbath was sanctified by God Himself.

זְמַן חֵרוּתֵנוּ / ***The season of our freedom***

R' Yerucham of Mir

We are accustomed to think that the time at which an event occurs is a matter of chance. But the fixing of the Festivals at particular periods of the calendar year shows, to the contrary, that the time determines that an event shall occur just then.

Shlomo HaMelech said: "Everything has its season; there is a time for each thing" (*Koheles* 3:11), to which the Midrash comments: "There was a particular time at which Adam was to enter *Gan Eden* (Paradise) and a time when he was scheduled to leave . . . and a time at which the Torah was to be given to Israel." This is difficult to fathom. Adam was the end-purpose of Creation, he was created to enter *Gan Eden*. Why then see the time of his entering as more than an incidental factor? He was banished from *Gan Eden*, because of his sin. Why do *Chazal* say that there was a specific time at which he was to leave? And the giving of the Torah after the Exodus followed upon the fifty days of counting (סְפִירָה) between *Pesach* and *Shavuos*. How, then, can it be said that it was given because of the specific time?

On all nights other than Friday, begin here;
on Friday night include all passages in parentheses.

By your leave, my masters and teachers:

Blessed are You, HASHEM, our God, King of the universe, Who creates the fruit of the vine.

Blessed are You, HASHEM, our God, King of the universe, Who has chosen us from all nations, exalted us above all tongues, and sanctified us with His commandments. And You, HASHEM, our God, have lovingly given us (Sabbaths for rest), appointed times for gladness, feasts and seasons for joy, (this Sabbath and) this Feast of Matzos, the season of our freedom (in love,) a holy convocation in memoriam of the Exodus from Egypt. For You have chosen and sanctified us above all peoples, (and the Sabbath) and Your holy festivals (in love and favor), in gladness and joy have You granted us as a heritage. Blessed are You, HASHEM, Who sanctifies (the Sabbath,) Israel, and the festive seasons.

All the potential effects that time can have were built into it upon its creation. And our service to Hashem is directed in such a way as to receive the outpouring of time's influence. *Chazal* expressed the same idea in different terms when they noted that Bilaam had the ability to determine the very moment when Hashem was "angry" and deliver his curse then. All the sacrifices which he offered (*Bamidbar* 23:1) were means by which he could determine that specific moment and use time most efficiently. That, too, is why the Torah emphasizes the date of the Flood: "In the six hundredth year of Noach's life, in the second month, on the seventeenth day of the month . . . all the fountains of the great deep were torn asunder" (*Bereishis* 7:11). The Flood was part and parcel of a specific time.

We are to strive to raise ourselves up at the particular time of the Festivals, each year, because they did not occur then accidentally. *Shabbos* occurs each seventh day, not by chance, but because Hashem "rested" then (*Bereishis* 2:3). The season of our freedom (זְמַן חֵרוּתֵנוּ) does not only celebrate an event which occurred thousands of years ago when we left Egypt; it is built into the particular date on the calendar, because on that date, in the here and now, too, Revelation takes place. All of the service of the *Seder* is designed to prepare us to leave the servitude to the physical, accept the freedom of the world of the spirit and receive that Revelation.

On Saturday night, add the following two paragraphs:

בָּרוּךְ אַתָּה יהוה אֱלֹהֵינוּ מֶלֶךְ הָעוֹלָם, בּוֹרֵא מְאוֹרֵי הָאֵשׁ.

בָּרוּךְ אַתָּה יהוה אֱלֹהֵינוּ מֶלֶךְ הָעוֹלָם, הַמַּבְדִּיל בֵּין קֹדֶשׁ לְחוֹל, בֵּין אוֹר לְחֹשֶׁךְ, בֵּין יִשְׂרָאֵל לָעַמִּים, בֵּין יוֹם הַשְּׁבִיעִי לְשֵׁשֶׁת יְמֵי הַמַּעֲשֶׂה. בֵּין קְדֻשַּׁת שַׁבָּת לִקְדֻשַּׁת יוֹם טוֹב הִבְדַּלְתָּ, וְאֶת יוֹם הַשְּׁבִיעִי מִשֵּׁשֶׁת יְמֵי הַמַּעֲשֶׂה קִדַּשְׁתָּ, הִבְדַּלְתָּ וְקִדַּשְׁתָּ אֶת עַמְּךָ יִשְׂרָאֵל בִּקְדֻשָּׁתֶךָ. בָּרוּךְ אַתָּה יהוה, הַמַּבְדִּיל בֵּין קֹדֶשׁ לְקֹדֶשׁ.

On all nights conclude here:

בָּרוּךְ אַתָּה יהוה אֱלֹהֵינוּ מֶלֶךְ הָעוֹלָם, שֶׁהֶחֱיָנוּ וְקִיְּמָנוּ וְהִגִּיעָנוּ לַזְּמַן הַזֶּה.

The wine should be drunk without delay while reclining on the left side. It is preferable to drink the entire cup, but at the very least, most of the cup should be drained.

ורחץ

The head of the household — according to many opinions, all participants in the Seder — washes his hands as if to eat bread, [pouring water from a cup, twice on the right hand and twice on the left] but without reciting a blessing.

הֲסִבָּה / *Reclining*

R' Yosef Leib Bloch of Telshe

The *Seder* has many tokens of remembrance: We eat in a reclining position in memory of our acquisition of freedom; we do not eat the bitter herbs (מָרוֹר) while reclining, because they are a token of our bitter slavery in Egypt; the *matzah, charoses* and the four cups of wine are all in memory of particular events. But they are all relatively modest tokens. Would not an elaborate audio-visual pageant have a far greater effect?

It seems that magnificent, one might say bombastic, spectacles, which, when they take place, appear to make a tremendous impression, have only a surface and passing influence. The immensity and scope of the performance do not penetrate in depth to affect the constant, fine

On Saturday night, add the following two paragraphs:

Blessed are You, HASHEM, our God, King of the universe, Who creates the illumination of the fire.

Blessed are You, HASHEM, our God, King of the universe, Who distinguishes between sacred and secular, between light and darkness, between Israel and the nations, between the seventh day and the six days of activity. You have distinguished between the holiness of the Sabbath and the holiness of a Festival, and have sanctified the seventh day above the six days of activity. You distinguished and sanctified Your nation, Israel, with Your holiness. Blessed are You, HASHEM, who distinguishes between holiness and holiness.

On all nights conclude here:

Blessed are You, HASHEM, our God, King of the universe, Who has kept us alive, sustained us, and brought us to this season.

The wine should be drunk without delay while reclining on the left side. It is preferable to drink the entire cup, but at the very least, most of the cup should be drained.

URECHATZ

The head of the household — according to many opinions, all participants in the Seder — washes his hands as if to eat bread, [pouring water from a cup, twice on the right hand and twice on the left] but without reciting a blessing.

---

emotions. The relatively minute actions, although they do not seem to have a visible effect, descend into the depths of the personality and awaken the hidden chords of feeling. Thus, on *Succos* the Torah tells us to offer seventy bulls, an overabundance of sacrifices, symbolizing the seventy nations of the world. But on the eighth day (שְׁמִינִי עֲצֶרֶת), we are to sacrifice a single lone bull: like a king who held a banquet for seven days in succession and invited all of the country. When the seven days had elapsed, he said to his dear friend, "We have paid our social obligations to all the citizens of the realm. Let the two of us sit and eat a simple meal together, a meal of fish and greens" (*Bamidbar Rabbah, Pinchas*). For when there is a sense of closeness, and when one wishes to arouse his inner feelings, he should not do so with expensive externals. Plant a single grain in a secluded spot; it will certainly bear fruit.

כַּרְפַּס

All participants take a vegetable other than maror and dip it into salt-water. A piece smaller in volume than half an egg should be used. The following blessing is recited [with the intention that it also applies to the maror which will be eaten during the meal] before the vegetable is eaten.

בָּרוּךְ אַתָּה יהוה אֱלֹהֵינוּ מֶלֶךְ הָעוֹלָם, בּוֹרֵא פְּרִי הָאֲדָמָה.

יַחַץ

The head of the household breaks the middle matzah in two. He puts the smaller part back between the two whole matzos, and wraps up the larger part for later use as the Afikoman. Some briefly place the Afikoman portion on their shoulders, in accordance with the Biblical verse recounting that Israel left Egypt carrying their matzos on their shoulders, and say בְּבֶהָלוּ יָצָאנוּ מִמִּצְרַיִם, 'In haste we went out of Egypt.'

בָּרוּךְ אַתָּה / Blessed are You

R' Yerucham of Mir

Blessings begin in the second person — *You* — the pronoun which indicates the one spoken to, the one who is present (נוֹכַח). They end in the third person — *He* — the one spoken about, the one not present (נִסְתָּר).

It is true that faith rests on reason and there is solid evidence present to support faith. But such faith can be shaken. It is but a stage on the way to the firm faith indicated by the prophet: "The righteous man shall live in his faith" (*Chavakuk* 2:4) — the faith which is a firm bar of steel which cannot be eroded.

Avraham's faith was at first a faith based on reason. He sought an answer to the basic question: "How can the world exist without one to govern it?" (*Bereishis Rabbah* 39). And he reached the height of faith with the Binding of Yitzchak (עֲקֵידַת יִצְחָק) — a faith without questions!

So, too, Israel in the desert had unquestioning faith. "Thus says HASHEM: I remember the affection of your youth, the love you bore as a bride when you followed after Me in the wilderness, in a land unsown" (*Yirmeyahu* 2:2). "And they had not made provisions for the way" (*Shemos* 12:39). "They traveled by HASHEM's command and by HASHEM's command they encamped" (*Bamidbar* 9:20). Forty years of faith without question! And with this they laid the foundations of the nation of Israel.

And the Redemption (גְּאוּלָה) of the future will come about in a like manner. All the troubles that *Chazal* enumerate in the period of *Mashiach's* footfall (עִקְבְתָא דִמְשִׁיחָא) will occur. "Torah will be forgotten in Israel" (*Shabbos* 138). "Those who fear sin will be abhorred; truth will be unknown; the face of the generation will be like that of the dog" (*Sotah* 49). All of these will shake the clearly seen belief based on reason and force man to place his

KARPAS

All participants take a vegetable other than maror and dip it into salt-water. A piece smaller in volume than half an egg should be used. The following blessing is recited [with the intention that it also applies to the maror which will be eaten during the meal] before the vegetable is eaten.

Blessed are You, HASHEM, our God, King of the universe, Who creates the fruits of the earth.

YACHATZ

The head of the household breaks the middle matzah in two. He puts the smaller part back between the two whole matzos, and wraps up the larger part for later use as the Afikoman. Some briefly place the Afikoman portion on their shoulders, in accordance with the Biblical verse recounting that Israel left Egypt carrying their matzos on their shoulders, and say בִּבְהִלוּ יָצָאנוּ מִמִּצְרָיִם, *'In haste we went out of Egypt.'*

---

faith on the unseen. They will bring him to the realization that "we have no one on whom to lean other than our Father in the Heavens" (*Sotah* 48). And this faith will deliver us.

אֱלֹהֵינוּ מֶלֶךְ הָעוֹלָם / *Our God, King of the universe*

R' Yerucham of Mir

In the format of our blessings we address ourselves first to our God (אֱלֹהֵינוּ), the God of Israel Who chose us to serve Him, and immediately thereafter we call Him, King of the universe (מֶלֶךְ הָעוֹלָם). Our morning prayers, too, reflect this same dual approach. We find the blessing "He creates the heavenly lights" (יוֹצֵר הַמְּאוֹרוֹת), which speaks of the Creation as a whole, followed by a "You have loved us with a great love" (אַהֲבָה רַבָּה), on the selection of Israel as the chosen people — the universal, side by side with the national.

The universe is a unified whole and it was created to serve man. "You established him (man) to rule over the creations of Your hands; You placed everything beneath his feet" (*Tehillim* 8:7). And when man serves Hashem he fulfills the purpose of Creation (*Berachos* 6b) and then it comes to his aid. When Adam was in *Gan Eden* (Paradise) the angels roasted heavenly meat before him and the serpent served as his messenger (*Sanhedrin* 59b). But with his sin, Creation itself fell from its former state. "Cursed is the earth on your account. It will give forth thorns and thistles for you" (*Bereishis* 3:17-18). In R' Shimon ben Shetach's day grains of wheat grew to the size of the kidneys of an ox. Some were preserved to show later generations with their smaller grains the effect of their sins (*Taanis* 23). And from the day the *Beis HaMikdash* was destroyed, fruits lost their taste (*Sotah* 48).

When man rises, he elevates the whole of creation. Thus, it was that the very rocks which Yaakov placed at his head quarreled with one another as

מַגִּיד

The broken matzah is lifted for all to see as the head of the household begins with the following brief explanation of the proceedings.

הָא לַחְמָא עַנְיָא דִי אֲכָלוּ אַבְהָתָנָא בְּאַרְעָא דְמִצְרָיִם. כָּל דִּכְפִין יֵיתֵי וְיֵכוֹל, כָּל דִּצְרִיךְ יֵיתֵי וְיִפְסַח. הָשַׁתָּא הָכָא, לְשָׁנָה הַבָּאָה בְּאַרְעָא דְיִשְׂרָאֵל. הָשַׁתָּא עַבְדֵי, לְשָׁנָה הַבָּאָה בְּנֵי חוֹרִין.

The Seder plate is removed and the second of the four cups of wine is poured. The youngest present asks the reasons for the unusual proceedings of the evening.

מַה נִּשְׁתַּנָּה הַלַּיְלָה הַזֶּה מִכָּל הַלֵּילוֹת?

שֶׁבְּכָל הַלֵּילוֹת אָנוּ אוֹכְלִין חָמֵץ וּמַצָּה, הַלַּיְלָה הַזֶּה – כֻּלּוֹ מַצָּה.

שֶׁבְּכָל הַלֵּילוֹת אָנוּ אוֹכְלִין שְׁאָר יְרָקוֹת, הַלַּיְלָה הַזֶּה – מָרוֹר.

שֶׁבְּכָל הַלֵּילוֹת אֵין אָנוּ מַטְבִּילִין אֲפִילוּ פַּעַם אֶחָת, הַלַּיְלָה הַזֶּה – שְׁתֵּי פְעָמִים.

שֶׁבְּכָל הַלֵּילוֹת אָנוּ אוֹכְלִין בֵּין יוֹשְׁבִין וּבֵין מְסֻבִּין, הַלַּיְלָה הַזֶּה – כֻּלָּנוּ מְסֻבִּין.

---

to which one should have the privilege of having the righteous Yaakov rest his head on it. Hence, it is that when we ask for our Redemption (גְּאוּלָה), we do so in the blessing which deals with the heavenly lights and all of creation: "Bring forth a new light on Zion, and may we all, soon, be worthy to enjoy its light." All of us, and the whole of creation along with us, will share, then, in the Revelation of the glory of Heaven.

הָשַׁתָּא הָכָא, לְשָׁנָה הַבָּאָה בְּאַרְעָא דְיִשְׂרָאֵל
Now, we are here; next year may we be in the Land of Israel

R' Yechezkel Levenstein

Is this declaration relevant, in our day and age, for that goodly part of the Jewish people who are fortunate to live in the land of Israel?

The prophet writes: צִיּוֹן בְּמִשְׁפָּט תִּפָּדֶה וְשָׁבֶיהָ בִּצְדָקָה – Zion will be redeemed in justice and those who return unto her in righteousness

MAGGID

The broken matzah is lifted for all to see as the head of the household begins with the following brief explanation of the proceedings.

This is the bread of affliction that our fathers ate in the land of Egypt. Whoever is hungry — let him come and eat! Whoever is needy — let him come and celebrate Pesach! Now, we are here; next year may we be in the Land of Israel! Now, we are slaves; next year may we be free men!

The Seder plate is removed and the second of the four cups of wine is poured. The youngest present asks the reasons for the unusual proceedings of the evening.

Why is this night different from all other nights?

1. On all other nights we may eat chametz and matzah, but on this night only matzah.

2. On all other nights we eat many vegetables, but on this night — we eat maror.

3. On all other nights we do not dip even once, but on this night — twice.

4. On all other nights we eat either sitting or reclining, but on this night — we all recline.

(*Yeshayahu* 1:27). The *Gaon of Vilna* sees this as envisioning a two-stage return. First, the land (Zion) will be redeemed and become a land of holiness. And then, those who return to her will become a nation of God. At present, even those in the Land of Israel must say: Now we are here — in the Israel of today; next year may we be in Israel — in the Israel which will be redeemed and sanctified. Now we are, as yet, slaves (עַבְדֵי) — in spirit; only after the redemption will we truly be a free people (בְּנֵי חוֹרִין).

מַה נִּשְׁתַּנָּה / *Why is this night different . . .*

The Alter of Kelm

The *Alter* wondered why we start the narrative of the Exodus from Egypt on the note of a question: *Why is this night different?* Why do we not begin to speak of the miracles immediately?

One day, while taking a stroll, he chanced upon a stone bench. It caused him to remember a Midrash which tells us that R' Yehudah approached the rock upon which R' Meir would sit while learning; he kissed the rock and compared it to Sinai where the Torah had been given.

The Seder plate is returned. The matzos are kept uncovered as the Haggadah is recited in unison. The Haggadah should be translated if necessary, and the story of the Exodus should be amplified upon.

עֲבָדִים הָיִינוּ לְפַרְעֹה בְּמִצְרָיִם, וַיּוֹצִיאֵנוּ יהוה אֱלֹהֵינוּ מִשָּׁם בְּיָד חֲזָקָה וּבִזְרוֹעַ נְטוּיָה. וְאִלּוּ לֹא הוֹצִיא הַקָּדוֹשׁ בָּרוּךְ הוּא אֶת אֲבוֹתֵינוּ

The *Alter* thought to himself that were the bench the seat of R' Meir and had he seen R' Yehoshua fall down at the foot of the rock and kiss it, he would never have forgotten the sight! For there is a world of difference between intellectually understanding an incident and seeing it happen before your eyes.

This led him to appreciate the power inherent in visualizing a scene, bringing a picture to life and brought him to a further thought. The process by which he had come to this appreciation was one of comparison: He had weighed what he had known (the *relating* of the story in the Midrash) as against the new light in which he viewed it (*visualizing* the incident). And this in turn gave rise to a specific methodology — one should always ask himself what he had thought previously and, then, what new factor was he now aware of. "That is why," he thought, "we ask *why is this night different*; what did we know previously and what is now different?"

[The need to "sense the picture," which lies behind the directive that "it is one's duty to regard himself as though he personally had gone out from Egypt," was also highlighted by the *Alter*.]

There are many proofs to show how important this "sense of the picture" is in fully implanting a matter into a person. Aharon the High Priest was certainly filled with fear of God and fear of sinning. It is he of whom *Chazal* say that the Torah praises him for carrying out Hashem's instructions to the letter "without a hair of a change." Yet, when the Torah wishes to warn him not to enter the Tent of Meeting indiscriminately, it informs him of this commandment, just after his two sons have died; it emphasizes the need to obey, lest his end be like theirs. *Rashi* compares this to a doctor who orders his patient to take medicine and adds, "Lest you die like so-and-so." This gives weight to his words. Even an Aharon needed such threats and examples! Everyone profits by the "looking" at a picture.

Moshe, the first among the prophets, also, no less than Aharon, was turned in the direction of a "picture." Before he was sent to Pharaoh to lead Israel up out of Egypt, the Holy One gave him three signs with which he was to approach the ruler of Egypt and the Children of Israel. Hashem, however, not only instructed Moshe as to what he was to do when he stood before his audience; He demonstrated the signs to Moshe. The *Ramban* notes that Moshe's faith became stronger when he witnessed the acts with his very own eyes.

The Seder plate is returned. The matzos are kept uncovered as the Haggadah is recited in unison. The Haggadah should be translated if necessary, and the story of the Exodus should be amplified upon.

We were slaves to Pharaoh in Egypt, But HASHEM our God took us out from there with a mighty hand and an outstretched arm. Had not the Holy One, Blessed is He, taken our fathers out

---

Visualization has awesome force. Without the ability to animate and picture things, man is blind and unfeeling, closed up in his shell. That is why *Chazal* have numbered the ability "to help bear the burden of another" (נוֹשֵׂא בְּעוֹל עִם חֲבֵרוֹ) among the desirable qualities for the study of Torah (*Avos* 6). Sympathy for another flows from the power of visualization, from one's ability to step out of the narrow, private world of the ego. Without such ability, a man would never be able to understand anything outside of his self.

The Torah chose to give details of only two episodes in the long eighty years of Moshe's life before he rose to become Israel's leader: the first — "he went out to his brothers and looked on their burdensome labors" (*Shemos* 2:11); the second is that at the well in Midian. These two incidents are Moshe's "identity card."

He left the palace to witness his fellow Jews at their tasks, and when he saw an Egyptian beating a Jew, he could not contain himself; he killed the oppressor. The reaction reflects his empathy. He felt the yoke of servitude in common with his brethren. Such was his power of visualization, that he felt the Egyptian's blows on his own back.

Later he was a stranger, a refugee who had fled to Midian. Yet, when he saw the local shepherds harassing helpless girls, although they were unknown to him: "Moshe rose up and saved them" (*Shemos* 2:17).

When one has the power to picture things, he will take up the burden of his fellow man. This power will take him out of his shell of selfishness and bring him to the feeling and contemplation which can lead to prophecy, Redemption and the Giving of the Torah at Sinai.

עֲבָדִים הָיִינוּ לְפַרְעֹה בְּמִצְרָיִם

We were slaves to Pharaoh in Egypt

R' Shlomo Harkavy of Grodno

The dynasty of the Pharaohs has long since disappeared and the empire of Egypt toppled long ago, but the statement is constantly relevant.

Egypt was in its time the world center of culture — "And Shlomo's wisdom was greater than all the wisdom of Egypt!" (*I Melachim* 5:10). But Egypt turned its wisdom in the direction of impurity (טוּמְאָה) and cultivated sorcerers and magicians; it was sunk deep in moral depravity and thus the Torah warns us: "You shall not do the deeds of the land of Egypt in which you dwelt" (*Vayikra* 18:3). And Israel, while there, had itself descended to

the all but final depth, the forty-ninth level (מ״ט שַׁעֲרֵי טוּמְאָה), and had almost completely intermingled with the Egyptians. Had that happened, the world would have continued to wallow in the muck of desire and defilement and we would have been an integral part of it all, of the impurity of Egypt under the direction of Pharaoh.

Such would have been the case "had not the Holy One, Blessed is He, taken our fathers out of Egypt." The Exodus involved removing "a nation from within a nation" (*Devarim* 4:34) — "like a man who slips out the fetus from the innards of an animal" (*Midrash Shochar Tov*) — from the state of a fetus, which lives within, and by virtue of, its mother, to that of an independent creature.

This was a new act of creation which raised us up in a single action from the extreme depths to the heights: "And I took you — and I brought you to Me" (*Shemos* 19:4). It was a conclusive break from their former impure behavior: "For as you have seen the Egyptians today, you shall not see them again ever" (*Shemos* 14:13).

עֲבָדִים הָיִינוּ. . . וַיּוֹצִיאֵנוּ ה׳ אֱלֹהֵינוּ
We were slaves. . . but HASHEM our God took us out

R' Yitzchak Blazer of Peterburg

Chazal have said: "The Holy One wished to bestow a bounty on Israel; therefore, He gave them the Torah and *mitzvos* in abundance" (*Makos* 23). And yet, what sort of a bounty is this with its multitudinous commands and prohibitions which spread themselves over all facets of our lives and intrude upon us at all times?

Such a question would be a proper one, if we were totally independent and the Creator would ask us to serve Him in some manner; we would most likely choose to do the least possible service and, if we were asked to do more, it would appear like an imposition and not a gift. However, the truth of the matter is that "we were slaves to Pharaoh in Egypt but HASHEM our God took us out from there" in order that we should serve Him and not Pharaoh: "They are My servants whom I took out of the land of Egypt" (*Vayikra* 25:55). Nothing belongs to us — not the work of our hands, not our lives, not our families. We are servants and ought to labor for our Master day and night. How fortunate we are that He, our Master, has granted us a Torah with its abundance of *mitzvos* and told us how to fill each moment with unceasing service to Him.

Just as to the servant, being a servant means that his very eating, sleeping, dressing and every act are part of his existence as a slave, so, too, when the Jew submits to the yoke of Heaven (קַבָּלַת עוֹל מַלְכוּת שָׁמַיִם), he is meant to dedicate his entire life to the service of his King and his G-d. Thus, on *Yom*

from Egypt, then we, our children, and our children's children would have remained enslaved to Pharaoh in Egypt. Even if we were all men of wisdom, under-

---

Kippur we confess to "the sin which we have sinned before You by throwing off Your yoke." For, at times, even at the moment of performing a *mitzvah*, we may forget the basic motif that we are not our own masters.

On the surface, the feeling of servitude might seem to make man unfortunate, and make the fulfillment of *mitzvos* all the more difficult. But, in truth, when a man knows that he must serve, he does not suffer an inner turbulence. It is the supposedly free man who must struggle with every prohibition and in every situation.

It is stated: "The road of the righteous is like a brilliant light and the path of the wicked like the darkness; they know not where they will stumble" (*Mishlei* 4:19). The way of the righteous is a well-built road. They are prepared for any deed, for they are servants at their allotted stations. David HaMelech slept no longer than a horse naps (*Succah* 26b) and, when Rav Chisda was asked by his daughter, "Don't you wish to rest longer?" he replied, "The time will come when I will rest for days without end" (*Eruvin* 65a). If a man has such an attitude, he does not feel that he is in a state of constant trial, nor does he sense the weight of his servitude.

But the path of the wicked is like the darkness. Each step is fraught with danger for them and may lead to their fall. They do not know what they will stumble against. Each *mitzvah* is a new trial and each possibility of sin presents a new trap set out for them. All this, because they do not feel the sense of servitude.

וְאִלּוּ לֹא הוֹצִיא הַקָּדוֹשׁ בָּרוּךְ הוּא אֶת אֲבוֹתֵינוּ מִמִּצְרַיִם

Had not the Holy One, Blessed is He, taken our fathers out from Egypt

R' Yechezkel Levenstein

The stress is on the role of the Holy One. The going out of Egypt was not only a miracle which broke the rules of nature — Hashem has no difficulty in turning water into blood, or sea to dry land; in bringing plagues of frogs, wild beasts, lice and boils. This miracle was on a far loftier plane. It was difficult to free Israel by the usually accepted patterns of nature — *Chazal* tell us that not a single slave could escape from Egypt. But beyond that, they should not have been freed by the legal canons of the Heavenly justice of the world above. The prosecution in Heaven against Israel argued and with truth: How are these (Israel) different from them (the Egyptians)? These worship idols and those worship idols (*Mechilta, Beshalach* 64). And it is a commonplace that Israel had sunk to the depths of impurity (מ״ט שַׁעֲרֵי טוּמְאָה). Indeed, when Moshe came to inform them of their impending Redemption, they asked, "On what grounds do we deserve to be delivered? All of Egypt is filled with our idol worship." Moshe answered: "Because the Holy One wishes to deliver you,

נְבוֹנִים, כֻּלָּנוּ זְקֵנִים, כֻּלָּנוּ יוֹדְעִים אֶת הַתּוֹרָה, מִצְוָה עָלֵינוּ לְסַפֵּר בִּיצִיאַת מִצְרָיִם. וְכָל הַמַּרְבֶּה לְסַפֵּר בִּיצִיאַת מִצְרַיִם, הֲרֵי זֶה מְשֻׁבָּח.

He does not look to see if you are deserving, as it said: 'He skips over the hills' " (*Shir HaShirim Rabbah* 5).

In the events of the Exodus, Hashem showed His absolute control of Creation; He was not bound, even by the rules of Heavenly justice. He does as He pleases. As *Chazal* say: "I will favor whomsoever I favor" (*Shemos* 33:19) — even though he is not worthy (*Berachos* 7a). When He wishes to turn evil into good, who can prevent Him, as it is stated: "If you have sinned how can you affect Him?" (*Iyov* 35:6).

We are told that although we are to mention the parting of the Red Sea each day, as well as the Exodus from Egypt, this is a recommendation prior to the fact (לכתחילה) and if one forgets to mention it, one's benediction is still valid. Only the remembrance of the Exodus is a requirement which cannot be bypassed in any way (מעכב בדיעבד), because it appears in the verse: "I am HASHEM, your God, Who took you out of Egypt from the house of slaves" (*Shemos* 20:2; see *Shemos Rabbah* 22:3).

The reason for the distinction is clear: The parting of the Red Sea was exciting, brought Israel to faith and song of praise and caused Yisro to convert: "The nations heard and trembled; sorrow seized the dwellers of Palestine (*Shemos* 15:14). But the Exodus revealed something more, that "I am HASHEM Your God." He alone rules all the worlds without restraint or hindrance.

Had not the Holy One, Blessed is He, taken our fathers out from Egypt, had we been required to wait until we were worthy to be redeemed on our own merits and by the rules of Heavenly justice, *we would have remained enslaved to Pharaoh* to this very day.

וַאֲפִילוּ כֻּלָּנוּ חֲכָמִים. . . מִצְוָה עָלֵינוּ לְסַפֵּר
Even if we were all men of wisdom . . .
it would still be an obligation upon us to tell about

R' Eliahu Dessler

The *Haggadah* was composed by *Chazal* as an instrument whereby we might fulfill the *mitzvah* that "you shall tell your son" — וְהִגַּדְתָּ לְבִנְךָ (*Shemos* 13:8). It must, then, reflect the best possible methods of teaching. We find the format of question and answer: "Why is this night different. . .? We were slaves to Pharaoh in Egypt." We offer motivation: we do things so that the children should wonder and ask. We provide concrete illustrations: "This *matzah* which we eat. . ." "Why do we eat these bitter herbs?" And vivid imaginative suggestions: "It is one's duty to regard himself as though he personally had gone out of Egypt." There is the breaking down of the whole into its

standing, experience, and knowledge of the Torah, it would still be an obligation upon us to tell about the Exodus from Egypt. The more one tells about the Exodus, the more he is praiseworthy.

---

components and concentration on each part: "Had he brought us out of Egypt but not executed judgments against them, it would have sufficed us." And the combination of the parts, so that we get the full effect of Hashem's bounty and deliverance: "How much more so should we be grateful to the Omnipresent. . . He brought us out of Egypt; executed judgments against the Egyptians. . .''

In short, the *Haggadah* can serve as a handbook of education in the spirit of the Torah.

❧ ❧ ❧

We must understand why "even if we were all men of wisdom. . . it would still be an obligation upon us to tell about the Exodus from Egypt." And not only relate it, but to do so in the specific manner which we mentioned above, through question and answer. Even if a man is all alone on the eve of the *Seder*, he must ask himself the questions and answer them (*Pesachim* 116a). What purpose can there be in questions to which the answers are known beforehand?

The *Seder* is not meant to impart a body of information to the brain; it is meant to implant the story in the heart. The mind may be that of a genius and the heart of that genius might be ignorant; the mind may be adult and the heart childish. The wisest and oldest among us must all speak to their hearts, in the way that one speaks to a youngster, using the whole range of the methods of teaching.

כֻּלָּנוּ זְקֵנִים / *All men . . . of experience*

The Alter of Kelm   *If we were all men of wisdom, understanding. . .* It is obvious that the wise know more than those who are not wise. But what plus can there be in *men of experience*, or age (זְקֵנִים), over a younger man? True, *Chazal* say that the mind of the wise becomes ever firmer with ever advancing age (*Kinnim* 3:6). But why is this so?

The wise man in his youth grasps matters theoretically, but as he grows older, that which was described becomes real and actual to him. For example, when young he understands, intellectually, that Providence works within Creation. With age he sees sin and punishment and gains insight into the principle of Hashem paying measure-for-measure (מִדָּה כְּנֶגֶד מִדָּה), that punishment fits the crime. All that he knows becomes real and actual to him and his senses and therefore it becomes fixed within him. The wisdom which was previously a cold, impersonal, abstract, intellectual perception becomes part of himself. *Chazal* describe the process: The eye sees, the

heart desires and the organs of action complete the deed. The seeing eye is intellectual understanding, the desirous heart is the implantation within the heart and that gives the push towards action. Such is the process for evil and, certainly, for good. The wise man with increasing years finds that his knowledge becomes truer and truer before his eyes; it takes root in his heart and creates a drive to fulfill *mitzvos*.

וְכָל הַמַּרְבֶּה לְסַפֵּר בִּיצִיאַת מִצְרַיִם, הֲרֵי זֶה מְשֻׁבָּח
The more one tells about the Exodus, the more he is praiseworthy

R' Yerucham of Mir The obligation to remember the Exodus tells us about the foundation of faith and how to acquire it. The *Ramban* (to *Shemos* 13:16) notes that many *mitzvos* were given in order to remember the going out of Egypt (*Pesach, Succos, tefillin, mezuzah* and others). From the time when first there were lapses in faith, there were those with mistaken ideas. Some denied the very existence of the Creator and claimed that there had been a world from time immemorial, that it was not a created entity. Others admitted to the existence of God, but said that He had no idea as to what happened on earth; or that He did know of our affairs, but did not involve Himself in them; He did not govern His creatures or reward and punish them. However, when God elects to choose a people and perform miracles for them, miracles which a prophet proclaims before they occur, all of these opinions vanish on the instant. Everyone can then clearly see that God exists, that He has ties with His creatures, that He governs nature unconditionally, bestows reward and metes out punishment. All this, we learn from the story of the Exodus.

If perhaps, we previously thought that there is a sharp and clear-cut distinction between the man of faith and the non-believer, the *Ramban* teaches us that faith, like kindness (חֶסֶד) and compassion (רַחֲמִים), possesses many intermediary levels between the extremes of complete faith and complete lack of faith. There are shades of belief. There were, and are, as we said, people who believed in the existence of God but did not accept the idea of reward and punishment. We may not be able to understand how one can divide one position (the existence of God) from the other (reward and punishment). But this is so, because faith reveals itself on different levels in various guises and behind varied veils.

Chazal demonstrate this scale of faith. As they put it: He who has sufficient for the needs of *today* and is concerned for the *morrow* may be numbered among those of little faith (*Sotah* 48). They refer to the God-fearing, pious Jew, who performs all the *mitzvos*, who believes in the Creator and in His Divine Providence, who believes that there is reward and punishment. But, if his faith and trust in Hashem does not prevent him from worrying about the next day, it has lost a bit of its luster; it is a *little* diminished and he is of *little* faith (קְטַן־אֱמוּנָה).

At the time of the Exodus, faith was writ large; it was shining and clear. R'

Moshe Cordovero writes, in his *Or Ne'erav*, that even a hypothetical conjecture (הֲוָא אֲמִינָא) is heresy and atheism, in matters of faith. At the moment of the Exodus, all such conjectures and all hints of skepticism ceased to exist. Faith shone forth, bright and revealed.

The going out of Egypt was meant to dispel any doubts and hesitations. Such clarity of faith is the goal of man. And he is bidden to labor constantly to preserve the image of the Exodus in all its brilliance and not allow it to be clouded over by even the thinnest of films, or have dust settle on it.

But how can we reach this goal? The *Ramban* tells us (ibid.) not to expect the Holy One to work such obvious miracles in each age for the benefit of the skeptics. Thus, we are commanded to perform many acts of remembrance of the Exodus and pass them on from generation to generation.

For it is a standing axiom that a man does not lie to his children. A man, when asked, will give his grandfather's name without hesitation, even though he never knew him. But he does not have the slightest doubt about the truth of his answer, because it is his father who told him about the member of the family. So, too, we pass on the account of the miracle of the Exodus to our children. They will accept it and it will become implanted within them. That is what lies behind: "that you might tell over in the ears of your son and your son's son" (*Shemos* 10:2).

In order that the lessons of faith which can be extracted from the Exodus should stand before our eyes in full life, we have been given many signs and commandments — *Pesach, Succos, tefillin,* etc. Both morning and evening we make daily mention of the Exodus. And the Torah has decreed that whoever eats leavened products (*chametz*) on *Pesach*, or avoids sacrificing the *Pesach*-offering (קָרְבַּן פֶּסַח) deserves the punishment of uprooting (*kares*), death at Heaven's hands. The point is clear; the lessons of the Exodus must be preserved.

The *Rambam* in his *Guide for the Perplexed* (מוֹרֶה נְבוּכִים) writes that the Torah has given a record of the treks and way stations of Israel in the desert wilderness at length, lest someone in the future might be skeptical about what had happened. In a like manner, the Torah has given a great number of *mitzvos* as tokens of remembrance of the Exodus, so that no one will doubt that it did, indeed, occur.

David HaMelech has said: "When a multitude of thoughts are within me, Your comfortings bring joy to my soul" (*Tehillim* 94:19); the more a man reviews his knowledge and thinks about his faith, the more they are absorbed and influence him. By multiplying the signs of remembrance, the radiance of faith becomes evident with every step, beyond a shadow of doubt. That is why *the more one tells about the Exodus, the more he is praiseworthy*. Every addition to, and review of, the story etches it more deeply on the soul.

The highest goal is the faith of R' Chanina ben Dosa. As the eve of *Shabbos* was approaching, he noticed that his daughter was sad. She had, in error,

מַעֲשֶׂה בְּרַבִּי אֱלִיעֶזֶר וְרַבִּי יְהוֹשֻׁעַ וְרַבִּי אֶלְעָזָר
בֶּן עֲזַרְיָה וְרַבִּי עֲקִיבָא וְרַבִּי טַרְפוֹן שֶׁהָיוּ
מְסֻבִּין בִּבְנֵי בְרַק, וְהָיוּ מְסַפְּרִים בִּיצִיאַת מִצְרַיִם כָּל
אוֹתוֹ הַלַּיְלָה. עַד שֶׁבָּאוּ תַלְמִידֵיהֶם וְאָמְרוּ לָהֶם,
רַבּוֹתֵינוּ הִגִּיעַ זְמַן קְרִיאַת שְׁמַע שֶׁל שַׁחֲרִית.

אָמַר רַבִּי אֶלְעָזָר בֶּן עֲזַרְיָה, הֲרֵי אֲנִי כְּבֶן
שִׁבְעִים שָׁנָה, וְלֹא זָכִיתִי שֶׁתֵּאָמֵר יְצִיאַת
מִצְרַיִם בַּלֵּילוֹת, עַד שֶׁדְּרָשָׁהּ בֶּן זוֹמָא, שֶׁנֶּאֱמַר,
לְמַעַן תִּזְכֹּר אֶת יוֹם צֵאתְךָ מֵאֶרֶץ מִצְרַיִם כֹּל
יְמֵי חַיֶּיךָ.¹ יְמֵי חַיֶּיךָ הַיָּמִים, כֹּל יְמֵי חַיֶּיךָ הַלֵּילוֹת.

___

filled the *Shabbos* lamps with vinegar rather than oil. R' Chanina said to her,
"Why are you perturbed? He Who has decreed that oil should burn, shall
tell the vinegar to burn." A miracle took place and the lamps burned until the
Shabbos was over and fire had been taken from them for *havdalah* (*Ta'anis*
25). Such faith, before which the natural order of things does not stand as a
mask, which sees that everything is in the hands of Divine Providence
(הַשְׁגָּחָה פְּרָטִית) at each moment, glows with the radiance of the faith of the
Exodus when water became blood and light became night. Whoever does
not reach such a level should realize that, in his eyes, the miracle of the
Exodus has become dim, and the Torah looks askance at him.

The *Ramban* (loc. cit.) in his concluding remarks states that the purpose of
the *mitzvos* and the goal of Creation is: to believe in Hashem and give praise
to Him for having created us; that is the reason for Creation and the Creator
had no other purpose. We gather in our synagogues to say before Him in
communal fashion, "We are your creatures." All of man's service to
Hashem turns on this cardinal point — to reach a pinnacle of revealed faith
that has nothing of hesitation or dimness about it, but a wondrous light — *as
though he personally had gone out of Egypt*.

שֶׁתֵּאָמֵר יְצִיאַת מִצְרַיִם
Having the Exodus from Egypt mentioned

The Alter of Kelm   We are told to remember the Exodus twice daily, at
day's outset and at its close.

Man passes through many trials in his waking hours; he is tested by his
nature (יֵצֶר), his will and the forces of necessity. One can weather these
trials, successfully, only by a quest for, and knowledge of, the truth.

If man knows and admits that Hashem governs the world and that he is

It happened that Rabbi Eliezer, Rabbi Yehoshua, Rabbi Elazar ben Azaryah, Rabbi Akiva, and Rabbi Tarfon were reclining (at the Seder) in Bnei Brak. They discussed the Exodus all that night until their students came and said to them: 'Our teachers, it is [daybreak] time for the reading of the morning Shema.'

Rabbi Elazar ben Azaryah said: I am like a seventy-year-old man, but I could not succeed in having the Exodus from Egypt mentioned every night, until Ben Zoma expounded it: 'In order that you may remember the day you left Egypt all the days of your life.'[1] The phrase 'the days of your life' would have indicated only the days; the addition of the word 'all' includes the nights as well.

1. *Devarim* 16:3.

God's servant, as we read at the end of *Shema* — "I have taken you out of Egypt to be a God to you" — he will easily pass the tests which are put to him. If he should go off the track, he will easily put himself back on the proper path. But if he does not make this true and honest calculation, he is like the merchant who, in his impatience to turn a quick profit, sets up crooked scales. He fools only himself.

The Torah shows us what happens when we do not take the true measure of things. Pharaoh stands as an example. He made a false reckoning which took only the present into consideration. When he felt the effects of the plagues, he agreed to free Israel; when he had a breathing spell, he once more hardened his heart.

Even when he finally did send Israel off, he regretted his decision and pursued them — right into the sea, which swept the Egyptians away and drowned them.

Remembrance of the Exodus teaches us that an honest and constant weighing leads us to the path of success; the plagues of Pharaoh show us the result of a false, small-minded reckoning for the moment only.

כֹּל יְמֵי חַיֶּיךָ / All the days of your life

The Alter of Kelm Rare things, such as gold and diamonds, cost much, but have little intrinsic worth, since we can live without them. The rarer and costlier the item, the less vital it is and, in truth, the less real worth it has.

Wine is a delicious and a relatively expensive drink. Yet, if one would be

וַחֲכָמִים אוֹמְרִים, יְמֵי חַיֶּיךָ הָעוֹלָם הַזֶּה, כֹּל יְמֵי
חַיֶּיךָ לְהָבִיא לִימוֹת הַמָּשִׁיחַ.

---

asked to sacrifice half of his possessions for it, he would forgo wine. Bread and water, on the other hand, are cheap. Yet when man needs them, he will part with all that he owns. It is marvelous to see that whatever man needs has been created in abundance and can be easily found. Bread, water, and air — without which we cannot exist — are available everywhere.

If Hashem created His world along these lines, it is plausible to think that His Torah was established in a parallel fashion. Thus, when we note that we are commanded to remember the Exodus (יְצִיאַת מִצְרַיִם) twice daily without any lapses, we should conclude that it is necessary for man, like breathing air. He cannot live without it in the spiritual sense. It is the foundation of faith. It emphasizes that Hashem conducts His world and rules over it; punishes the wicked and brings redemption to those whom He loves. He who does not pay attention to the topic of the Exodus is not alive.

לְהָבִיא לִימוֹת הַמָּשִׁיחַ
. . . includes the era of the Messiah

R' Yerucham of Mir Ben Zoma was of the opinion that there would no longer be an obligation to remember the Exodus once the Messiah would have come. The prophet tells us as much: "Behold, days are coming," sayeth HASHEM, "and no longer will they say, 'By HASHEM who took the children of Israel up out of Egypt,' but, 'By HASHEM who took the children of Israel up out of all the lands to which I thrust them' " (*Yirmeyahu* 23:7-8). The other Sages felt that the requirement to remember the Exodus would not lapse, but it would assume a role secondary to that of the future Redemption. It may be compared to the man who encounters a wolf in his path and is saved from it, and speaks continually of the incident, but if he afterwards meets up with a lion and is spared, he will speak continually about his deliverance from the lion. And if at a later date he comes upon a serpent and escapes, he will forget about both the wolf and lion, and tell about his adventure with the serpent. So, too, later troubles cause Israel to forget the former ones (*Berachos* 12b).

When we are told that the Redemption-to-be will be the more important incident and the Exodus less so, our first thought is that the miracles of the Redemption-to-be and its results will be so wondrous that those of the Exodus will pale in comparison. But then, the parable would be inaccurate. The parable put the emphasis on the troubles (the wolf, lion and serpent) and not on the deliverance from them (a seemingly more appropriate parable would be that of a man who was happy, because he had earned a profit of a thousand pieces of gold and, later, forgot the joy he had experienced upon gaining the thousand, when he made a million).

> **But the Sages declare that 'the days of your life' would mean only the present world; the addition of 'all' includes the era of the Messiah.**

But, in truth, there is a qualitative, not a quantitative, difference between the miracles of the Exodus and the Redemption-to-come. The miracles of the Exodus were departures from the natural order of things — light turned to darkness, the sea to dry land — and everyone saw "I am Hashem in the midst of the earth" (*Shemos* 8:18), the sole Ruler of nature, Who does as He pleases. But in the future, all eyes will open wide to see and realize that all that exists, the natural process included, is in itself miraculous. And this will become clearer and clearer from the very troubles themselves — a single lamb, Israel, survives in the midst of seventy wolves, the nations of the world (*Yoma* 69); in every generation they rise up to annihilate us, but the Holy One saves us from their hand.

This conception of the difference between the miracle within the framework of nature and that which lies beyond the natural process underlies the dual pronouncement which Hashem made to Moshe just prior to the Exodus. Moshe asked: "And they will say to me, 'What is His Name?' What shall I say to them?" (*Shemos* 3:13). Israel will ask what kind of program for governing the world will Hashem follow when He reveals Himself to deliver us. And Hashem told Moshe to reply, "I Will Be (אֶהְיֶה) sent me to you" (ibid. v. 14). This represents the revelation of Hashem through obvious miracles, which are clearly miracles to everyone, such as occurred in Egypt. But in addition, the Holy One informed Moshe of another program within the framework of which He conducts the affairs of the world — I Will Be Who Will Be (אֶהְיֶה אֲשֶׁר אֶהְיֶה) — which is explained to mean: Just as I was with them in this exile, I will be with them in other exiles (*Berachos* 9). The *Ramban* interpreted this to mean: I will be with them in all their troubles; they will call out to Me and I will answer them.

The miracle of "I am with them in all their troubles" and of "they will call out to Me and I will answer them" is no less a miracle than those of the Exodus, even though there is a vast difference between them. The miracle of continued Jewish survival in exile is a concealed (נִסְתָּר) miracle. But because it is not obvious it is an even greater miracle. For it shows that there is really no such thing in the world as a "natural" order. When this basic idea is widely accepted in the future, the obvious miracles of the Exodus, which are so easily seen, will pale into relative insignificance against this "secret" miracle.

Truth to tell, the "secret" miracle (נֵס נִסְתָּר) and "'obvious" miracle (נֵס גָּלוּי) are distinct only from the usual human perspective. The man of faith, however, will see a miracle in the process of nature; the heretic, unfortunately, will shut his eyes tight and stop up his heart to even the most obvious of miracles.

בָּרוּךְ הַמָּקוֹם, בָּרוּךְ הוּא. בָּרוּךְ שֶׁנָּתַן תּוֹרָה לְעַמּוֹ יִשְׂרָאֵל, בָּרוּךְ הוּא. כְּנֶגֶד אַרְבָּעָה בָנִים דִּבְּרָה תוֹרָה: אֶחָד חָכָם, וְאֶחָד רָשָׁע, וְאֶחָד תָּם, וְאֶחָד שֶׁאֵינוֹ יוֹדֵעַ לִשְׁאוֹל.

כְּנֶגֶד אַרְבָּעָה בָנִים דִּבְּרָה תוֹרָה
Concerning four sons does the Torah speak

The Alter of Novharodok   The wicked son (רָשָׁע) is not the heretic who denies the existence of Hashem and the validity of His Torah. He, seemingly, is the kind who believes in God and performs the *mitzvos*. He just misses here, and compromises there. He does not see the need for the scrupulous adherence to every minute detail, nor does he think that he is able to change his temperament. After all, he cannot understand that there is any need to do so. He asks, "Why do you make a (difficult) labor of this? — מָה הָעֲבוֹדָה הַזֹּאת לָכֶם." To his mind, Judaism is not a religion of the extreme.

He is told: "Had he been there, he would not have been redeemed." The entire "going out of Egypt" (יְצִיאַת מִצְרַיִם) was an act of sacrifice, an act of the extreme. It involved drastic about-faces and changes from the normal patterns of behavior. "We shall do" (נַעֲשֶׂה) preceded "We shall hear" (נִשְׁמָע). It was a period in which "You (Israel) followed after Me (Hashem) in the desert, in a land unsown" (*Yirmeyahu* 2:2); a period in which the questions "What shall we eat? How shall we live?" were left unasked. Whoever feared the extreme, whoever refused to alter his pattern of life-as-usual remained behind in Egypt. And in our day and age, too, whoever refuses to master his traits is mastered by them and chained within them for all time.

❀ ❀ ❀

The wise son (חָכָם) knows that his personal considerations must yield to the demands of the Torah. He asks how he might best uphold the testimonies, statutes and laws without permitting the influence of outside factors, or allowing false compromises. He asks how, for example, one might reach the level of R' Yehudah the son of R' Ilai.

R' Yehudah found a break in the fence surrounding his vineyard and thought about repairing the breach. But remembering that it was *Shabbos* and the thought was not proper to the day, he decided that he would never mend the fence (*Shabbos* 150). Yet the improper thought merely passed through his mind and one is allowed to *think* of weekday matters on *Shabbos* (*Shulchan Aruch, Orach Chaim* 307:14). Nevertheless, R' Yehudah determined to leave the damage untouched in the future. Furthermore, he declared the vineyard ownerless, lest a trespasser enter and violate the

Blessed is the Omnipresent; Blessed is He. Blessed is the One Who has given the Torah to His people Israel; Blessed is He. Concerning four sons does the Torah speak: a wise one, a wicked one, a simple one, and one who is unable to ask.

---

commandment against stealing. And this, though the vineyard was his source of income. But how could his decision, in any way, correct that improper thought which had come and gone on its way?

R' Yehudah, however, understood that as long as the thought would not be implemented, it would float free and not leave its mark and would not harm him. And if, besides, because of that random thought, he would never mend his fence, he would gain a fuller appreciation of the gravity of *Shabbos*.

Were someone to have asked him, "What about the future? Doesn't the income from the vineyard provide you with the possibility of studying Torah and elevating yourself?" he would have answered, "Had I repaired the damage, I would have caused the thought to come to life and brought an immediate decline of the spirit in its wake. I could not sacrifice the present for a spiritual gain in the future. A proper future cannot be based on a shaky present." R' Yehudah was willing to sacrifice what might be, for a perfect moment of the here and now.

The story has an amazing ending. With the close of *Shabbos* a miracle occurred. A fruit tree grew, stopping up the break in the fence, and R' Yehudah and his family were to enjoy its fruits. Because he had declared his vineyard ownerless and decided to depend on a miracle, a miracle did happen.

The wise son asks: "How can one reach that lofty state where only the testimonies, statutes and laws have significance?" And we reply: "One may not eat dessert after the final taste of the Passover offering" — we have no personal considerations over and above the Torah.

❧ ❧ ❧

The third son is the simpleton (תָּם). He agrees with the desired goal and knows that personal desires should be suppressed; that one should dedicate himself completely to Hashem's service. What he does not understand is the constant need for systematic study of *mussar* (ethics) and unceasing labor towards the desired goal. When he views the totality of the laws of *Pesach*, he asks, "What's this?" He imagines that there is an easy shortcut without toil.

And you will say to him, "With a strong hand did HASHEM take us out of Egypt." If you think that there is a way of reducing the route, why, then, were the strong arm, the ten plagues and the other varied wonders and miracles necessary? Why did the Holy One not slay the firstborns

חָכָם מָה הוּא אוֹמֵר? מָה הָעֵדֹת וְהַחֻקִּים
וְהַמִּשְׁפָּטִים אֲשֶׁר צִוָּה יהוה אֱלֹהֵינוּ
אֶתְכֶם?¹ וְאַף אַתָּה אֱמָר לוֹ כְּהִלְכוֹת הַפֶּסַח,

immediately, and free Israel? This shows what great stock we should place
in persuasion. We see how the will works to harden Pharaoh's heart. Even
after a plague, he stubbornly refuses to release Israel. And when he became
aware of the hand of Hashem and did send them forth, he pursued them
and, finally, drowned in the sea. Man needs a strong arm when he labors to
control his will.

The worst of the four sons is the one who does not know how to ask
(שֶׁאֵינוֹ יוֹדֵעַ לִשְׁאוֹל). He knows nothing. He is unaware of Torah, or of
overcoming one's will. He is completely imprisoned within the shell of self
and everything he does is for himself only. With such a one, you must open
him up (אַתְּ פְּתַח לוֹ). Make a window in that shell of his; let him see wherein
he wallows. Let him know that his life is a race for the meaningless. He
wishes to grasp all the honor and wealth of the world; what he has, he does
not wish to have. He desires that which is beyond him and in striving for it,
he loses that which he already possesses. The opening you make for him will
take him out of his private shell of Egypt to a spiritual redemption.

מָה הָעֵדֹת וְהַחֻקִּים
What are the testimonies, decrees . . .

The Alter of Kelm Man finds great difficulty withstanding the flood
brought on by his desires and will. As *Chazal* have said:
The soul of man lusts for robbing and the carnal (*Chagigah* 11); the majority
of mankind commit robbery (*Bava Basra* 165).

The Torah says: "Do not put HASHEM, your God, to the test as you tested
[Him] at Massah" (*Devarim* 6:16). The *Ramban* feels that such testing of
Hashem was treated as a sin which they had committed, because it had
already been verified to them by signs and wonders that Moshe was the
prophet of God who spoke in God's name, and that what he said was true;
it was, then, not befitting to demand further tests. The Torah continues:
"Do, indeed, preserve the commandments of HASHEM, His testimonies and
decrees" — the *Ramban* sees that the stress is on the *testimonies*, those
commandments which bear witness to the miracles which were carried out
for Israel's sake, *mitzvos* such as the *Pesach*-offering, *matzah* and *succah* —
"that it might be well for you and you will come and inherit the good land
which HASHEM swore to your ancestors" (ibid. vs. 17-18). This is the sense of
the flow of the *pesukim*, says the *Ramban*: A man who saw the miracles
with his own eyes would not put Hashem to the test. He would believe in
Him and fulfill the decrees (חֻקִּים) which he does not understand. Therefore,
we ought to keep watch over the *mitzvos*, the commandments which bear

The wise son — what does he say? 'What are the testimonies, decrees, and ordinances which HASHEM, our God, has commanded you?'[1] Therefore explain to him the laws of the Pesach offering:

1. *Devarim* 6:20.

witness to the miracles of Divine Providence (עֵדֹת) and because of them, we will also fulfill the decrees, trusting that He will grant us benefits and keep His promise made to our forefathers.

This presents us both with a basic idea and a practical guide on how to overcome the blandishments of the evil will (יֵצֶר הָרָע) and the trials of life. We must absorb the testimonies to God's Providence and His miracles — such as *Pesach* and *Succos* — which are well known and are passed on from generation to generation. Are they not, as yet, present and with us? Egypt still exists. *Shabbos*, which points to the renewal of Creation, is alive and well; as the *Kuzari* noted, the day of *Shabbos* bears its Hebrew name in all languages. I have investigated the matter and find that his statement still stands true. The Temple Mount (הַר הַבַּיִת) and *Eretz Yisrael* are still with us. The Western Wall (כֹּתֶל מַעֲרָבִי) still stands. And not long ago some Temple vessels (כְּלֵי מִקְדָּשׁ), which are still to be found in their vaults, were sent from Rome to an exhibition in Chicago along with a letter from the evil Titus in which he boasts of his might in conquering such a Temple. He was a tyrannical, powerful ruler and if he says that the conquest of the second *Beis HaMikdash* required great might, it certainly did. How much more power was required to overcome the first *Beis HaMikdash!*

If man will labor to implant the *testimonies*, his faith will become both tangible and anchored within him: He will be able to build watch towers and fortifications upon their firm foundations. Nothing will turn him astray — and indeed, all that occurs is a difficult trial.

The Torah testifies to the possibility that a false prophet will come and will work signs and portents and Heaven forbid that we listen to him: "For HASHEM your God tries you to know whether you love HASHEM" (*Devarim* 13:4). Hashem brings these trials to pass, because He demands that man establish his faith on a firm foundation. He wishes that intelligence, the precious gift which He bestowed on man, not go to waste. For intelligence is a fortified city, a strong wall which all trials cannot breach. With contemplation of the testimonial commandments, man lays the foundation of his faith on his intelligence. Then it is that he can obey the decrees (חֻקִּים) and withstand all trials and temptations with ease.

וְהַחֻקִּים וְהַמִּשְׁפָּטִים /*Decrees and ordinances*

R' Avraham Grodzinski of Slobodka

The ordinances (מִשְׁפָּטִים) are defined as laws which rest on rational precepts. Decrees (חֻקִּים) are those which do not have a humanly under-

stood reason, such as the prohibitions against eating pork — חֲזִיר, or wearing clothes which contain a mixture of linen and wool — שַׁעַטְנֵז; the freeing of a childless widow from marriage with a brother-in-law — חֲלִיצָה; the purification rites of the former leper — טָהֳרַת הַמְצֹרָע (*Yoma* 67b). The Midrash also says: Our evil nature (יֵצֶר הָרָע) casts doubts on four matters and all are called decrees (חֻקִּים) — the levirate marriage (יִבּוּם); the prohibitions against hybrids (כִּלְאַיִם); the goat sent off into the wilderness on *Yom Kippur* (שָׂעִיר הַמִּשְׁתַּלֵּחַ לַעֲזָאזֵל) and the Red Heifer (פָּרָה אֲדֻמָּה). They are decrees, because each contains contrary elements. A brother's wife is normally forbidden. But if she is left a childless widow, her brother-in-law is *commanded* to marry her. It is forbidden to wear a mix of linen and wool. Yet it is permitted to attach the strand of blue wool of the *tzitzis* (צִיצִית) to a linen garment (*Yalkut Shimoni, Vayikra* 16).

We are given the impression that there are relatively few decrees. But this seems to fly in the face of the facts. The Midrash considers the Red Heifer a matter of decree, because of the seeming contradiction built into its laws; it (or rather its ashes) is meant to purify the defiled and nevertheless, whoever is involved in the process of preparing the ashes or the purification becomes impure himself. True, the law is not understandable, but is it less so than all the other laws of purity and impurity? Do we understand the degrees, distinctions, ways of becoming defiled and the attaining of purity after a waiting period of specific days by immersion in the still waters of a *mikveh* or the running waters of a spring? A whole order, a sixth of the *mishnayos* is devoted to these matters and they are a closed book, beyond our comprehension. All of *Taharos* is a matter of decree. So, too, the order of *Kadashim* which deals with animal- and meal-offerings (קָרְבָּנוֹת וּמְנָחוֹת). Much has been written on it in the way of original Torah insight (חִידּוּשׁ) and the works are filled with good sense and sound conjecture (סְבָרָא), wisdom and brilliance; with definitions, comparisons and distinctions. Each detail is explained well and reflects marvelous understanding. But the overarching principle is locked away and sealed from us. What is holiness? How does the non-sacred become holy? How can an object be deprived of its holiness through redemption (פִּדְיוֹן) or unwarranted use (מְעִילָה)? The whole topic of the holy is a matter of decree. And can the order of *Moed* (מוֹעֵד) be said to present laws based on reason? Do the thirty-nine types of work (ל״ט מְלָאכוֹת) prohibited on *Shabbos* and all their derived forms fall under the heading of law based on reason? Or the order of *Nashim* (נָשִׁים)? By what chemistry does the unmarried girl become a married woman? The married woman a divorcee? And the order of *Zeraim* (זְרָעִים)? Tithes (תְּרוּמוֹת) and tenths (מַעַשְׂרוֹת), hybrids (כִּלְאַיִם) and *orlah* (עָרְלָה) are all decrees.

Even the order of *Nezikin* (נְזִיקִין), which seems to be completely a matter of reasoned law — damages, claims and payments — is very much a matter

that one may not eat dessert after the final taste of the Pesach offering.

---

of decree, not only with regard to the laws of the high courts (סַנְהֶדְרִין) and witnesses but also with respect to punishments and fines and even, perhaps, the modes of acquisition (קִנְיָן) and their distinctions. The Torah in its overall makeup is decree; there is hardly a law based on reason. And yet the Midrash found only four decrees.

The idea is novel. We do not usually think that the Torah, filled with the boundless wisdom of Heaven, is basically composed of decrees. Novel and incorrect.

Torah is wisdom and flows from the source of all wisdom. It was given to man and the very giving testifies that those who accepted it are wise: "And they will say: This great nation is none other than a wise and understanding people" (*Devarim* 4:6). Men are bound to remark about the depth of its wisdom, as it is said: "He gives wisdom to the wise" (*Daniel* 2:21). It is as the Midrash says. The entire order of *Taharos* has only a single decree of which the reason is beyond us — that of the Red Heifer; in all the order of *Moed* the only decree is the *Yom Kippur* goat sent off into the wilderness, which causes the nations to err and imagine that we do as they do (see *Ramban* to *Vayikra* 16:8); in the order of *Nashim*, only the levirate marriage and in *Zeraim* only the chapters of the hybrids; in all of *Kadashim* and *Nezikin* there is not a single decree.

It is *we* who do not understand the reasoned structure of the Torah, because we are lacking in intelligence. And we lack intelligence, because we do not make an effort to grasp it. *Chazal* have pointed this out: If you have labored and not found [what you seek], do not believe [that you have labored] (*Megillah* 6). Even that which you think you have discovered is not true discovery.

The facts prove this. We cannot distinguish between a rational law (מִשְׁפָּט) and a Divine decree (חוק). Such inability to differentiate is the fruit of lack of knowledge (the *havdalah* which divides or differentiates *Shabbos* at its close from the weekdays is placed in the blessing of *Shemoneh Esrei* which speaks of Hashem's granting understanding. For without understanding we cannot make differentiations — *Yerushalmi Berachos* 5:2). The inability to differentiate between principles, even the most basic principles, is a far more serious problem than the inability to distinguish between details.

And yet, we don't have the slightest idea as to the essence of the *holy* or *purity*. We take them up and study them. But we are like the blind man who speaks about light — its benefits and the ways it sheds its illumination. We have a mental block; we are open, so to speak, at the edges and plugged up within. Were we not to experience this, we would not believe it. But the block is there. After all the thought and examination, labor and creative

רָשָׁע מָה הוּא אוֹמֵר? מָה הָעֲבֹדָה הַזֹּאת לָכֶם?[1] לָכֶם וְלֹא לוֹ, וּלְפִי שֶׁהוֹצִיא אֶת עַצְמוֹ מִן הַכְּלָל, כָּפַר בְּעִקָּר – וְאַף אַתָּה הַקְהֵה אֶת שִׁנָּיו וֶאֱמָר לוֹ, בַּעֲבוּר זֶה עָשָׂה יהוה לִי בְּצֵאתִי מִמִּצְרָיִם.[2] לִי וְלֹא לוֹ, אִלּוּ הָיָה שָׁם לֹא הָיָה נִגְאָל.

---

ideas, when we look at our store of knowledge we find that it is very, very superficial and shallow.

רָשָׁע מָה הוּא אוֹמֵר
The wicked son — what does he say?

_____
R' Yitzchak Waldshein
_____

The Torah formulates the questions of all but the wicked son in a similar fashion: "When your son shall ask you saying" (כִּי יִשְׁאָלְךָ בִּנְךָ לֵאמֹר). Each asks a question which expects an answer (we find, for example, "And I pleaded with Hashem saying — 'give me an answer' — *Sifri Devarim* 3). The wicked son however does not ask: "And it will be when your sons *say* to you, 'What is this service (עֲבֹדָה) to you?'" This is not a true question and he seeks no answer. He only wishes to mock!

מָה הָעֲבֹדָה הַזֹּאת לָכֶם
Of what purpose is this work to you?

_____
R' Yerucham of Mir
_____

Many have wondered how the question of the wicked son differs from that of the wise son. But there is also another problem. The Torah has given a full and dispassionate answer to the wicked son: "And you will say, 'It is the *Pesach* sacrifice to HASHEM, Who passed over the houses of the Children of Israel in Egypt . . . and He saved our houses'" (*Shemos* 12:27). Yet, we have a different answer given in the *Haggadah*. The question of the wicked son, like that of the wise son, is a serious question which has a reasonable answer; that answer is given in the Torah. But, by formulating two similar questions, the Torah indicates that, at times, even though the question is a necessary one and deserves an answer, we should bend an ear and pay attention to the tone and nuances in which the question is posed.

The heretic questions principles of faith and so, too, does Rav Saadia Gaon. But there is an essential difference. Rav Saadia's faith is firmly rooted and does not depend on the answers to the questions. It is indeed written: "know the God of your father" (*I Divrei HaYamim* 28:9). We are meant to probe the principles of faith, but with the understanding that He is "the God of your father"; do not veer away from the faith of your father.

The wicked son — what does he say? 'Of what purpose is this work to you?'[1] He says, 'To you,' thereby excluding himself. By excluding himself from the community of believers, he denies the basic principle of Judaism. Therefore, blunt his teeth and tell him: 'It is because of this that HASHEM did so for me when I went out of Egypt.'[2] 'For me,' but not for him — had he been there, he would not have been redeemed.

1. *Shemos* 12:26.   2. 13:8.

The wicked son asks, "Of what purpose is this work to you?" This question springs forth from the throat of the wicked. It is as though his taking part in the service depends on the answer. Let him know this is improper. Chastise him; blunt his teeth. Tell him that had he been there, he would not have been redeemed. This will shake him up and he will realize that he asked a wicked man's question. This answer will be sufficient.

The wise man asks, "What are the testimonies, decrees and ordinances which Hashem, our God, has commanded you?" He accepts Hashem's Divinity, but wishes to understand it. Explain the laws to him. Have him understand, just as he wishes to do.

הַקְהֵה אֶת שִׁנָּיו / Blunt his teeth

R' Yehudah Leib Chasman

The four sons should not be understood as four distinct personalities. The traits exemplified by them all struggle within each of us. One moment we are the wise son, the next the wicked one; one instant the simple son, the next we are unable to ask.

The Torah has ways and means to strengthen us in each of our states. And for each trait there is a reasonable answer, other than for the trait of the "wicked son," whose teeth we are to blunt. What sort of an answer is that?

Know that a spark of Jewishness still glows, even within the wicked man. "He shall not repel the wayward one" (*II Shmuel* 14:14). And to the degree that he is as yet joined to his people, Israel, there is hope. Only by excluding himself from the community of believers, he denies the basic principle of Judaism. But in his innermost heart, he knows that there is no true basis to his heresy and, given a shock, he will return to whence he came.

"Blunt his teeth." Have him lose his sense of taste, both physical and spiritual. The serpent caused man to sin through desire for the fruit of the tree of knowledge; the serpent's punishment was the loss of his sense of taste — "And you shall eat dust." The wicked man, who knows the truth in his heart of hearts, cannot withstand his will and is pulled along by his desires. "Blunt his teeth;" he will lose his taste for following his desires, and will repent.

תָּם מָה הוּא אוֹמֵר? מַה זֹּאת? וְאָמַרְתָּ אֵלָיו, בְּחֹזֶק יָד הוֹצִיאָנוּ יהוה מִמִּצְרַיִם מִבֵּית עֲבָדִים.[1]

וְשֶׁאֵינוֹ יוֹדֵעַ לִשְׁאוֹל, אַתְּ פְּתַח לוֹ. שֶׁנֶּאֱמַר, וְהִגַּדְתָּ לְבִנְךָ בַּיּוֹם הַהוּא לֵאמֹר, בַּעֲבוּר זֶה עָשָׂה יהוה לִי בְּצֵאתִי מִמִּצְרָיִם.[2]

יָכוֹל מֵרֹאשׁ חֹדֶשׁ, תַּלְמוּד לוֹמַר בַּיּוֹם הַהוּא. אִי בַּיּוֹם הַהוּא, יָכוֹל מִבְּעוֹד יוֹם, תַּלְמוּד

There can also be a spiritual loss of taste, a loss of a drive for the things of the spirit, a loss of longing for the spiritual. When a man suffers such a loss, his soul licks at the dust.

We warn the wicked man that if, heaven forbid, he reaches that depth, there is no hope for redemption. This is , in reality, a warning to each and everyone, to the "wicked" within himself. He must blunt his desires and take care, lest the longing to rise be extinguished, lest he lick dust, in a spiritual sense, and sever the last thread and lose hope for the Redemption.

וְהִגַּדְתָּ לְבִנְךָ / *You shall tell your son*

R' Yerucham of Mir

Judaism is, in its essence, a tradition (מְסוֹרֶת) handed down from father to son, from teacher to pupil — "And you shall tell your son."

When the angel revealed himself to Gideon and said, "Brave hero, Hashem is with you," Gideon replied, "Excuse me, my lord, is Hashem with us? Then why has all this happened to us? Where are all the wonders of which our fathers have told us, saying that Hashem took us up out of Egypt? And now He has abandoned us and given us into the palm of Midian!" (*Shoftim* 6:12-13). *Rashi*, there, explains that it was *Pesach* and Gideon told the angel, "Yesterday my father recited the *Hallel* (song of praise) before me and I heard him say, 'When Israel went forth from Egypt . . .' and now He has abandoned us." Gideon speaks as if all his knowledge is a hand-me-down. He, on his own, knows nothing — "Our fathers told us wonders;" "Yesterday my father recited the *Hallel*." And so it is. The basis for everything is the tradition handed down by the fathers and faith in what the wise say.

The purpose of the Revelation at Sinai was: "so that the people will hear when I speak to you (Moshe) and will believe in you, too, forever" (*Shemos* 19:9). This will happen because: "You shall make them known to your sons and your sons' sons. The day on which you stood before HASHEM your God

The simple son — what does he say? 'What is this?' Tell him: 'With a strong hand did Hashem take us out of Egypt, from the house of bondage.'[1]

As for the son who is unable to ask, you must initiate the subject for him, as it is stated: You shall tell your son on that day: 'It is because of this that Hashem did so for me when I went out of Egypt.'[2]

One might think that the obligation to discuss the Exodus commences with the first day of the month of Nissan, but the Torah says: 'You shall tell your son on that day.' But the expression 'on that day' could be understood to mean only during the day-

---

1. *Shemos* 13:14.   2. 13:8.

---

at Chorev'' (*Devarim* 4:9-10). The tradition is handed down from generation to generation. R' Eliezer the Great said of himself: I have learned much Torah and it is no more than what a dog can lap up of the water of the sea; I have taught much Torah and yet my pupils have taken away from me no more than does the make-up brush when it is drawn from the tube (*Sanhedrin* 68). And yet it is told of this same R' Eliezer that once when he sojourned in the Galil he was asked thirty questions concerning the laws of *Succah*. To twelve he replied, "I have heard (the answer)" and to eighteen he said, "I have not heard." They said, "Is all of what you have to say excerpts taken only from that which you have heard?" To which he answered, "You force me to say something which I have not heard from my teachers, (namely,) I have never said anything which I did not hear from my teacher."

Torah is just that — tradition and inheritance! "The Torah which Moshe commanded us is an inheritance handed down to the congregation of Yaakov'' (*Devarim* 33:4)!

יָכוֹל מֵרֹאשׁ חֹדֶשׁ, תַּלְמוּד לוֹמַר בַּיּוֹם הַהוּא
*One might think that the obligation to discuss the Exodus
commences with the first day of the month of Nissan,
but the Torah says: You shall tell your son on that day.*

R' Eliahu Dessler   We are accustomed to think that the Torah commanded us to set aside one day of the year to tell the story of the Exodus at length. And we search the calendar for an appropriate date.

But it is really the other way around. It is the date, on which the Exodus from Egypt occurred, which creates the opportunity and aids in feeling, and implanting, the sense of the miracles and their message. That day possesses

לוֹמַר בַּעֲבוּר זֶה. בַּעֲבוּר זֶה לֹא אָמַרְתִּי אֶלָּא בְּשָׁעָה שֶׁיֵּשׁ מַצָּה וּמָרוֹר מֻנָּחִים לְפָנֶיךָ.

מִתְּחִלָּה, עוֹבְדֵי עֲבוֹדָה זָרָה הָיוּ אֲבוֹתֵינוּ, וְעַכְשָׁו קֵרְבָנוּ הַמָּקוֹם לַעֲבוֹדָתוֹ.

---

a special quality which makes it a time to contemplate the deliverance from Egypt, whereas on all other days we are satisfied with a short reminder and nothing more. Even if we were to enlarge upon it on other days, it would not have its proper effect. For this reason, too, we relate the story at night when *matzah* and *maror* lie before you. It is then, when you stand at the very hour when the event took place in Egypt, with the same articles of *mitzvah* of long ago before your eyes, that the picture is complete. Then it is that under the spell of the totality of impressions, we have the feeling of *as though he, personally, had gone out from Egypt*.

Yet, why indeed is there a particular effect, if we develop, enlarge upon and explain the tale of the Exodus on this date or another; or when *matzah* and *maror* lie before you or not?

Shlomo HaMelech said: "the wise man shall listen and add to his knowledge" (*Mishlei* 1:5), to which the Midrash comments: This is Moshe. The Holy One said: Make a serpent for yourself and place it on a pole and it will be that whoever is bitten (by the plague of desert snakes) and sees it shall live (*Bamidbar* 21:9). Moshe was perplexed and did not know of what material to make the serpent. He decided to form it out of bronze because in the Holy Tongue we have a play on words (serpent — נָחָשׁ; bronze — נְחֹשֶׁת). And thus Moshe added to his store of learning (*Yalkut Shimoni, Yehoshua* 15).

Was Moshe interested in wit, in poetical expression, or wordplay? The directive was to lift the serpent aloft on a pole. This was meant to impress upon Israel that it was not the serpents which had brought death to the people, but sin (*Berachos* 33). They were to lift their eyes heavenward and repent (*Rosh Hashannah* 29). Why was the byplay of language used?

However, the more complete the artistry, the greater will be the effect of an action. And language makes its impression on a man. The repetitive phrase (נְחַשׁ נְחֹשֶׁת) might very well be the factor which would arrest, for a moment, the frantic gallop of his life and give pause to his confusion of soul. It would allow an idea to pierce through to his heart. He would realize that the punishment of serpents falls from Heaven. Language, like each addition which is the fruit of thought, creates and completes a whole world of the spirit. [Perhaps the phrase bronze serpent (נְחַשׁ נְחֹשֶׁת) contains a less obvious aspect. The serpent may allude to the primordial snake in *Gan Eden* which goaded Eve into sinning and which represents man's evil nature (יֵצֶר הָרָע) and, as in the verse: "your forehead is brazen" (*Yeshayahu* 48:4), the bronze symbolizes stiff-neckedness.]

time; therefore the Torah adds: 'It is because of this that HASHEM did so for me when I went out of Egypt.' The pronoun 'this' implies something tangible, thus, 'You shall tell your son' applies only when matzah and maror lie before you — at the Seder.

Originally our ancestors were idol worshipers, but now the Omnipresent has brought us near to His

---

בַּעֲבוּר זֶה . . . בְּשָׁעָה שֶׁיֵּשׁ מַצָּה וּמָרוֹר מֻנָּחִים לְפָנֶיךָ
Because of this . . . when matzah and maror lie before you

R' Yerucham of Mir   The *mitzvos* of the *Seder* night are designed to have a man "regard himself as though he personally had gone out from Egypt." We would imagine that this feeling is engendered by the study of what has been written on the topic and contemplation of the miracles which occurred. But whoever thinks so has no idea as to what the process of education is. Knowledge does shed light, but it is the language of the mind. It cannot speak to the emotions or effect a change in a man. Action, however, is the language of the body. And it is the acts of the *mitzvos* which can bring about change. "You shall keep the *mitzvos* and do them" — וַעֲשִׂיתֶם אֹתָם (*Vayikra* 19:37), it is as if you create (literally, make) yourselves — עֲשִׂיתֶם אֶת עַצְמְכֶם (*Sanhedrin* 99).

Shlomo HaMelech in speaking of the education of the child says: "Bring up each youngster in the way best suited for him" — not by imparting knowledge, giving lofty lectures, but in accordance with his nature and character. And then: "even when he becomes old, he will not turn away from it" (*Mishlei* 22:6). In a like manner, when the adult educates himself, he must train the "youngster" within himself, his rash impulses. They can only be trained by the language of unceasing action.

Hence both the learned and the unlearned must observe the act of retelling the story of the Exodus from Egypt. And no matter how comprehensive the narration: "whoever has not explained the following three things on Passover has not fulfilled his duty, namely: *Pesach* — the Passover offering; *Matzah* — the Unleavened Bread; *Maror* — the Bitter Herbs. These refer to acts of eating. These acts will bring a man to see himself as one of those who left Egypt in the Exodus. "The more one tells about the Exodus, the more he is praiseworthy" (הֲרֵי זֶה מְשֻׁבָּח). We might, perhaps, understand this as the more does he become improved (שֶׁבַח may be a praise or improvement); the more he does, the greater the effect on him for the good.

קֵרְבָנוּ הַמָּקוֹם לַעֲבוֹדָתוֹ
The Omnipresent has brought us near to His service

R' Yerucham of Mir   These words give the whole of the purpose of our deliverance from Egypt in abbreviated form. We were

שֶׁנֶּאֱמַר, וַיֹּאמֶר יְהוֹשֻׁעַ אֶל כָּל הָעָם, כֹּה אָמַר
יהוה אֱלֹהֵי יִשְׂרָאֵל, בְּעֵבֶר הַנָּהָר יָשְׁבוּ אֲבוֹתֵיכֶם
מֵעוֹלָם, תֶּרַח אֲבִי אַבְרָהָם וַאֲבִי נָחוֹר, וַיַּעַבְדוּ

---

taken out from under the hand of Pharaoh to be free; free to serve Hashem.

This attitude is reflected in the *Ramban's* comments on the verse: "Fear HASHEM your God and serve Him" (*Devarim* 6:13) — your relationship to Him should be at all times like that of a bought slave who constantly serves his master; who sees his own needs as secondary to those of his lord. And the principle is stated quite explicitly: "Because the Children of Israel are servants to Me; they are My servants whom I have taken out of the land of Egypt" (*Vayikra* 25:55); I have taken them out so that they might be free for, and given over to, My service. *Pesach* is called 'the time of our freedom' (זְמַן חֵרוּתֵנוּ). We are *free* to be, in the terms of the opening phrase of the *Hallel*, servants of Hashem (עַבְדֵי ה׳), which *Chazal* interpret, by adding: and not slaves of Pharaoh (*Megillah* 14a). Our freedom from Pharaoh was given to us on the condition that we be servants of Hashem.

When we recite the *Shema*, we pronounce the paragraph of *Shema* (שְׁמַע יִשְׂרָאֵל), with which we accept upon ourselves the yoke of Heaven's Majesty (קַבָּלַת עוֹל מַלְכוּת שָׁמַיִם), before the paragraph of *Vehaya im shamoa* (וְהָיָה אִם שָׁמֹעַ). That represents the acceptance of the yoke of *mitzvos* (קַבָּלַת עוֹל מִצְוֹת) which can only follow and not precede the acceptance of God's kingdom (*Berachos* 13). With the departure from Egypt, Israel as a nation also accepted the Majesty of Hashem first, and afterwards took upon themselves the *mitzvos* when they received the Torah.

The cardinal principle which we should grasp on *Pesach* is: *and now the Omnipresent has brought us near to His service* — a thought upon which we should contemplate throughout *Pesach* and, most especially, during prayer, and while reciting the *Shema* and *Hallel*.

אֱלֹהֵי יִשְׂרָאֵל / God of Israel

The Alter of Kelm

The whole of creation belongs to God; He is the Master of the universe. Yet He is called אֱלֹהֵי יִשְׂרָאֵל — "God of Israel" and we are called the עַם ה׳ — "nation of HASHEM" (*Yechezkel* 36:20). Why is there this particular relationship between God and Israel?

Now, not everyone who sits before a great teacher can be thought of as his pupil — R' Chaim of Volohzin would say that he was not fit to be called a student of the *Gaon* of Vilna, because he had not learned enough from him. So, too, the nations of the world are not fit to be called "nations of God." For they hardly recognize His greatness, nor follow His commands.

If a man would contemplate himself, he would be overwhelmed by the degree to which he shakes off the yoke of Heavenly dominion and by how

service, as it is written: Joshua said to all the people, 'So says HASHEM, God of Israel: Your fathers always lived beyond the Euphrates River, Terach the father of Avraham and Nachor, and they served other

---

little he conducts himself in the ways of the Torah. Alas and alack! Is he really fit to be called a "man of God" or can God be truly "his" God?

תֶּרַח אֲבִי אַבְרָהָם / *Terach the father of Avraham*

R' Eliahu Dessler

Why introduce Terach into the *Haggadah*?

Chazal explain that when the Torah directs us "to love Hashem with all your heart" (*Devarim* 6:5), we are to involve both wills — the evil inclination as well as the good (*Berachos* 61). At times, by witnessing wickedness and retreating from it, a man is aroused to turn to the good with greater drive. Evil becomes a force which propels him to the good.

The prophet Ovadiah, who was a minister in the court of Achav, was the one best suited to prophesy about Edom. "Let Ovadiah who lived in the company of two evil people (Achav and Izevel) and did not learn from their wicked ways come and say prophecy on Esav (the forefather of Edom) who dwelt in the company of two upright individuals (Yitzchak and Rivkah) and did not learn from their actions" (*Sanhedrin* 39).

Esav symbolizes evil at its worst; his heavenly representative (שַׂר) is Satan; his descendants are the Amalekite. Such evil can only develop in one who dwelt with the upright. Every attempt to educate him foundered against that stubbornness which implanted the evil in him until it reached the depths which it did.

Ovadiah, in contrast, who lived among the wicked, did not learn from their actions. They drove him to hate falsehood to the utmost and to turn to the holy.

Our teacher, Moshe, the prince of prophets who ascended to Heaven and received the Torah, could not have reached such heights had he not been brought up in Pharaoh's palace, in the very heart of the temple of impurity. That itself drove him towards the holy, so much so, that he became the "man of God." The people of Israel who were to receive the Torah did not prepare themselves for such an eventuality in some heavenly atmosphere. To the contrary, because they were sunk in the ultimate corruption (מ״ט שַׁעֲרֵי טוּמְאָה) of the Egyptian exile, they were driven to cry out to Hashem (*Shemos* 2:23). That cry began the process of severance from Egypt which led to their receiving the Torah. The Redemption of the future, too, will come to a generation in which all are worthy of it, or all are sinners (*Sanhedrin* 98). It is the completely wicked, in particular, who can rise up and up, if they are powerfully driven by repentance (תְּשׁוּבָה). For then they see to what a state of degradation their association with evil has brought them.

We open the account of the Exodus with a reference to the greatness of

אֱלֹהִים אֲחֵרִים. וָאֶקַּח אֶת אֲבִיכֶם אֶת אַבְרָהָם
מֵעֵבֶר הַנָּהָר, וָאוֹלֵךְ אוֹתוֹ בְּכָל אֶרֶץ כְּנָעַן, וָאַרְבֶּה
אֶת זַרְעוֹ, וָאֶתֶּן לוֹ אֶת יִצְחָק. וָאֶתֵּן לְיִצְחָק אֶת
יַעֲקֹב וְאֶת עֵשָׂו, וָאֶתֵּן לְעֵשָׂו אֶת הַר שֵׂעִיר לָרֶשֶׁת
אוֹתוֹ, וְיַעֲקֹב וּבָנָיו יָרְדוּ מִצְרָיִם.[1]

Avraham, the son of Terach. Terach served idols in the generation of a
Nimrod who rebelled against his Creator, in an age which was the
culmination of the "ten generations which had angered Hashem" (*Avos*
5:2). When Avraham became aware of his Creator and fully perceived the
terrible evil which surrounded him, he rose to a state of holiness which can
never be done away with.

וָאֶקַּח אֶת אֲבִיכֶם / Then I took your father

[Avraham was the first who, on his own, wondered about the origins of
creation and sought out the Creator. *Chazal* compare him to a man who sees
a palace alit and asks, "Can there be such a palace without an owner?" The
lord of the palace looks out and says to him, "I am he!" By this image the
initiative came from our forefather Avraham, yet the account in *Yehoshua* tell
us: "Then I took your father" (*Yehoshua* 24:3). It was *I* who caused him to
wonder and be aroused and find Me out. "Then I took your father Avraham
from beyond (מֵעֵבֶר — literally, *across, the other side of*) the river" — like a
father who *crosses* his child from one side of the road to the other.]

R' Yehudah Leib Chasman   It was not enough that Avraham came to
realize that the Creator existed. He had to
uproot himself and break his former ties. The "Go you forth (לֶךְ לְךָ) from
your land and your birthplace and your father's home" (*Bereishis* 12:1) was
one of the ten trials of our forefather Avraham.

But he was not alone in this. His nephew Lot was also involved in the
same trial. On the surface, Lot's test was the more difficult, because he had
not been given a Divine command and, nevertheless, went forth. Lot pulled
up his roots and went forth. However, he went beyond what was required;
he went all the way to Sodom!

It is insufficient to move only in terms of space — from one place to
another; from Ur Kasdim to Eretz Yisrael, or from home to the *yeshivah*.
There must be a qualitative uprootal. One must sever oneself from the
essence and atmosphere of what was to become a new person, a *yeshivah*
student, a *ben yeshivah* — a son of the *yeshivah*. Our forefather Avraham
was commanded to leave not only his *country* — the physical surroundings,
but also his "birthplace and father's home" — his former set of mind. Lot's
change was a change of locale; he did not change his essential self. And

gods. Then I took your father Avraham from beyond the river and led him through all the land of Canaan. I multiplied his offspring and gave him Yitzchak. To Yitzchak I gave Yaakov and Esav; to Esav I gave Mount Seir to inherit, but Yaakov and his children went down to Egypt."[1]

1. Yehoshua 24:2-4.

---

when he faced a trial — a trifling desire for good pasture — he descended to Sodom.

וָאֶתֵּן לְיִצְחָק אֶת יַעֲקֹב וְאֶת עֵשָׂו
To Yitzchak I gave Yaakov and Esav

The Alter of Novharodok The topic of Esav is a puzzling one. What is the difference between Yaakov and Esav? We are told that Esav came from the field and he was faint. Yaakov was cooking lentils and Esav asked, "Fill me, I beg you, with some of this red, red (אָדֹם) stuff" (ibid. 25:30). Therefore he called him Edom (אֱדוֹם — Red). Is a man given a name that will ring down through the generations because of a chance luckless expression? And what is, indeed, improper about the expression? Let us assume that it is improper. Yet, *Chazal* tell us Esav committed five serious sins on that day — among them, he denied the existence of God; he murdered; he committed adultery. But it is the innocent meal of the dish of lentils which gives him his name Edom, the Red. Yaakov had long aspired to possess the birthright of the firstborn. Yet, how did he know that he had chanced upon an opportune moment and Esav would agree to the sale?

There is, however, a single answer which can be suggested to clear up all the questions and difficulties. All the bad faults arise through some superficial illusion, or false, external glitter. And a man rushes in haste and does not pause for a moment to examine the sight and see the lie at its core. Were he to examine and analyze things as they really are, he would not be taken in by external coloration, which leads him astray.

For example, *Chazal* say that on that day, when Esav came faint and weary from the fields, our forefather Avraham had passed away and Yaakov cooked the lentils for the occasion as they were a food customarily given to mourners. The lentils are symbolic of mourning. They are round, representing the wheel of life which turns round and round with its continually returning lamentation; they are smooth without a break, a "mouth," like the mourner who has no "mouth" and sits in silence. But such symbolism has meaning to one who contemplates. Esav sees nothing of this; he sees only the obvious — the colorful red outer covering which draws attention. If that is what he's like, he'll certainly agree to sell his birthright — a matter of the spirit — for the here-and-now dish of lentils. He is interested in the

בָּרוּךְ שׁוֹמֵר הַבְטָחָתוֹ לְיִשְׂרָאֵל, בָּרוּךְ הוּא. שֶׁהַקָּדוֹשׁ בָּרוּךְ הוּא חִשַּׁב אֶת הַקֵּץ, לַעֲשׂוֹת כְּמָה שֶׁאָמַר לְאַבְרָהָם אָבִינוּ בִּבְרִית בֵּין

---

superficial and the momentary. "Therefore, he called him Edom."

R' Yehudah Leib Chasman: *Chazal* say that Yaakov and Esav divided the worlds between them. Yaakov chose the World-to-Come — עוֹלָם הַבָּא; Esav the world of here-and-now — עוֹלָם הַזֶּה (*Tana D'Vei Eliahu Zuta* 19). But this should not be taken at face value. Does not Israel have any pleasure from this world? The Torah itself writes that if one follows its precepts he will gain all that is good in both worlds!

What is meant is that, in all things, Esav sees only the outer world and Yaakov penetrates to the inner essence of things, to the World-to-Come facet in this world.

We can give a parable. It is as if a man were to see a field high with grain, ears bulging. He imagines that the farmer has sweated laboriously for what he gazes upon. But all that he sees will become chaff and hay; the wind will make off with it. It is only the small grains hidden in the ears standing on the high stalks — that which the man cannot see — which is important. It is for them that the owner of the field labored; for them he plowed and planted. It is they which he will harvest and store and from them he will prepare his bread.

❦ ❦ ❦

Yaakov and Esav stand apart. Esav is "the man of the field" and Yaakov "dwells in the tents" (*Bereishis* 25:27). Esav stands without and Yaakov within. Esav goes afield led by outer appearances, by the color and glitter; Yaakov examines things and chooses the inner essence.

R' Yerucham of Mir — Yaakov and Esav represent two approaches towards worship of, and service to, God. Thus, Yitzchak's love for Esav (*Bereishis* 25:28) was not without rhyme or reason. He loved him, because Esav represented basic evil. For it is through bending evil, our evil inclination (יֵצֶר הָרָע), to our will that we serve God.

That thought lies behind the following Rabbinic interpretation: וַיַּרְא אֱלֹהִים אֶת כָּל אֲשֶׁר עָשָׂה וְהִנֵּה טוֹב מְאֹד — And God saw all that He had made and behold it was very good (*Bereishis* 1:31) — behold it was very good, this is the good spirit (יֵצֶר טוֹב); *and* behold it was very good, this (implied by the added *and*) is the evil spirit (*Bereishis Rabbah*). The interpretation is of apiece with their comment that we are to fulfill the commandment to love God through both the evil and good inclinations (*Berachos* 54a), a comment on the verse וְאָהַבְתָּ אֵת ה' אֱלֹהֶיךָ . . . בְּכָל לְבָבְךָ — And you shall love the Lord your God with all your heart (*Devarim* 6:11).

It is fitting that our forefather Yitzchak, in particular, should have fathered

Blessed is He Who keeps His pledge to Israel; Blessed is He! For the Holy One, Blessed is He, calculated the end of bondage in order to do as He said to our father Avraham at the Covenant between

---

Esav, the essence of evil, and loved him. For it is Yitzchak — who represents Law (דִּין) as opposed to mercy (רַחֲמִים), who begged God to send him suffering — of whom it is appropriate to speak of serving God through the medium of evil, since Law (or Strict Justice) is related to evil.

The Torah describes Esav as red and hairy; וַיֵּצֵא הָרִאשׁוֹן אַדְמוֹנִי כֻּלּוֹ כְּאַדֶּרֶת שֵׂעָר . . . — "And the first came forth completely red, like a hairy cloak" (Bereishis 25:25). And Yaakov in contrast was אִישׁ חָלָק — "a smooth-skinned man" (ibid. 27:11). Red is a color that reminds one of blood and an exacting Law and Justice; smooth and hairy (or rough), like the two sides of fabric. The reverse, hairy side is more prone to catch dust. And so, too, evil and the evil inclination are more prone to be clinging when the Divine Presence is but darkly felt (הֶסְתֵּר פָּנִים), when God applies the measure of Law and Justice.

וַיְהִי עֵשָׂו אִישׁ יֹדֵעַ צַיִד אִישׁ שָׂדֶה וְיַעֲקֹב אִישׁ תָּם . . . — And Esav was one who knows of hunting, a man of the field and Yaakov was straightforward, a dweller in tents (Bereishis 25:27). Two different approaches.

There is the way of the man of the field who wishes to embrace the outer world, to risk catching the dust — and hopes to shake it off. Yitzchak wished to give his blessing to Esav, to this way of life. But experience shows that whoever leaves the tent — the study hall (בֵּית הַמִּדְרָשׁ) — for the more open spaces — the street, the world — does not shake off the dust, but sinks into it. He does not read the newspaper accounts, recording the seamy side of life, as an ethical text to strengthen his service to God. On the contrary, he becomes more and more scarlet with sin.

The blessings were given to Yaakov the tent dweller, engaged in the pursuit of Torah. For the cloak of Torah is smooth surfaced, not hairy; dust and dirt do not cling to it.

חִשַּׁב אֶת הַקֵּץ / He calculated the end

R' Yerucham of Mir We are directed to learn proper behavior from the ways of the Holy One (Shabbos 133b). Let us learn how He administers punishment.

It is written: כִּי לֹא עִנָּה מִלִּבּוֹ . . . — For He does not oppress willingly (Eichah 3:33). God does not wish to punish; He wishes to benefit man. But man prevents God from being kind. And when that kindness is delayed, God looks out expectantly for the moment that He can bring it to pass. As it is written: לֵיל שִׁמֻּרִים הוּא לַה' — the night (of Pesach) was one of watching for God (Shemos 12:42) — a night of watchful expectancy. From the day that it had been decreed that they would go into exile, throughout those few hundred years, God kept watch. He watched for that moment to arise in

הַבְּתָרִים, שֶׁנֶּאֱמַר, וַיֹּאמֶר לְאַבְרָם, יָדֹעַ תֵּדַע כִּי גֵר יִהְיֶה זַרְעֲךָ בְּאֶרֶץ לֹא לָהֶם, וַעֲבָדוּם וְעִנּוּ אֹתָם, אַרְבַּע מֵאוֹת שָׁנָה. וְגַם אֶת הַגּוֹי אֲשֶׁר יַעֲבֹדוּ דָּן אָנֹכִי, וְאַחֲרֵי כֵן יֵצְאוּ בִּרְכֻשׁ גָּדוֹל.[1]

---

which He might take them out quickly, with haste (*Ramban* to *Shemos* 12:42). And it was because of that hopeful watching that He made a calculation which brought an early Redemption as *Chazal* have explained in their interpretation to the verse: קוֹל דּוֹדִי הִנֵּה זֶה בָּא מְדַלֵּג עַל הֶהָרִים מְקַפֵּץ עַל הַגְּבָעוֹת — The sound of my love on his way can be heard; he skips on the hills and leaps over the heights (*Shir HaShirim* 2:8).

This shows us how we are to behave.

Hope to be helpful. Even when punishment is decreed, promise redemption (as it is written): . . . יָדֹעַ תֵּדַע כִּי גֵר יִהְיֶה זַרְעֲךָ . . . אַרְבַּע מֵאוֹת שָׁנָה . . . וְאַחֲרֵי כֵן יֵצְאוּ בִּרְכֻשׁ גָּדוֹל — Know, indeed, that your seed shall be a sojourning stranger . . . four hundred years . . . and thereafter they shall go out with great wealth (*Bereishis* 15:13-14). During the entire period of punishment, hope and look forward for the delivery of the punished and wish to bring it about before its time. When the redemption arrives, put it into force immediately with great haste; *Chazal* interpret בְּחִפָּזוֹן — "with haste" (*Shemos* 12:11) — the haste of the Divine Presence — שְׁכִינָה (*Mechilta* to *Shemos* 12:11). God himself acted in haste, as it were.

גֵר יִהְיֶה זַרְעֲךָ . . . וַעֲבָדוּם וְעִנּוּ אֹתָם
Your offspring will be aliens . . .
they will serve them and they will oppress them

R' Avraham Grodzinski of Slobodka

Why did Heaven decree that Israel be enslaved by Egypt?

The sufferings which man experiences may be divided into two categories. There are those which are meant as correctives or warnings. "If a man sees that afflictions have come upon him, let him examine his actions" (*Berachos* 5). When Achashverosh removed his signet ring and gave it to Haman, thereby putting the fate of the Jews in his hands, he aroused a greater sense of repentance than did all the exhortations of the prophets (*Megillah*). This is especially true when the affliction is a punishment which fits the sin — מִדָּה כְּנֶגֶד מִדָּה (*Sanhedrin* 90). "Shimshon followed after the desires of his eyes, therefore his eyes were put out; Avshalom took overly much pride in his hair, therefore he hung from his hair" (*Sotah* 9).

But there is suffering which can be described as "afflictions which cleanse" (*Yoma* 86). These are the sufferings such as may come in the wake of repentance; they are meant as an atonement. Such are the sufferings of

the Parts, as it is stated: He said to Avram, 'Know with certainty that your offspring will be aliens in a land not their own, they will serve them and they will oppress them four hundred years; but also upon the nation which they shall serve will I execute judgment, and afterwards they shall leave with great possessions.'[1]

---

1. *Bereishis* 15:13-14.

Gehinnom. For "all who descend into *Gehinnom*, rise" (*Bava Metzia* 58). The Egyptian exile is suffering of such sort.

❧ ❧ ❧

Avraham asked: "How will I know that I will inherit the land" (*Bereishis* 15:8). In the framework of the answer to his question he was told that his descendants would go down into Egypt. To understand this as part of an answer to the question we must examine the question itself.

Eretz Yisrael has a lofty spiritual quality: "The Land of Israel upon which HASHEM your God's eyes are fixed" (*Devarim* 11:12). "There is no study of Torah like the study of Torah in *Eretz Yisrael*" (*Bereishis Rabbah* 16). There is a greater value assigned to *mitzvos* when performed in *Eretz Yisrael* (*Ramban* to *Vayikra* 18:25). The service of the *Beis HaMikdash* has validity only in *Eretz Yisrael* and *Eretz Yisrael* is the seat of prophecy (*Moed Katan* 25). "For HASHEM has chosen Zion; He desired (it) as a resting place for Himself" (*Tehillim* 132:13).

Because of this lofty quality, *Eretz Yisrael* cannot suffer sinners to occupy her; it vomited out the nations which had settled on her (*Vayikra* 18:25). And the *Ramban* states that Sodom and Amorah were destroyed, because they were located in *Eretz Yisrael*. The people of Israel, themselves, are warned to refrain from sin, lest they be exiled like those who came before them (*Vayikra* 26:33).

But their exile differs from that of the other nations. The land is theirs, even when they are in exile; other nations do not have true sovereignty over it (*Vayikra* 26:32) and they were destined to return to it. Even in their exile they make a blessing: "that You gave our forefathers a desirable, good and broad land as their inheritance."

Avraham was troubled. "How will I know that I will inherit" — how will that quality be implanted in my descendants, so that their basic nature will be upright and they would always be able to preserve the elevated spiritual bond with the land?

And thereupon the Holy One replied that the necessary quality would be implanted in them in the Egyptian Exile. It was not because they will improve themselves there; we are told that Israel sank to the depths of immorality; that they had to be drawn forth as the fetus comes forth from the womb of an animal (*Shochar Tov* 107). It was implanted by the

affliction and sufferings. And these work their way in a very specific manner.

❧ ❧ ❧

The evil nature (יֵצֶר הָרָע) has two aspects — that of will and that of desire. Desire is related to the physical self, the body. A man has drives and inclinations, which he satisfies through physical pleasures. The greater the sense of the physical, the more it clouds the purity of the soul and stands in the way of its aspirations. Suffering of the body weakens these desires and reins them in. It shows that life is possible without the pleasures. And by limiting the sense of the physical, the soul is released from close quarters and servitude.

But there is the other facet of the evil nature of man — will.

Antoninus asked Rebbe (R' Yehudah HaNassi): When does the evil nature enter the human personality — at the time of conception or at birth? Rebbe replied that this already occurred with conception; to which Antoninus commented, that were this true, the fetus in its earliest stages would kick its way out of the mother. The evil nature comes not with conception, but with birth. Rebbe was able to find evidence to the view of Antoninus from a verse: לַפֶּתַח חַטָּאת רֹבֵץ — "Sin lies at the opening" — at birth (Sanhedrin 91).

Their discussion was not about the evil nature as it relates to desires. For the fetus has no unfulfilled desires which would make it kick out at the mother to leave the womb. It lacks nothing; it has no idea as to what exists in the outside world. The leaving of the mother at such an early date is tantamount to an act of suicide, for it is hardly likely to survive.

They were thinking of the evil nature in terms of will. Man's ego, his sense of self does not tolerate authority; it is unable to bear restraints. It is prepared to have the fetus kick at the mother, throw off the yoke of submission and enter into the unknown — even if the act is suicidal. Such is the nature of the will.

It must be harnessed and put under the yoke. The paragraph of Shema (שְׁמַע) precedes that of Vehayah im shamoa (וְהָיָה אִם שָׁמֹעַ) — in the reciting of Krias Shema — so that one may receive upon himself first the yoke of the kingship of Heaven and then the yoke of the mitzvos (Berachos 13). The yoke of kingship is for the rebellious will, that of the mitzvos in order to check the desires.

There were two parts to the decree concerning the Exile in Egypt. After Yitzchak was born, the patriarchs and their descendants were under foreign rule — "Your offspring will be aliens for four hundred years in a land which is not their own." And they were subject to bitter servitude for eighty-six years — "They will serve them and they will oppress them." The decree was designed to restrain the two forces of desire and will. The lack of sovereignty for four hundred years weakened the will for freedom without bounds; the eighty-six years of acute suffering wore down the desire. The heart was cleansed. And even though they sank into the depths of corruption in Egypt, when they saw the miracles they were able to emerge. But the hearts of the

Egyptians remained unchanged; they had hearts of stone and like stone sank to the depths of the Red Sea.

With the two-pronged effect of foreign rule and affliction, Israel weakened the force of the evil nature within for all time. This enabled them to receive *Eretz Yisrael* for all time.

וְאַחֲרֵי כֵן יֵצְאוּ בִּרְכֻשׁ גָּדוֹל
And afterwards they shall leave with great possessions

The Alter of Kelm   Is wealth good or bad? On the one hand, we see that Avraham was promised that his descendants would leave the land of their bondage with great wealth; the *gemara* views the one who enjoys "two tables" (שְׁנֵי שֻׁלְחָנוֹת) — who is both learned and wealthy — as truly fortunate (*Berachos* 5). But on the other hand: Poverty is a fine attribute for Israel (*Chagigah* 9). How does one reconcile these two contrary views?

Riches and poverty are means and they must be judged by their results. If "the rich man will answer with insolence" (*Mishlei* 18:23), if wealth breeds insolence (and of the insolent it is said: "All the insolent are loathed by HASHEM" — *Mishlei* 16:5), it is evil. Then "poverty is a fine attribute for Yisrael," if it will bring them to be humble. But if the rich man is modest and humble he will, certainly, be superior to the poor man. For his wealth will provide the means to do good. The Divine Presence rests only on the man who is wise, heroic and wealthy (*Nedarim* 38). Moshe Rabbeinu was living proof; he became wealthy from the chips of the second set of Tablets which he chiseled out of precious stone. And do not *Chazal* say that a handsome home and lovely furnishings enlarge a man's soul? It was to achieve this enlargement of soul that Moshe was destined to be brought up in the royal household of Pharaoh (*Ibn Ezra* to *Shemos* 2:3).

Just as wealth can be a positive good for the perfected man, poverty can degrade the lowly one even further. *Chazal* note that poverty pushes a man to disregard his own principles and the will of his Creator (*Eruvin* 41b). If he does not submit to his Creator through his neediness, but is one of the prideful poor, he shows a trait which the Holy One hates (*Pesachim* 113).

Chazal say that when one has the opportunity to study Torah and does not, the Holy One brings "disgusting" afflictions upon him (*Berachos* 5). What might such afflictions be? We have been warned that whoever wastes his time and does not study Torah when he is rich will find that he will eventually come to the state where he will waste his time and not study Torah in his poverty (*Avos* 4:9). The affliction and punishment of poverty will not achieve the end of returning him to the study of Torah. Such afflictions which do not change the man and better him are "disgusting" afflictions.

Wealth is indeed a great good, if it does not, Heaven forbid, corrupt. If one does suffer from poverty, let him at least take care that it work an improvement, that it bring him to be modest and humble. For if it does not, he will be doubly afflicted; his troubles will be "disgusting" afflictions.

The matzos are covered and the cups lifted as the following paragraph is proclaimed joyously. Upon its conclusion, the cups are put down and the matzos are uncovered.

וְהִיא שֶׁעָמְדָה לַאֲבוֹתֵינוּ וְלָנוּ, שֶׁלֹּא אֶחָד בִּלְבָד עָמַד עָלֵינוּ לְכַלּוֹתֵנוּ. אֶלָּא שֶׁבְּכָל דּוֹר וָדוֹר עוֹמְדִים עָלֵינוּ לְכַלּוֹתֵנוּ, וְהַקָּדוֹשׁ בָּרוּךְ הוּא מַצִּילֵנוּ מִיָּדָם.

צֵא וּלְמַד מַה בִּקֵּשׁ לָבָן הָאֲרַמִּי לַעֲשׂוֹת לְיַעֲקֹב אָבִינוּ, שֶׁפַּרְעֹה לֹא גָזַר אֶלָּא עַל הַזְּכָרִים, וְלָבָן בִּקֵּשׁ לַעֲקוֹר אֶת הַכֹּל. שֶׁנֶּאֱמַר:

אֲרַמִּי אֹבֵד אָבִי, וַיֵּרֶד מִצְרַיְמָה וַיָּגָר שָׁם בִּמְתֵי מְעָט, וַיְהִי שָׁם לְגוֹי, גָּדוֹל עָצוּם וָרָב.[1]

וַיֵּרֶד מִצְרַיְמָה – אָנוּס עַל פִּי הַדִּבּוּר.

וַיָּגָר שָׁם – מְלַמֵּד שֶׁלֹּא יָרַד יַעֲקֹב אָבִינוּ לְהִשְׁתַּקֵּעַ בְּמִצְרַיִם, אֶלָּא לָגוּר שָׁם. שֶׁנֶּאֱמַר, וַיֹּאמְרוּ אֶל פַּרְעֹה, לָגוּר בָּאָרֶץ בָּאנוּ, כִּי אֵין מִרְעֶה לַצֹּאן אֲשֶׁר לַעֲבָדֶיךָ, כִּי כָבֵד הָרָעָב בְּאֶרֶץ כְּנָעַן, וְעַתָּה יֵשְׁבוּ נָא עֲבָדֶיךָ בְּאֶרֶץ גֹּשֶׁן.[2]

בִּמְתֵי מְעָט – כְּמָה שֶׁנֶּאֱמַר, בְּשִׁבְעִים נֶפֶשׁ

וְהִיא שֶׁעָמְדָה / *It is this that has stood*

R' Moshe Rosenstein of Lomza

What is it that has stood by our fathers and us? The *Alter* of Kelm said that this referred to the Exodus from Egypt. Each and every one, in each and every generation, in each and every situation, can learn his all from the Exodus; he can see therein all his deeds and all that which occurs in his life and the whole panorama of our nation's history.

In a word: The Exodus and its events were the preface to all that was to happen to Yisrael and they have stood by our fathers and us in each generation.

בְּשִׁבְעִים נֶפֶשׁ / *With seventy persons*

R' Eliahu Dessler

The works of the *kabbalah* tell us that the Egyptian Exile was meant to repair the damage done by the sin of

The matzos are covered and the cups lifted as the following paragraph is proclaimed joyously. Upon its conclusion, the cups are put down and the matzos are uncovered.

It is this that has stood by our fathers and us. For not only one has risen against us to annihilate us, but in every generation they rise against us to annihilate us. But the Holy One, Blessed is He, rescues us from their hand.

Go and learn what Lavan the Aramean attempted to do to our father Yaakov! For Pharaoh decreed only against the males, Lavan attempted to uproot everything, as it is said:

An Aramean attempted to destroy my father. Then he descended to Egypt and sojourned there, with few people; and there he became a nation — great, mighty and numerous.[1]

Then he descended to Egypt — compelled by Divine decree.

He sojourned there — this teaches that our father Yaakov did not descend to Egypt to settle, but only to sojourn temporarily, as it says: They (the sons of Yaakov) said to Pharaoh: 'We have come to sojourn in this land because there is no pasture for the flocks of your servants, because the famine is severe in the land of Canaan. And now, please let your servants dwell in the land of Goshen.'[2]

With few people — as it is written: With seventy

---

1. *Devarim* 26:5.   2. *Bereishis* 47:4.

Adam. But the Talmud says that the giving of the Torah at Sinai served that purpose (*Shabbos* 146).

From that fateful day when man was expelled from *Gan Eden* (Paradise), until he will have mended himself in the end of days (אַחֲרִית הַיָּמִים), the history of the human race turns about the central pivot of Adam's sin. Before the sin, man's world was a world of the spirit. The concrete and physical was a mere covering of true existence. And man knew how to extract the spiritual from all that was concrete. When he ate from "the tree of knowledge" (עֵץ הַדַּעַת), Adam brought on a radical change. The state of the world fell, so that it seemed as if the physical was the true existence, so much so, that even the world of the spirit was understood in the language and terms of pleasure. From the world of *Gan Eden*, in which he had been directed to the spiritual, Adam was thrown into the world of "my power and the strength of my hand

יָרְדוּ אֲבֹתֶיךָ מִצְרָיְמָה, וְעַתָּה שָׂמְךָ יהוה אֱלֹהֶיךָ כְּכוֹכְבֵי הַשָּׁמַיִם לָרֹב.[1]

have produced this wealth for me" (*Devarim* 8:17), into the world of "by the sweat of your brow, you shall eat bread" (*Bereishis* 3:19).

To change this, the wheel must be turned back; the world of the spirit must be once more seen from within the world of the concrete. Our forefather, Avraham began the process. He used his great wealth as an instrument for kindness (חֶסֶד), the generous hospitality towards guests. And through this kindness he made men aware of their Creator. Yitzchak continued in his father's path and Yaakov brought it to perfection — "and Yaakov came to perfection" (וַיָּבֹא יַעֲקֹב שָׁלֵם — literally, whole; *Bereishis* 33:18).

But the efforts of single individuals are not sufficient to reverse the effects of Adam's sin. For Adam is not only an individual, he is the father of mankind and all of the souls of the future are contained within him (*Shemos Rabbah*).

The seventy souls who went down into Egypt represent a more all-embracing picture than that of a group of individuals. The number seventy is used in a number of instances — there are seventy aspects to the Torah; Moshe appointed seventy elders; there are seventy members of the Sanhedrin and seventy nations. Seventy spells out comprehensiveness. The subjects of the Torah are surveyed from seventy angles and the seventy members of the Sanhedrin review all sides of an issue. The seventy nations represent the whole world of inclinations and traits. When the family of Yaakov reached the number seventy, they went down into Egypt to repair the damage done by Adam's sin.

Egypt represents the fullest effect of Adam's sin. All of the "wisdom of Egypt" (*I Melachim* 5:10) was used to enhance the rule of the concrete. They used the spiritual for their own purposes. Through magic and sorcery, they submerged themselves within animal desire, the "abominations of Egypt" (תּוֹעֲבוֹת מִצְרַיִם) and the depths of immorality (מ"ט שַׁעֲרֵי טֻמְאָה).

Israel, too, descended to those depths but preserved its identity: they did not alter their names — a name indicates the inner self; they did not alter their clothes — their outward appearance; they did not alter their tongue — the bond which tied them together. Despite the press of slavery and oppression, they multiplied to the number of sixty myriads (these six hundred thousand were the basic souls of the people of Israel; all other Jews are branches of the basic souls). They kept their identity, cried out to Hashem to deliver them, believed in Moshe as a messenger of God, saw the signs and wonders and followed after Hashem in the unsown desert, without taking along provisions (*Shemos* 12:39).

They exchanged the physical for the spirit and were found worthy to receive the Torah all bound together as closely as if they were a single soul. And then the evil nature was eradicated from within them and the venom of

persons, your forefathers descended to Egypt, and now HASHEM, your God, has made you as numerous as the stars of heaven.[1]

1. *Devarim* 10:22.

---

the serpent ceased to work. Even the angel of death removed himself from their midst (*Avodah Zarah* 3). They were worthy and withstood temptation, mending the damage caused by Adam's sin. Had they entered *Eretz Yisrael* in that state, the final Redemption would have occurred and the world would have been restored to its original condition.

But they sinned with the Golden Calf and were found unworthy. They plummeted from on high; the evil nature found its way back; the angel of death returned. The world of the concrete once more assumed its mask of true reality and paraded its blandishments. Man was forced to follow the long road of thousands of years. And we must suffer through the exiles, scattered among the seventy nations. We must contend with all that they represent and discover their lack of worth, until that time when all will be completely restored with the Redemption, may it come in the near future.

כְּכוֹכְבֵי הַשָּׁמַיִם לָרֹב
As numerous as the stars of heaven

R' Nasan Tzvi Finkel, the Alter of Slobodka

Man is a superior being, the crowning achievement of Creation. And since each should think that the world was created solely for his sake (*Berachos* 6b), he must strive for the highest and not be content with less.

When God wished to have an angel lead the people of Israel, after the sin of the Golden Calf, Moshe insisted that the people would remain where they were. He said: אִם אֵין פָּנֶיךָ הֹלְכִים אַל תַּעֲלֵנוּ מִזֶּה — "If Your Presence does not go (with us), do not carry us up from here" (*Shemos* 33:15). It is better to remain in the desolate desert than to be satisfied with less than the height of bliss which accompanies direct contact with the Creator.

So, too, the Midrash comments on the verse: וְהִנְּכֶם הַיּוֹם כְּכוֹכְבֵי הַשָּׁמַיִם לָרֹב — And behold, you are today *as numerous as the stars of heaven* (*Devarim* 1:10); Moshe asked God, "Why did You not compare Your children to the sun and the moon which are greater than the stars?"

And the Holy One replied, "In truth, the sun and moon are destined to suffer shame as it is said: וְחָפְרָה הַלְּבָנָה וּבוֹשָׁה הַחַמָּה, 'And the moon will be ashamed and the sun humiliated' (*Yeshayahu* 24:23) but the stars will not be shamed. Of Israel, too, it is said: וִידַעְתֶּם כִּי בְקֶרֶב יִשְׂרָאֵל אָנִי . . . וְאֵין עוֹד וְלֹא יֵבֹשׁוּ עַמִּי לְעוֹלָם — 'And you will know that I am in the midst of Israel . . . and there is no other and My people will never suffer shame' " (*Yoel* 2:27; *Devarim Rabbah* 1:14).

Astounding! We know how brilliant the sun is and how bright the moon;

וַיְהִי שָׁם לְגוֹי – מְלַמֵּד שֶׁהָיוּ יִשְׂרָאֵל מְצֻיָּנִים
שָׁם.
גָּדוֹל עָצוּם – כְּמָה שֶׁנֶּאֱמַר, וּבְנֵי יִשְׂרָאֵל פָּרוּ
וַיִּשְׁרְצוּ וַיִּרְבּוּ וַיַּעַצְמוּ בִּמְאֹד מְאֹד, וַתִּמָּלֵא הָאָרֶץ
אֹתָם.[1]

how necessary and beneficial they are to the world. It is difficult to conceive a more powerful image for light, splendor and the good. And yet, Israel is not to be compared to them, because sometime in the future, thousands of years hence, they will suffer shame. The nation of God must be likened to that which lacks nothing at all and has not a hint of a taint.

כְּכוֹכְבֵי הַשָּׁמַיִם / As the stars of heaven

R' Moshe Rosenstein of Lomza

For years, I have wondered if anyone exists, or once existed who truly understands the inner essence and workings of the billions of stars at which we gaze. Possibly, each star is a world in itself — God alone knows.

But the Torah indicates that they were all created for the needs of our world. And I seek someone who knows how they influence this world of ours. I have not found, nor will I ever find, that someone. But, now, my soul is at rest and my mind tranquil, for I have discovered not their inner essence, but the spiritual value which they have for us.

It is a basic principle of the Torah that we are bound to value every individual. For "Each man must say: the world was created for my sake" (*Sanhedrin*). Yet, the thought steals to mind, "How is it possible to view each man as a world in himself? When we see that man is as numerous as the fish in the sea, are we to truly think that each is worthy to have God create the world for his sake? How can we imagine that God would make a covenant with each and every one?"

But when we gaze upwards, to the heavens, towards the billions of stars, and realize that each is a world in itself, immense and important, then we can believe that, even if the people of the world are like the sands of the shores, each is a world in himself. God created all for his sake and he is worthy to hear the word of God and enter into His covenant.

שֶׁהָיוּ יִשְׂרָאֵל מְצֻיָּנִים שָׁם
The Israelites were distinctive there

The Alter of Kelm

The *Ramban* writes that the Torah has commanded us to remember and know that there is an ordered process of reward and punishment: "And know that HASHEM, your God, is God, the faithful God, Who keeps the covenant with, and the kindness

There he became a nation — this teaches that the Israelites were distinctive there.

Great, mighty — as it says: And the children of Israel were fruitful, increased greatly, multiplied, and became very, very mighty; and the land was filled with them.[1]

---

1. *Shemos* 1:7.

---

towards, those who love Him and keep His commandments" (*Devarim* 7:9). And the source of this knowledge is indicated in the previous *pasuk*: "Because HASHEM loved you . . . He took you out . . . and delivered you from the house of slaves, from the hand of Pharaoh, king of Egypt." There they saw with their own eyes that those who kept guard over the *mitzvos* were rewarded. Yisrael kept the *mitzvos* of Hashem and were delivered from their servitude; they went out from darkness to great light. The Egyptians who rebelled against Hashem were beset by plagues and drowned in the sea.

But how can Yisrael in Egypt be considered "observers of *mitzvos*?" We are accustomed to think of them as sunk in the depths of corruption (מ"ט שַׁעֲרֵי טֻמְאָה). They had no *mitzvos* through which they might be redeemed until *milah* (circumcision) and the *korban Pesach* (the *Pesach* sacrifice) were given to them.

Yet, we should not be amazed. Yisrael were slaves to Pharaoh and the Egyptians. Servants by nature submit to their masters and ape their ways. They are fearful and ashamed of keeping other customs. Yisrael, however, as *Chazal* point out, were "distinctive there in language, dress and personal names" (*Yalkut Shimoni* I:773). They did not speak Egyptian; they did not dress like Egyptians; they did not bear Egyptian names. All this was done to strengthen the traditions which they had received from their fathers who had recognized the Creator. They did not want to be swept away by, and intermingled with, the Egyptians and their loathsome ways.

It is unbelievable that a nation of downtrodden slaves who have labored at lowly tasks — producing bricks and mortar — for over two hundred years would not have left off continuously renewing their ties to the past. But there they were standing their guard, rejecting their masters' culture on three cardinal points that help make up the bonds of society — language, clothing and names. Small wonder, then, that they are called "keeper of the *mitzvos*" and that it is from their deliverance we learn of the process of reward and punishment.

וּבְנֵי יִשְׂרָאֵל פָּרוּ וַיִּשְׁרְצוּ וַיִּרְבּוּ

And the children of Israel were fruitful, increased greatly, multiplied

---

R' Yechezkel Levenstein

If we do nothing more than look at the obvious meanings of the Torah, we will bolster our faith.

וָרָב – כְּמָה שֶׁנֶּאֱמַר, רְבָבָה כְּצֶמַח הַשָּׂדֶה
נְתַתִּיךְ, וַתִּרְבִּי וַתִּגְדְּלִי וַתָּבֹאִי בַּעֲדִי עֲדָיִים, שָׁדַיִם
נָכֹנוּ וּשְׂעָרֵךְ צִמֵּחַ, וְאַתְּ עֵרֹם וְעֶרְיָה; וָאֶעֱבֹר עָלַיִךְ
וָאֶרְאֵךְ מִתְבּוֹסֶסֶת בְּדָמָיִךְ, וָאֹמַר לָךְ, בְּדָמַיִךְ חֲיִי,
וָאֹמַר לָךְ, בְּדָמַיִךְ חֲיִי.[1]

"The children of Israel were fruitful, increased greatly, multiplied and
became very, very mighty" (*Shemos* 1:7). *Chazal* say that women gave birth
to six at a time (שִׁשָּׁה בְּכֶרֶס אֶחָד). The Egyptians had the newborn males cast
into the river. They decreed that the Israelites had to sleep in the fields where
they worked, in order to limit the rate of childbirth (*Shemos Rabbah* 1). But
all their schemes came to naught.

Let us examine the record at the simplest level. Our forefathers descended
into Egypt in a group of seventy souls. After a stay of two hundred and ten
years they went out of Egypt with a multitude which numbered six hundred
thousand men from the age of twenty to sixty. Add on children and the aged
and double the sum to include women. If they gave birth to six at a time, there
were many, many infants. The sum grows, so much so, that there are those
who estimate that twenty million souls left Egypt. *Chazal* have said that
four-fifths of Israel perished in Egypt during the three days of the plague of
darkness. That would give us a sum of one hundred million descendants of
the original seventy souls who descended into Egypt!

What was the point of such a population explosion? The Midrash tells us:
Hashem said to the Egyptians: I told Avraham that I will multiply his children
like the stars; you scheme to prevent their increase. Let us see whose will
prevails, Mine or yours. Immediately the Torah tells us: "As they oppressed
them so they multiplied and spread" (ibid. v. 12).

Our faith is supported by our senses. See how certain Hashem's
promise is.

וְאַתְּ עֵרֹם וְעֶרְיָה / But you were naked and bare

R' Yehudah Leib Chasman　　Hashem wished to take Israel out of Egypt but
He found them naked, without *mitzvos* (fulfill-
ment of commandments) which would make them worthy of redemption.
And so He gave them the commandments of the sacrifice of the *Pesach*
offering and circumcision (*Mechilta, Shemos* 12:6).

Man must accept Hashem's dominion, but intellectual submission is not
enough. He must also harness his desires and his limbs in Hashem's
service. This can be done by fulfilling the entire range of commandments,
which take in the whole of man. And they act in a two-fold manner; he who
fulfills them avoids harm and his deeds are fine and noble.

Numerous — as it says: I made you as numerous as the plants of the field; you grew and developed, and became charming, beautiful of figure; and your hair grown long; but you were naked and bare. And I passed over you and saw you downtrodden in your blood and I said to you: 'Through your blood shall you live!' And I said to you: 'Through your blood shall you live!'.[1]

1. *Yechezkel* 16:7,6.

The prophet says: "And you grew and matured and were adorned with jewels . . . and you were naked and exposed" (*Yechezkel* 16:7). What a marvelous image! A handsome developed figure bedecked with bracelets and rings — but otherwise naked! For, indeed, Israel in Egypt did possess positive qualities; they had not given up their names, their mode of dress, or their language. But this "jewelry" did not prevent them from sinking together with the Egyptians to the forty-ninth depth of impurity (מ״ט שַׁעֲרֵי טֻמְאָה), because they lacked the "clothes" of the commandments. Just as clothes cover the entire body, so do the commandments encompass all the organs and desires. Clothes have a dual purpose; they ward off the cold and, at the same time, invest the wearer with a respectful and handsome appearance. In a like manner, the commandments ward off the harm which could be caused by a man's desires and direct him to acts which are proper and useful.

The Holy One wished to redeem Israel and gave them the two commandments. Through them they became worthy of redemption; through circumcision, which the *Ramban* says weakens desire, and through the blood of the slaughter of the *Pesach* sacrifice — the lamb which was worshipped as a god by the Egyptians. These two commandments symbolize the entire body of the Torah commandments. For they aim at harnessing the intellect and the drives to the service of Hashem. Through them Israel became worthy of redemption and were given the complete Torah. As the prophet puts it: "And I said to you, 'Through your blood shall you live' " (*Yechezkel* 16:6).

וָאֹמַר לָךְ בְּדָמַיִךְ חֲיִי

And I said to you, 'Through your blood shall you live'

The Alter of Kelm

"Through your blood shall you live" (*Yechezkel* 16:6). Because they fulfilled commandments with the placing of the blood of the *Pesach* sacrifice on their doorposts and by circumcising their sons, they were taken out of Egypt (*Shemos Rabbah* 17:3).

See how great is the reward for fulfilling a commandment. We see how greatly a proper act is repaid elsewhere, also. Avraham, our forefather, played host to the angels and ordered that a *bit* of water (מְעַט מַיִם) be brought for them (*Bereishis* 18:4). Because he did so, God brought forth the well which

וַיָּרֵעוּ אֹתָנוּ הַמִּצְרִים, וַיְעַנּוּנוּ, וַיִּתְּנוּ עָלֵינוּ עֲבֹדָה קָשָׁה.[1]

וַיָּרֵעוּ אֹתָנוּ הַמִּצְרִים – כְּמָה שֶׁנֶּאֱמַר, הָבָה נִתְחַכְּמָה לוֹ, פֶּן יִרְבֶּה, וְהָיָה כִּי תִקְרֶאנָה מִלְחָמָה, וְנוֹסַף גַּם הוּא עַל שֹׂנְאֵינוּ, וְנִלְחַם בָּנוּ, וְעָלָה מִן הָאָרֶץ.[2]

וַיְעַנּוּנוּ – כְּמָה שֶׁנֶּאֱמַר, וַיָּשִׂימוּ עָלָיו שָׂרֵי מִסִּים, לְמַעַן עַנֹּתוֹ בְּסִבְלֹתָם, וַיִּבֶן עָרֵי מִסְכְּנוֹת לְפַרְעֹה, אֶת פִּתֹם וְאֶת רַעַמְסֵס.[3]

וַיִּתְּנוּ עָלֵינוּ עֲבֹדָה קָשָׁה – כְּמָה שֶׁנֶּאֱמַר, וַיַּעֲבִדוּ מִצְרַיִם אֶת בְּנֵי יִשְׂרָאֵל בְּפָרֶךְ.[4]

וַנִּצְעַק אֶל יהוה אֱלֹהֵי אֲבֹתֵינוּ, וַיִּשְׁמַע יהוה אֶת קֹלֵנוּ, וַיַּרְא אֶת עָנְיֵנוּ, וְאֶת עֲמָלֵנוּ, וְאֶת לַחֲצֵנוּ.[5]

וַנִּצְעַק אֶל יהוה אֱלֹהֵי אֲבֹתֵינוּ – כְּמָה שֶׁנֶּאֱמַר, וַיְהִי בַיָּמִים הָרַבִּים הָהֵם, וַיָּמָת מֶלֶךְ מִצְרַיִם, וַיֵּאָנְחוּ בְּנֵי יִשְׂרָאֵל מִן הָעֲבֹדָה,

---

supplied the nation of Israel with water for forty years in the dry desert. And then He brought them to the land of Israel: אֶרֶץ נַחֲלֵי מָיִם, עֲיָנֹת וּתְהֹמֹת יֹצְאִים בַּבִּקְעָה וּבָהָר, "A land of rivers of water, of fountains and depths flowing in valley and hill" (*Devarim* 8:7). In the future, too, a living stream will come forth from Jerusalem (*Zechariah* 14:8). See what reward was given to countless generations for that bit of water. See how great is the reward for fulfilling a commandment.

הָבָה נִתְחַכְּמָה לוֹ
Let us deal with them wisely

<u>R' Yerucham of Mir</u> When we read the *Ramban* to the verse (*Shemos* 1:10), we imagine that we are reading a current newspaper. In Egypt, too, they put on trial any Egyptian who had murdered a Jewish child. But, all of a sudden, no witnesses can be found to testify

The Egyptians did evil to us and afflicted us; and imposed hard labor upon us.[1]

The Egyptians did evil to us — as it says: Let us deal with them wisely lest they multiply and, if we happen to be at war, they may join our enemies and fight against us and then leave the country.[2]

And afflicted us — as it says: They set taskmasters over them in order to oppress them with their burdens; and they built Pisom and Raamses as treasure cities for Pharaoh.[3]

They imposed hard labor upon us — as it says: The Egyptians subjugated the children of Israel with hard labor.[4]

We cried out to HASHEM, the God of our fathers; and HASHEM heard our cry and saw our affliction, our burden and our oppression.[5]

We cried out to HASHEM, the God of our fathers — as it says: It happened in the course of those many days that the king of Egypt died; and the children of Israel groaned because of the servitude

---

1. *Devarim* 26:6. 2. *Shemos* 1:10. 3. 1:11. 4. 1:13. 5. *Devarim* 26:7.

---

to the act of murder — exactly what happens in our day, during the turbulence in Russia and elsewhere! More than three thousand years have passed from the time of the Egyptian servitude and, nevertheless, whatever has been handed down to us about that period is as fresh as if we were seeing our own day before our eyes.

A thorough examination tells us that the long list of Jew haters is a basic mystery to us. The hatred of the non-Jew to the Jew is bound up with another mystery — the hatred of the evil towards the good. "God created this as opposed to that" (*Koheles* 7:14). If good exists, evil too must exist; if there are Jews, there must be Jew-haters. Each generation has its thirty-six righteous men (ל"ו צַדִּיקִים) and, perforce, there is a sufficient number of enemies of the Jews.

Chazal have given us the source of this hatred: Why was the mountain called Sinai? because hatred (*sinah*) descended from there to befall Yisrael (*Shabbos* 89). When Yisrael received the Torah and the good became implanted in them, at that time, too, the hatred of the nations towards Yisrael made its way down into the world.

וַיִּזְעֲקוּ, וַתַּעַל שַׁוְעָתָם אֶל הָאֱלֹהִים מִן הָעֲבֹדָה.[1]

וַיִּשְׁמַע יהוה אֶת קֹלֵנוּ – כְּמָה שֶׁנֶּאֱמַר, וַיִּשְׁמַע אֱלֹהִים אֶת נַאֲקָתָם, וַיִּזְכֹּר אֱלֹהִים אֶת בְּרִיתוֹ אֶת אַבְרָהָם, אֶת יִצְחָק, וְאֶת יַעֲקֹב.[2]

וַיַּרְא אֶת עָנְיֵנוּ – זוֹ פְּרִישׁוּת דֶּרֶךְ אֶרֶץ, כְּמָה שֶׁנֶּאֱמַר, וַיַּרְא אֱלֹהִים אֶת בְּנֵי יִשְׂרָאֵל, וַיֵּדַע אֱלֹהִים.[3]

וַיֵּאָנְחוּ . . . וַיִּזְעָקוּ / ***And groaned . . . and cried***

R' Yechezkel Levenstein

The desire for Redemption (גְאוּלָה) is the pre-condition for Redemption. All had been prepared, as it were, in Heaven, but until there was that cry, Israel could not be taken out of Egypt.

Chazal tell us that many, many Jews were found to be unworthy and perished during the days of the plague of Darkness (*Shemos Rabbah* 14:3). And, yet, this requires an explanation. For Hashem, Himself, testifies that Israel are believers and the sons of believers (*Shabbos* 97a). And these believers witnessed eight wondrous plagues which befell the Egyptians. This should have strengthened their belief. But they were found unworthy, because they lacked the strong desire to be redeemed. Without that desire, Redemption could not be realized.

We should see this as exemplifying a basic principle in our approach to life. If we wish to be granted anything by Hashem, we must be driven by a powerful desire to obtain it.

The description of the way in which the *Pesach* sacrifice is to be eaten demonstrates this sense of readiness and desire: "And so you shall eat it, your loins girded, shoes on your feet, staff in hand; and you should eat it in haste" (*Shemos* 12:11) — completely prepared for an immediate exodus, waiting only for the sign. Then, and only then, we are worthy to receive that sign!

וַיִּזְעָקוּ וַתַּעַל שַׁוְעָתָם / ***And cried . . . their cry . . . rose up***

R' Yerucham of Mir

When man calls out to Hashem, Hashem reveals Himself to him, as it is written: "Wheresoever My name will be mentioned, I will come to you and bless you" (*Shemos* 20:21). The whole process — the Exodus, Israel's selection as the nation of God and the giving of the Torah — all began with a crying out to Hashem. For the Name of Hashem is the key to all deliverance.

The Midrash dramatizes this thought with a parable: Hashem brought Israel into the mouth of a trap on the shore of the Red Sea. They were surrounded by the Egyptians, the desert and the sea; like a king who passes

and cried; their cry because of the servitude rose up to God.[1]

HASHEM heard our cry — as it says: God heard their groaning, and God recalled His covenant with Avraham, with Yitzchak, and with Yaacob.[2]

And saw our affliction — that is the disruption of family life, as it says: God saw the Children of Israel and God took note.[3]

1. *Shemos* 2:23. 2. 2:24. 3. 2:25.

by and hears a princess cry out, "Save me from the bandits." The king heard and saved her. After a while he wished to marry her, but she refused to speak to him. He set loose the bandits on her and, once again, she cried out for his help. "Ah," said the king, "that is what I longed for, to hear your voice." So, too, when Israel was enslaved in Egypt, they called out to Hashem and He saved them. He wished to hear their voice, once more, and therefore set Pharaoh loose to pursue them (*Shemos Rabbah* 21).

We are accustomed to think that the purpose of Israel's prayer was to obtain freedom from the affliction; that it would have been preferable not to suffer and not be required to pray. Yet, here, we see that it is the other way around — the sufferings were imposed to elicit prayer. For deliverance does not only involve removal of distress. The deliverance is a manifestation of Divine Revelation and that comes in the wake of the prayer, born of the pains of affliction.

This sheds a new light on the process of miracles. The Holy One stops up all the natural avenues of escape; man is forced to pray and, then, Hashem performs the miracle. The Holy One saved our forefather, Avraham, from within the fiery furnace, so that he would cry out, "Father, save me" from within the bowels of the furnace. And so, too, our ancestors were childless. Hashem waited until Avraham was one hundred years old and Sarah ninety. And when nature could surely no longer hold forth hope, then He blessed them with a child. For Hashem desires the prayers of the upright (*Shir HaShirim Rabbah* 2:32).

This should bring relief to us, at all times of exile and persecution, which surround us from all sides. As David HaMelech puts it: "They surrounded me, indeed, they surrounded me — yet I cut them down with the Name of HASHEM"(*Tehillim* 118:11). The *surrounded* is meant to bring forth the "I cut them down with the Name of HASHEM." The *straits* (מִן הַמֵּצַר) are meant to produce the *I called out to HASHEM* (קָרָאתִי יָּהּ) (ibid. v. 5), the *let Me hear your voice* (הַשְׁמִיעִנִי אֶת קוֹלֵךְ) (*Shir HaShirim* 2:14).

וַיֵּדַע אֱלֹהִים / *And God took note*

R' Yerucham of Mir

" 'For I know their pains' — this is similar to the verse, 'and God took note [lit., 'knew']' — It means:

וְאֶת עֲמָלֵנוּ – אֵלּוּ הַבָּנִים, כְּמָה שֶׁנֶּאֱמַר, כָּל הַבֵּן הַיִּלּוֹד הַיְאֹרָה תַּשְׁלִיכֻהוּ, וְכָל הַבַּת תְּחַיּוּן.[1]

וְאֶת לַחֲצֵנוּ – זוֹ הַדְּחַק, כְּמָה שֶׁנֶּאֱמַר, וְגַם רָאִיתִי אֶת הַלַּחַץ אֲשֶׁר מִצְרַיִם לֹחֲצִים אֹתָם.[2]

I have set My heart to noticing and understanding their pains and I have not shut My eyes, nor stopped up My ears to their outcry" (*Rashi* to *Shemos* 3:7).

Previously, Hashem had donned His judge's robes (מִדַּת הַדִּין); of such instances it is said: "and I shall, indeed, hide My face" (*Devarim* 31:18). When Hashem hides His face, so to speak, He does not hear, see, or know. But the moment that the True Judge becomes Hashem, the Merciful (מִדַּת הָרַחֲמִים), He immediately hears, sees and knows — and the Redemption comes, immediately. "I have indeed seen the affliction of My nation and I have heard their outcry, for I know their pains" (*Shemos* 3:7). "And I have come down to save them from the hand of Egypt" (ibid. v. 8).

The distinction between judgment — דִּין, and mercy — רַחֲמִים (which reflects itself in Exile as against Redemption) is that of the potential as against the actual. For example, Yisro suggests that Moshe choose judges who are brave, fear *Elokim*, are truthful and hate injustice (literally, hate gain; see *Shemos* 18:21 and *Ramban*). It is conceivable that a man may be brave, fear God, be truthful and, nevertheless, not hate injustice. The other virtues are passive aspects of the internal man, his "potential," as it were. Yet, though he has this potential, he may see injustice taking place before his eyes and bear it in silence. But the hater of injustice cannot stand by; that virtue shows itself in practice, not potential; he must root out the evil. Mercy (רַחֲמִים) is an active virtue. Hashem's "self-containment" is possible when He "hides His face." But when mercy replaces judgment (מִידַּת הַדִּין), He cannot bear Israel's suffering or turn away from their cries, for even an instant, and the Redemption follows suit.

Our teacher, Moshe, was chosen as the agent who was to bring the Redemption. He was eighty years old when the task was thrust upon him. Tradition has many wonderful tales to tell about Moshe as a warrior, as a king, in prison and discovering the marvelous staff (*Yalkut Shimoni*). But the Torah limits itself to only a few stories of his youth which demonstrate a particular trait.

He had been brought up amid luxury in Pharaoh's court, but " 'he went out to his brothers and saw their sufferings' — he set his eyes and heart to feel sorrow for them" (*Rashi, Shemos* 2:11). He noted their suffering with a sharp reaction and could not remain indifferent; he would lend a shoulder and aid each one (*Shemos Rabbah* 1).

Our burden — refers to the children, as it says: Every son that is born you shall cast into the river, but every daughter you shall let live.[1]

Our oppression — refers to the pressure expressed in the words: I have also seen how the Egyptians are oppressing them.

1. *Shemos* 1:22. 2. 3:9.

When he saw the Egyptian beating a fellow Jew, he killed him and hid the body in the sand (*Shemos* 2:12). Nor did he limit himself to correcting injustice between Jew and non-Jew. When two Jews quarreled: "He said, 'Wicked man, why will you beat your friend?'" (*Shemos* 2:13). And even when the dispute is between non-Jews, and he no longer appears in the costume of a prince of the realm, Moshe intervenes. He has come to a strange country as a refugee fleeing pursuit. But when he sees the shepherds of Midian harassing their fellow countrywomen, the daughters of Yisro: "And Moshe arose and saved them" (*Shemos* 2:17).

A common line runs through these incidents. Moshe is depicted as a hater of injustice. This, like mercy (מִדַּת הָרַחֲמִים), is an active, not a potential or passive trait. When Moshe sees injustice, he cannot contain himself; he rushes to the rescue. It is he who is chosen to deliver Israel: "A messenger worthy of Him who sent him" (*Sifra* — conclusion of *Bechukosai*).

כָּל הַבֵּן הַיִּלּוֹד הַיְאֹרָה תַּשְׁלִיכֻהוּ
Every son that is born you shall cast into the river

R' Yehudah Leib Chasman Providence (הַשְׁגָּחָה) mocked Pharaoh; it was the king himself who reared the leader who was to save Israel. True, it was the workings of Providence, but nevertheless, we cannot help but wonder at the extreme foolishness of Pharaoh who, instead of doing away with the Jewish infant which his daughter has found, allows her to bring it home. This, despite the warning of his astrologers that the future Jewish leader was about to be born at that time.

He has passed an all-encompassing and cruel decree, a decree which one does not enact lightly. He knows that the safety of his kingdom and even the security of his throne depend on the strict adherence to the decree. But, since it is his own daughter who has happened upon the infant, and a beautiful baby it is, he does not want to cause her pain by removing the object of her delight. He is blinded by this frivolous consideration and does not have the force of will to overcome it. Such is the nature of man!

וַיּוֹצִאֵנוּ **יהוה מִמִּצְרַיִם בְּיָד חֲזָקָה, וּבִזְרֹעַ נְטוּיָה, וּבְמֹרָא גָּדֹל, וּבְאֹתוֹת וּבְמֹפְתִים.**[1]

וַיּוֹצִאֵנוּ יהוה מִמִּצְרַיִם – לֹא עַל יְדֵי מַלְאָךְ, וְלֹא עַל יְדֵי שָׂרָף, וְלֹא עַל יְדֵי שָׁלִיחַ, אֶלָּא הַקָּדוֹשׁ בָּרוּךְ הוּא בִּכְבוֹדוֹ וּבְעַצְמוֹ. שֶׁנֶּאֱמַר, וְעָבַרְתִּי בְאֶרֶץ מִצְרַיִם בַּלַּיְלָה הַזֶּה, וְהִכֵּיתִי כָל בְּכוֹר בְּאֶרֶץ מִצְרַיִם מֵאָדָם וְעַד בְּהֵמָה, וּבְכָל אֱלֹהֵי מִצְרַיִם אֶעֱשֶׂה שְׁפָטִים, אֲנִי יהוה.[2]

וְעָבַרְתִּי בְאֶרֶץ מִצְרַיִם בַּלַּיְלָה הַזֶּה – אֲנִי וְלֹא מַלְאָךְ. וְהִכֵּיתִי כָל בְּכוֹר בְּאֶרֶץ מִצְרַיִם – אֲנִי וְלֹא שָׂרָף. וּבְכָל אֱלֹהֵי מִצְרַיִם אֶעֱשֶׂה שְׁפָטִים – אֲנִי וְלֹא הַשָּׁלִיחַ. אֲנִי יהוה – אֲנִי הוּא, וְלֹא אַחֵר.

אֲנִי וְלֹא מַלְאָךְ / *I and no angel*

The Alter of Slobodka

The sin which brought on the descent into Egypt and the taint which had to be removed were so slight (as was the punishment) that they were beyond the comprehension of even an angel. Hence, an angel was not sent to deliver Israel from its bondage.

The Exile was the result of our forefather Avraham's question: "How will I know that I will inherit the land?" (*Bereishis 15:8; Nedarim* 32). That question cast a minor blemish on the picture of his faith. And the faith of a righteous man (צַדִּיק) is his very life — "And the righteous man *lives* through his faith" — וְצַדִּיק בֶּאֱמוּנָתוֹ יִחְיֶה (*Chavakuk* 2:4). When his faith is at all reduced, this touches on his life and liberty and imposes some degree of servitude.

Yet Avraham, who posed the question, was the first and foremost of the faithful. The Torah itself bears witness to his faith two verses earlier: "And he believed in HASHEM and He accounted it to him as righteousness" (*Bereishis* 15:6). This is the view for all time: "and You found his heart faithful to You" (*Nechemiah* 9:8). Thus, whatever failing in faith was attributed to Avraham would be so minute that it would escape detection by even an angel.

Just as the sin was microscopic, so, too, was the punishment extraordinarily delicate. The four hundred years began with the birth of Yitzchak, who never left the boundaries of *Eretz Yisrael* proper. And when Yaakov and his

HASHEM brought us out of Egypt with a mighty hand and with an outstretched arm, with great awe, with signs and wonders.[1]

HASHEM brought us out of Egypt — not through an angel, not through a seraph, not through a messenger, but the Holy One, Blessed is He, in His glory, Himself, as it says: I will pass through the land of Egypt on that night; I will slay all the firstborn in the land of Egypt from man to beast; and upon all the gods of Egypt will I execute judgments; I, HASHEM.[2]

'I will pass through the land of Egypt on that night' — I and no angel; 'I will slay all the firstborn in the land of Egypt' — I and no seraph; 'And upon all the gods of Egypt will I execute judgments' — I and no messenger; 'I, HASHEM' — it is I and no other.

---

1. *Devarim* 26:8.   2. *Shemos* 12:12.

---

sons went down into Egypt, they were treated royally. Even the eighty-six years of servitude had a redeeming factor; they were a period of miracles. The women gave birth in the field and angels brought up the children and protected them (*Shemos Rabbah* 1). It was a punishment which could not be judged by the standards of an angel. And, indeed, when the time of Redemption drew near, an angel — the heavenly representative of Egypt (שַׂר שֶׁל מִצְרַיִם) — charged that Israel had not yet received the full punishment due them (*Yalkut, Beshalach*). But, when the sin is such that only the Holy One Himself can discern it, the punishment, too, is such that only He can note it. Only He will know when Israel has made up the minute lack in faith by witnessing the awe-inspiring miracles (*Shemos* 14:34). And, hence, only He can be the Redeemer.

לֹא עַל יְדֵי מַלְאָךְ / Not through an angel

R' Eliahu Dessler   The man who is spiritually elevated sees the hand of Hashem everywhere. Every facet of nature sends him a message of ethical importance. Others require obvious miracles, angels, or the prophecy of seers. Still others are so spiritually dull that their hearts are closed to even miracles and prophecy. So it was with Pharaoh when faced with the prophecies of Moshe and the miracles in Egypt. And thus it was that, when Eliahu on Mount Carmel begged that fire descend from the heavens onto his sacrifice, he prayed for a twofold miracle: "Answer me, HASHEM, answer me" (*I Melachim* 18:37). Answer me — have fire descend from Heaven; answer me — let them not say that I used witchcraft (*Berachos* 9b).

בְּיָד חֲזָקָה – זוֹ הַדֶּבֶר, כְּמָה שֶׁנֶּאֱמַר, הִנֵּה יַד יהוה הוֹיָה בְּמִקְנְךָ אֲשֶׁר בַּשָּׂדֶה, בַּסּוּסִים בַּחֲמֹרִים בַּגְּמַלִּים בַּבָּקָר וּבַצֹּאן, דֶּבֶר כָּבֵד מְאֹד.[1]

וּבִזְרֹעַ נְטוּיָה – זוֹ הַחֶרֶב, כְּמָה שֶׁנֶּאֱמַר, וְחַרְבּוֹ שְׁלוּפָה בְּיָדוֹ, נְטוּיָה עַל יְרוּשָׁלָיִם.[2]

וּבְמֹרָא גָּדֹל – זוֹ גִּלּוּי שְׁכִינָה, כְּמָה שֶׁנֶּאֱמַר, אוֹ הֲנִסָּה אֱלֹהִים לָבוֹא לָקַחַת לוֹ גוֹי מִקֶּרֶב גּוֹי, בְּמַסֹּת, בְּאֹתֹת, וּבְמוֹפְתִים, וּבְמִלְחָמָה, וּבְיָד חֲזָקָה, וּבִזְרוֹעַ נְטוּיָה, וּבְמוֹרָאִים גְּדֹלִים, כְּכֹל אֲשֶׁר עָשָׂה לָכֶם יהוה אֱלֹהֵיכֶם בְּמִצְרָיִם לְעֵינֶיךָ.[3]

The Zohar explains that an angel was not sent to take Israel out of Egypt because the Egyptians were in such a state of spiritual impurity (טוּמְאָה) that they would have impaired the holiness (קְדוּשָׁה) of even an angel. The Divine Presence Itself was needed to effect the Exodus.

The Egyptians were of those who are so unfeeling that even an angel's presence cannot move them. Hashem Himself was needed to impart great fear (מֹרָא גָּדֹל). And *Chazal* have, indeed, interpreted that great fear as the revelation of the Divine Presence (גִּלּוּי שְׁכִינָה).

וּבְמֹרָא גָּדֹל זוֹ גִּלּוּי שְׁכִינָה
With great awe — alludes to the Revelation of the Shechinah

R' Avraham Joffen   At first glance these are diametrically opposed to one another. Great awe is the depth of trembling and terror; Revelation is the height of bliss and spiritual attainment. And yet they are not unrelated. Man has the power to use ultimate evil as a springboard to the ultimate good, or good as a path to evil. Israel, through the terror of the plague of the firstborn (מַכַּת בְּכוֹרוֹת), rose to grasp Divine Revelation; through the fear of death at the parting of the Red Sea (קְרִיעַת יַם סוּף), they reached a peak of faith: "And the nation feared HASHEM — and they believed in HASHEM . . ." (*Shemos* 14:31).

R' Akiva would weep when he reached the verse which forbids one to communicate with the dead; to fast and lie in a cemetery so that an evil spirit rests on him. He noted that if one fasts for an impure purpose and the evil spirit which he seeks will come to rest on him, how much more so will the one who fasts to achieve purity gain his goal (*Sanhedrin* 65b). The complete man learns to ascend from the very source from which the evil man draws sin. And the wicked man seeks out the evil in the source of the good.

With a mighty hand — refers to the pestilence, as it is stated: Behold, the hand of HASHEM shall strike your cattle which are in the field, the horses, the donkeys, the camels, the herds, and the flocks — a very severe pestilence.[1]

With an outstretched arm — refers to the sword, as it says: His drawn sword in His hand, outstretched over Jerusalem.[2]

With great awe — alludes to the revelation of the Shechinah, as it says: Has God ever attempted to take unto Himself a nation from the midst of another nations by trials, miraculous signs, and wonders, by war and with a mighty hand and outstretched arm and by awesome revelations, as all that HASHEM your God did for you in Egypt, before your eyes?[3]

---

1. *Shemos* 9:3.   2. *I Divrei Hayamim* 21:16.   3. *Devarim* 4:34.

This it was that led Eliahu (when he had fire descend from on high to his altar on Mount Carmel) to pray: "Answer me — let them not say that I used witchcraft" (*Berachos* 9b). For Divine Revelation, itself, can be turned to evil purpose.

Haman, the unspeakable, cast the fear of death onto the people of Israel with his terrible decree of extermination. But Mordechai gathered his students and taught them the *halachos* (laws) dealing with the *omer* (the measure of barley which is cut from the new crop). When the fear of death loomed over them, learning Torah strengthened their desire to serve their Creator and raised their hopes of salvation. Haman saw this and understood that victory would not be his. "Your small measure of the *omer*," he said, "has driven off my ten thousand coins of silver" (*Esther Rabbah* 10:4).

גִּלּוּי שְׁכִינָה
Revelation of the Shechinah

R' Avraham Grodzinski of Slobodka

Revelation of the *Shechinah* is the essence of the Redemption from Egypt! With the exodus from Egypt, a new creation came into being. In the beginning of things, when the world was created, man came into being. When Egypt was left behind, the Jews, a new species, were created. And that which characterized the new species was the wherewithal to bear Revelation of the *Shechinah*.

Chazal say that the army of Sancheriv which besieged Jerusalem perished in a unique way — they heard the song of the angels and their souls left their

וּבְאֹתוֹת – זֶה הַמַּטֶּה, כְּמָה שֶׁנֶּאֱמַר, וְאֶת הַמַּטֶּה הַזֶּה תִּקַּח בְּיָדֶךָ, אֲשֶׁר תַּעֲשֶׂה בּוֹ אֶת הָאֹתֹת.[1]

וּבְמֹפְתִים – זֶה הַדָּם, כְּמָה שֶׁנֶּאֱמַר, וְנָתַתִּי מוֹפְתִים בַּשָּׁמַיִם וּבָאָרֶץ

As each of the words דָּם, blood, אֵשׁ, fire, and עָשָׁן, smoke, is said,
a bit of wine is removed from the cup, with the finger or by pouring.

דָּם וָאֵשׁ וְתִמְרוֹת עָשָׁן.[2]

דָּבָר אַחֵר – בְּיָד חֲזָקָה, שְׁתַּיִם. וּבִזְרֹעַ נְטוּיָה, שְׁתַּיִם. וּבְמֹרָא גָּדֹל, שְׁתַּיִם. וּבְאֹתוֹת, שְׁתַּיִם. וּבְמֹפְתִים, שְׁתַּיִם. אֵלּוּ עֶשֶׂר מַכּוֹת שֶׁהֵבִיא הַקָּדוֹשׁ בָּרוּךְ הוּא עַל הַמִּצְרִים בְּמִצְרַיִם, וְאֵלּוּ הֵן:

---

bodies (*Sanhedrin* 92). Yet Israel, an entire people, witnessed the Divine Presence *(Shechinah)* and, not only survived, but were redeemed. An entire people sang in praise: "*This* is my God and I will exalt Him" *(Shemos* 15:2) — *this*, as if pointing a finger *(Sotah* 11), with full awareness. An entire nation heard: the voice of HASHEM speaking to it from the midst of the fire — and remained alive *(Devarim* 4:33).

And this nation, this newly created entity, has a lofty task — to come close to the Creator: "and you shall walk in His ways" *(Devarim* 28:9) — you shall be like Him *(Shabbos* 133b), a demand for achievement without limit, greater and greater awareness, higher and higher. Through the Revelation of the *Shechinah* which brought them into being, through this awareness of Hashem, they gained the possibility of becoming like the Creator, so to speak.

It is this interpretation which lies behind the verse which tells us that Hashem took Israel out of Egypt as: "a nation from within a nation" *(Devarim* 4:34) — like one who removes a fetus from the innards of an animal *(Mechilta, Beshalach*). Israel and Egypt were of one species, of the same human flesh and blood. And, then, Israel became newly made and distinct. They were a people deemed worthy to experience Revelation of the *Shechinah* and that in turn, allowed them to fully savor: "I am HASHEM, your God . . . Who has taken you out of the land of Egypt" *(Shemos* 20:2).

Each time a Jew learns the story of Israel's exodus from Egypt, he should sense the Revelation of the *Shechinah* and feel that he can and must be like Hashem. For Revelation and being like Hashem are dependent on one another. With each added dimension of a man's awareness of Hashem's holiness, his own holiness rises in the eyes, so to speak, of Hashem. He

With signs — refers to the miracles performed with the staff as it says: Take this staff in your hand, that you may perform the miraculous signs with it.[1]

With wonders — alludes to the blood, as it says: I will show wonders in the heavens and on the earth

As each of the words דָּם, blood, אֵשׁ, fire, and עָשָׁן, smoke, is said, a bit of wine is removed from the cup, with the finger or by pouring.

Blood, fire, and columns of smoke.[2]

Another explanation of the preceding verse: [Each phrase represents two plagues,] hence: mighty hand — two; outstretched arm — two; great awe — two; signs — two; wonders — two. These are the ten plagues which the Holy One, Blessed is He, brought upon the Egyptians in Egypt, namely:

_____
1. Shemos 4:17. 2. Yoel 3:3.

perceives Hashem and is himself seen by the Great Perceiver. That is why we are commanded to make mention of the going out of Egypt twice daily — morning and evening, so that we might climb the successive rungs of: "You shall be holy, because I HASHEM am holy" (Vayikra 19:2) — one rung after another.

עֶשֶׂר מַכּוֹת / The ten plagues

The Alter of Kelm The Ten Commandments begin: "I am HASHEM your God, Who has taken you out of the land of Egypt" (Shemos 20:2). The Torah, by placing the Exodus from Egypt here, gives us a new perspective in our conception of the Creator. Previously, we knew that Hashem created the whole of the universe for man's benefit: "You placed everything beneath his (man's) feet" (Tehillim 8:7) and each man should feel that the world is created for his sake (Berachos 6). But the miracles of the ten plagues cast a different light on Creation and the Creator. Not only was the world *created* for each individual, so that he might serve Hashem, it is *recreated* for each individual at each and every moment.

Take the plague of blood (מַכַּת דָּם), for example. Both Jew and Egyptian draw water from the same source. The Jew draws up water; the Egyptian, blood. The Egyptian asks the Jew for a bit of water and it turns to blood when it reaches his hand. He says to the Jew, "Let's both drink together from your cup." The Jew drinks water; the Egyptian sips blood (Yalkut, Shemos 7).

When, then, we drink a cup of water, that water was created specifically for us. Miraculously, it is not blood. And when we recite the blessing over water: ". . . that all came into being by His word," let us be aware that it is because He has decided that it should be water, that it is, indeed, water.

As each of the plagues is mentioned, a bit of wine is removed from the cup.
The same is done by each word of Rabbi Yehudah's mnemonic.

דָּם. צְפַרְדֵּעַ. כִּנִּים. עָרוֹב. דֶּבֶר. שְׁחִין. בָּרָד. אַרְבֶּה. חֹשֶׁךְ. מַכַּת בְּכוֹרוֹת.

Similarly, during the plague of darkness (מַכַּת חֹשֶׁךְ), the sun did shine and the Jew looked about him with open eyes — but for the Egyptian there was darkness. The sun shines or does not shine for each soul, individually. And in the plague of hail (מַכַּת בָּרָד), Egypt experienced a storm, the likes of which it had never known, and, a bare pace away, in the land of Goshen, there was no hail. The stormy Red Sea swept away the Egyptians; Israel walked on dry firm land.

Although these were not recurring phenomena, they do serve to teach us an unchanging principle. Each Jew upon arising each morning must bless Hashem: ". . . Who spreads forth the earth upon the waters," because the earth is spread out at each moment, for each one, in particular. He must make the blessing: ". . . Who creates the (heavenly) lights," because the sun shines for him, privately. And when rain falls we bless Him: "for each and every drop" (*Taanis* 6b), because each detail of nature is a recurring miracle, which takes place at that instant for the man who benefits from it.

Hence it is that in the *Kiddush* of Friday evening we say that *Shabbos*, too, reminds us of our Exodus from Egypt. For, although the *Shabbos* has been given to us, to remember that Hashem created the world, our going out of Egypt showed us that the act of Creation is renewed daily for each person. It follows that we ought to, each of us, recreate our personalities continuously, to be worthy of the ongoing creation.

R' Yerucham of Mir How was it, indeed, possible that an inanimate staff should turn into a snake, water to blood, day to darkness; that fire and water combine in the plague of hail (בָּרָד)?

The ten plagues show us that all of creation is a single entity which expresses itself in different forms. But all are, in essence, one and the same and all have been brought into existence by a single Creator. The variety of forms is only external. That is why the bitter waters of Marah can become sweet and a living stream of water gush forth from the rock.

This teaches us that a man may not say, "I am as I am and cannot change. I am full of anger; I am lazy; I am a sinner." For it is possible to transform the nature of all things — from good to evil and from evil to good. That is the basis for *teshuvah* (repentance).

The Midrash expressly states this: When the Holy One wished to eradicate Israel, Moshe said, "Did you not tell me at Marah that, if I were to pray, you would turn the bitter waters to sweet? Now, too, change the bitterness of Israel and cure them" (*Shemos Rabbah* 43:3).

As each of the plagues is mentioned, a bit of wine is removed from the cup.
The same is done by each word of Rabbi Yehudah's mnemonic.

1. Blood 2. Frogs 3. Vermin 4. Wild Beasts 5. Pestilence 6. Boils 7. Hail 8. Locusts 9. Darkness 10. Plague of the Firstborn.

This is the lesson of the ten plagues. Man's task is to change his nature to the better.

דָּם צְפַרְדֵּעַ / Blood, frogs

R' Yosef Leib Bloch of Telshe   Why did Hashem devise deeds that could be imitated by the magicians?

Hashem revealed his powers through that which is found in our world — blood, frogs and lice. This allowed Pharaoh to err and assume that they were only the stuff of common magic. Would it not have been preferable to create new suns and gigantic frightful monsters? Pharaoh and his people could not, then, have fallen into error.

Man is a microcosm, a small world in himself (עוֹלָם קָטָן) and each facet of his nature is reflected in some being and specific power in the greater world that surrounds him. That greater world, in entirety, is a single perfect whole. Nothing is lacking; nothing is extraneous and without purpose. This is what King Shlomo meant when he said: "There is nothing new under the sun" (Koheles 1:9) — creation is already perfect and lacks nothing to make it perfect.

If new beings had been created for the plagues, they would not have been understood by man, nor would they have made an impression upon him. For man already possesses all that might bring him to an awareness of truth; everything has already been created.

R' Yerucham of Mir   The Creator was, in effect, demanding of Pharaoh that he distinguish between an act of Hashem and the trick performance of the magicians. An act of Hashem is on such a large scale that one cannot possibly mistake it. The magicians turned a cup of water to blood; Hashem transformed the waters of the rivers, the lakes, the canals and the wells (Shemos Rabbah 9).

This is characteristic not only of the plagues in Egypt, but of all the acts of Hashem. Creation itself bears witness that it is His understanding which underlies its existence: "Our Master is great and with immense power; there is no limit to His understanding" (Tehillim 147:5). Nature teaches us about its Creator. For nature has no limits and each of its facets is made up of innumerable parts and each part reveals boundless wisdom and understanding. All the parts and all the facets point to their Creator and demand of us: "Praise the name of Hashem, for His Name is on high alone; praise Him on earth and in heaven" (Tehillim 148:13). The very scale is so great that it denies man the possibility of ignoring it.

רַבִּי יְהוּדָה הָיָה נוֹתֵן בָּהֶם סִמָּנִים:

דְּצַ"ךְ • עֲדַ"שׁ • בְּאַחַ"ב.

The cups are refilled. The wine that was removed is not used.

רַבִּי יוֹסֵי הַגְּלִילִי אוֹמֵר: מִנַּיִן אַתָּה אוֹמֵר שֶׁלָּקוּ הַמִּצְרִים בְּמִצְרַיִם עֶשֶׂר מַכּוֹת וְעַל הַיָּם לָקוּ חֲמִשִּׁים מַכּוֹת? בְּמִצְרַיִם מָה הוּא אוֹמֵר,

R' Yehudah Leib Chasman The magicians, in truth, were unable to completely duplicate the acts of Moshe. Pharaoh himself was aware of this. For the tricksters could not remove the plagues and Pharaoh was forced to plead with Moshe to do so.

Nevertheless, Pharaoh needed but a weak excuse in order to continue shutting his eyes to the truth; the limited powers of the magicians served that purpose. Such is the nature of men.

The Torah says: "Sin lies at the door" (*Bereishis* 4:7). Sin spreads itself before a man, clear as can be. And yet, he falls victim to it, because there is a door, an opening, a way out — some weak rationalization which calms his conscience. Everyone sees the hand of Hashem in the workings of Creation, but not all trust in Him implicitly — because of a door. They say, "Look, nature possesses movement. Nature must be an independent force."

R' Yechezkel Levenstein When Moshe and Aharon made their first appearance before Pharaoh, they did so without asking prior permission. And they made a rebellious demand: "Send forth my people" (*Shemos* 5:1). *Chazal* describe the clearly miraculous way in which they arrived. Pharaoh was in the midst of a banquet and they slipped by the patrols of the guards and their attendant lions (*Yalkut Shimoni* 176). Pharaoh was so impressed that he did not have them executed as rebels against the crown. And yet he did not agree to free Israel.

And then, at their next meeting, Aharon threw down the staff which turned to a serpent. That put Pharaoh's back up and he summoned the magicians to do likewise. "And the staff of Aharon swallowed up the staves of the magicians" (*Shemos* 7:12).

The order of events is instructive. Pharaoh could easily have seen the truth with the first trial. It would have been natural to admit that the first appearance of Moshe and Aharon before him was a miracle. But once he had hardened his heart, he was presented with a situation — the incident of the serpent — in which it was less likely to see the marvel; the magicians could just as easily turn staves into serpents. And yet in the second incident, or trial of Pharaoh, there was still a clear element of the miraculous; Aharon's staff

Rabbi Yehudah abbreviated them
by their Hebrew initials:
D'TZACH, ADASH, B'ACHAB

The cups are refilled. The wine that was removed is not used.

Rabbi Yose the Galilean said: How does one derive that the Egyptians were struck with ten plagues in Egypt, but with fifty plagues at the Sea? — Concerning the plagues in Egypt the Torah states:

---

scored a clear victory. It swallowed those of the magicians. And with this further hardening of his heart, Pharaoh was presented with an even lesser miracle — water was transformed to blood. Lesser, because the magicians followed suit. And this was not followed by a miraculous victory of Moshe and Aharon over the magicians.

Man should know that such is the nature of trials which are sent from Heaven. It becomes harder and harder to withstand them, if one does not make the supreme effort to successfully withstand the first trial!

רַבִּי יְהוּדָה הָיָה נוֹתֵן בָּהֶם סִמָּנִים
R' Yehudah abbreviated them by their Hebrew initials

The Alter of Kelm What did R' Yehudah gain with his abbreviated symbols? He gained a great deal. He did not need to utter the full names of the foul plagues.

וְעַל הַיָּם לָקוּ חֲמִשִּׁים מַכּוֹת . . . חֲמִשִּׁים וּמָאתַיִם מַכּוֹת
With fifty plagues at the sea . . . two hundred and fifty

R' Eliahu Dessler *Chazal* have this remarkable difference of opinion as to the number of plagues the Egyptians absorbed at the Red Sea (fifty, two hundred or two hundred and fifty). We can understand the basis for such a controversy, if we realize that every act of the Creator can be considered in many ways, as if on a ladder of many rungs. And each level offers a different view and a different impression.

At the parting of the Red Sea (קְרִיעַת יַם סוּף), Israel contemplated the entire range of rungs and rose to the height of song of praise; but the hearts of the Egyptians were closed and sealed and they sank into the sea.

So, too, we can look at the Exodus from Egypt as a whole and it is possible to see it in innumerable detail — with each fine point a whole Redemption in itself.

How many kindnesses Hashem has done for us . . . had He done but this, it would have been enough for us. A single detail would have been sufficient for us to feel, for the whole of our lives, the thanks due Him!

וַיֹּאמְרוּ הַחַרְטֻמִּם אֶל פַּרְעֹה, אֶצְבַּע אֱלֹהִים הִוא.[1] וְעַל הַיָּם מָה הוּא אוֹמֵר, וַיַּרְא יִשְׂרָאֵל אֶת הַיָּד הַגְּדֹלָה אֲשֶׁר עָשָׂה יהוה בְּמִצְרַיִם, וַיִּירְאוּ הָעָם אֶת יהוה, וַיַּאֲמִינוּ בַּיהוה וּבְמֹשֶׁה עַבְדּוֹ.[2]

אֶצְבַּע אֱלֹהִים . . . הַיָּד הַגְּדֹלָה
The finger of God . . . the great hand

R' Yosef Leib Bloch of Telshe

It perhaps grates on the ear to hear the phrase "finger of God," or "His hand of five fingers." But such phrases demonstrate an important principle.

All the varied worlds, from those which are most spiritually elevated down to our own earth, are joined together and reflect each other. For example, in our daily conversation we speak of a "great man," a man who is "head and shoulders above all others." We don't refer to his physical stature, but to his loftiness of soul. We draw a parallel between the dimension of the physical and that of the spirit. In a similar manner, in the upper world, which reaches to the very seat of Creation, we find the same factors which we find here, on earth, and the same terms are used — even though it is clearly evident that the essence described, though parallel, is spiritual in nature and eons removed from its "fellow" on earth.

The Midrash provides us with an example which clarifies the parallelism. A poor, pious scholar (תַּלְמִיד חָכָם) had no money with which to provide himself with his *Shabbos* needs. He prayed and Heaven sent him a diamond. He bought the necessary provisions and, when he arrived home, he told his wife what had happened. She refused to eat until he promised to return the diamond to heaven, so that their share in the World-to-Come not be diminished. A greater miracle was needed to return the diamond. For Heaven gives, but does not receive.

The story raises a number of questions: Why a diamond; why would their share be reduced by a significant degree; why is a miracle needed to return the diamond — why do they not, simply, forgo the benefit and throw it into the sea?

The answer is that the wise scholar was destined to be poor in the here and now of this world. Riches were prepared for him in the World-to-Come — purified, spiritual wealth. For in that world the righteous take pleasure from the radiance of the Divine Presence (*Berachos* 17a).

We really don't know what that radiance and bliss is; we can but give it an image. If we are to translate light, brilliance, purity and great value into the terms of our world we have defined a diamond. And that is what our story tells us. This wise man's share in the World-to-Come, the heavenly radiance, was reduced into the concrete form of a diamond. He could not, then, merely throw the diamond away. He had to pray that the diamond would

The magicians said to Pharaoh, 'It is the finger of God.'[1] However, of those at the Sea, the Torah relates: Israel saw the great 'hand' which HASHEM laid upon the Egyptians, the people feared HASHEM and they believed in HASHEM and in His servant Moshe.[2]

1. *Shemos* 8:15. 2. 14:31.

pass back over the road it had taken; that it return to its former spiritual state of heavenly radiance. Such a return from the concrete to the spiritual does, indeed, require a greater miracle than the transformation of the spiritual to the concrete.

Not only are the worlds parallel and each world is a mirror image of the world above it, but true existence is to be found there, in the upper world. We have been created in God's image. And whatever we possess is a reflection of higher powers of true existence — of the Finger, the Hand and the Eye of Divine Rule. Such an understanding sheds light on many otherwise obscure matters and helps answer many of the questions which are raised. It is one of the foundations in the study of *kabbalah* (mysticism).

וַיִּירְאוּ הָעָם אֶת ה׳, וַיַּאֲמִינוּ בַּה׳
The people feared HASHEM and they believed in HASHEM

R' Yerucham of Mir

When Moshe first announced the Redemption to the Jews in Egypt we are told: "And the people believed" (*Shemos* 4:31). Afterwards they saw the terrifying plagues which afflicted the Egyptians. Yet only later, when they passed through the parted waters of the Red Sea do we find that: "the people feared HASHEM" and only then "they believed in HASHEM."

In truth, they had faith earlier, too. But that was a faith that touched their intellect only. They were, indeed, impressed when they contemplated the ten plagues, but even this was a matter of the mind. Faith and fear had not yet penetrated to the heart and the personality. However, with the parting of the sea, when Israel, themselves, stood in danger of death and were saved, they felt the emotion of fear and then their faith became a matter of feeling.

When Achashverosh removed his ring and gave it to Haman, he was more effective than all the prophets who had exhorted Israel (*Megillah* 14). The prophets spoke to their minds; the edict of Haman shook their souls.

"The man whose wisdom surpasses his good deeds is like a many-branched tree with few roots. It is uprooted with the coming of a wind" (*Avos* 3:17). For wisdom bears fruit. It is clearly visible and admirable. But good deeds are like the roots which guarantee that the tree will live on.

וַיִּירְאוּ . . . וַיַּאֲמִינוּ / *. . . feared . . . and they believed*

[R' Yisrael of Salant noted that the verse does not follow a natural pattern. For it would seem that faith in the Creator should precede fear of Him.

כַּמָּה לָקוּ בְאֶצְבַּע? עֶשֶׂר מַכּוֹת. אֱמוֹר מֵעַתָּה, בְּמִצְרַיִם לָקוּ עֶשֶׂר מַכּוֹת, וְעַל הַיָּם לָקוּ חֲמִשִּׁים מַכּוֹת.

רַבִּי אֱלִיעֶזֶר אוֹמֵר. מִנַּיִן שֶׁכָּל מַכָּה וּמַכָּה שֶׁהֵבִיא הַקָּדוֹשׁ בָּרוּךְ הוּא עַל הַמִּצְרִים בְּמִצְרַיִם הָיְתָה שֶׁל אַרְבַּע מַכּוֹת? שֶׁנֶּאֱמַר, יְשַׁלַּח בָּם חֲרוֹן אַפּוֹ – עֶבְרָה, וָזַעַם, וְצָרָה, מִשְׁלַחַת מַלְאֲכֵי רָעִים.[1] עֶבְרָה, אַחַת. וָזַעַם, שְׁתַּיִם. וְצָרָה, שָׁלֹשׁ. מִשְׁלַחַת מַלְאֲכֵי רָעִים, אַרְבַּע. אֱמוֹר מֵעַתָּה, בְּמִצְרַיִם לָקוּ אַרְבָּעִים מַכּוֹת, וְעַל הַיָּם לָקוּ מָאתַיִם מַכּוֹת.

The following are attempts to find an answer to the problem.]

R' Moshe Rosenstein of Lomza The verse speaks to those who argue that they do not keep the commandments because of their doubts. They are not certain as to whether or not the Creator exists.

Let us assume that they are telling the truth. But don't they, nevertheless, fear to sin? Great personalities did have faith and there is overwhelming evidence to support that faith. Perhaps the truth lies with the believers.

However, man wishes to give himself over to his desires; he shuts his eyes and hardens his heart. The Torah tells him that, if fear lest those who do believe have the truth would cause him to rein in his desires, he would reach complete faith. For then, the desires would not turn him away from seeing the truth.

R' Yerucham of Mir Man's fear of Hashem should, ideally, precede faith based on reason. One who sees flames, instinctively draws back, before he contemplates and weighs the results of a possible burn. That is what is meant by the precept: "You shall fear HASHEM your God" (*Devarim* 6:13) — fear, pure and simple.

Our forefather, Avraham, was the first of the faithful. But only after the binding of Yitzchak on the altar (עֲקֵדַת יִצְחָק) does the Torah say: "Now I know that you fear HASHEM" (*Bereishis* 22:12). For, then, he did not have a shadow of a thought, a hesitation of mind; he felt fear in every fiber of his being.

Let us give a concrete illustration. When a commanding officer asks for

How many plagues did they receive with the finger? Ten! Then conclude that if they suffered ten plagues in Egypt [where they were struck with a finger], they must have been made to suffer fifty plagues at the sea [where they were struck with a whole hand].

Rabbi Eliezer said: How does one derive that every plague that the Holy One, Blessed is He, inflicted upon the Egyptians in Egypt was equal to four plagues? — for it is written: He sent upon them his fierce anger: wrath, fury, and trouble, a band of emissaries of evil.[1] [Since each plague in Egypt consisted of] 1) wrath, 2) fury, 3) trouble and 4) a band of emissaries of evil, therefore conclude that in Egypt they were struck by forty plagues and by the sea two hundred!

_____
1. Tehillim 78:49.

---

volunteers for a dangerous mission, those who have weighed the issues and are willing to risk their lives step forward. But in time of war, we see that all the soldiers charge the enemy under fire without giving the matter thought; they are "soldiers in line of battle." Fear of Hashem should be like that. There should be no intellectual assessment of faith. We should be "soldiers serving the Creator."

שֶׁהֵבִיא הַקָּדוֹשׁ בָּרוּךְ הוּא עַל הַמִּצְרִים
That the Holy One, Blessed is He, inflicted upon the Egyptians

_____
R' Abba Grossbard of Ponoviez
_____

It is surprising that Israel only experienced faith after witnessing the fall of the Egyptians and not earlier when they, themselves, had been saved. Similarly the first verse of the Song of Praise at the Red Sea (שִׁירַת הַיָּם) is : "horse and rider He has thrown into the sea" (Shemos 15:1). It does not begin with the parting of the sea before the people of Israel. And in the prayers in the blessing which precedes the Shemoneh Esrei we also speak first of "the wicked, You drowned," before "You caused dear ones to pass over."

This teaches us that heavenly signs and wonders are not etched on a man's heart, as long as his pride and sense of self stand between him and his Creator. As long as the pride of "Egypt" stands, belief does not fix itself in the consciousness — and the song of thanks and praise does not burst forth. When they had seen: "the great hand which Hashem had brought against the Egyptians," the annihilation of human pride, then faith became rooted within them.

רַבִּי עֲקִיבָא אוֹמֵר. מִנַּיִן שֶׁכָּל מַכָּה וּמַכָּה שֶׁהֵבִיא הַקָּדוֹשׁ בָּרוּךְ הוּא עַל הַמִּצְרִים בְּמִצְרַיִם הָיְתָה שֶׁל חָמֵשׁ מַכּוֹת? שֶׁנֶּאֱמַר, יְשַׁלַּח בָּם חֲרוֹן אַפּוֹ, עֶבְרָה, וָזַעַם, וְצָרָה, מִשְׁלַחַת מַלְאֲכֵי רָעִים.[1] חֲרוֹן אַפּוֹ, אַחַת. עֶבְרָה, שְׁתַּיִם. וָזַעַם, שָׁלֹשׁ. וְצָרָה, אַרְבַּע. מִשְׁלַחַת מַלְאֲכֵי רָעִים, חָמֵשׁ. אֱמוֹר מֵעַתָּה, בְּמִצְרַיִם לָקוּ חֲמִשִּׁים מַכּוֹת, וְעַל הַיָּם לָקוּ חֲמִשִּׁים וּמָאתַיִם מַכּוֹת. **כַּמָּה מַעֲלוֹת טוֹבוֹת לַמָּקוֹם עָלֵינוּ.** אִלּוּ הוֹצִיאָנוּ מִמִּצְרַיִם, וְלֹא עָשָׂה בָהֶם שְׁפָטִים, **דַּיֵּנוּ.**

כַּמָּה מַעֲלוֹת טוֹבוֹת / So many favors

R' Yitzchak Waldshein of Ostrowze

At each stage we would have shouted, "Enough." We would have been satisfied and would not have imagined that there was anything more to ask for. Even "had He brought us before Mount Sinai, but not given us the Torah," we would have said, "Enough." We would have been overwhelmed by the lofty occasion and been content. But the kindness of Hashem is so great and complete that He did not take our limited vision into consideration. He removed the feeling of "Enough." Now, we realize that standing before Sinai pales before the experience of receiving the Torah.

"Had he brought us out of Egypt, but not executed judgments against the Egyptians — it would have sufficed us." We would have thought that it was sufficient to be saved. We would not have thought of how Divine Revelation and Honor might be made clear to all, by the punishment of the Egyptians. But the Holy One brought this to pass and also "executed judgments against their gods" to show the meaninglessness and emptiness of idolatry. "He had slain their firstborn" to reveal Hashem's Divine Providence (הַשְׁגָּחָה פְּרָטִית) in a marvelous manner. "He had given us their wealth." We feared to take it, lest the Egyptians pursue us to recover it. But Hashem wished us to rely completely on Him and not be afraid. "He had split the Sea" to show His great hand and strike the final blow to the Egyptians. "He had led us through it on dry land"; not even our shoes were muddied. Was there, ever, a more all-encompassing deliverance?

We must learn from this ascending catalogue of favors that when we bring up children, we are not to be satisfied with the minimum. We must not stop at their cry of "Enough." We must teach with such a full scope

Rabbi Akiva said: How does one derive that each plague that the Holy One, Blessed is He, inflicted upon the Egyptians in Egypt was equal to five plagues? — For it is written: He sent upon them His fierce anger, wrath, fury, trouble, and a band of emissaries of evil.[1] [Since each plague in Egypt consisted of] 1) fierce anger, 2) wrath, 3) fury, 4) trouble and 5) a band of emissaries of evil, therefore conclude that in Egypt they were struck by fifty plagues and by the sea two hundred and fifty!

The Omnipresent has bestowed so many favors upon us!

Had He brought us out of Egypt, but not executed judgments against the Egyptians,
it would have sufficed us.

---

that they will be ashamed of their early "Enough."

R' Yechezkel Levenstein Would we really have been content with the assembly before Sinai, had we not been given the Torah? If He had supplied our wants for the forty years in the desert and not brought us into the land of Israel, would we have truly been satisfied?

The *Alter* of Kelm explained that "It would have sufficed us" (דַּיֵּנוּ) expresses the idea that each of these miracles in itself is "enough," sufficient, to strengthen our faith. Man can build his whole world of faith on the strength of a single wondrous act.

Yisro heard about the parting of the Red Sea and came and converted (*Rashi* to *Shemos* 18:1). When Moshe stood before Pharaoh, the king demanded a heavenly sign. And Hashem said, "His request is in place." When Pharaoh persisted in his stubbornness after witnessing the transformation of staff to serpent and the swallowing of the staves of the magicians, Hashem began to afflict him (*Shemos Rabbah* 8). This shows that a single miracle is deemed sufficient to bring us to belief.

Shlomo HaMelech has indicated as much: "A good report puts fat on the bone" (*Mishlei* 15:30); a single message of good tidings can put fat on all the dry bones of man. Hashem multiplied His favors and rained down a shower of miracles upon us to strengthen us in our faith.

אִלּוּ הוֹצִיאָנוּ מִמִּצְרַיִם . . . וְלֹא נָתַן לָנוּ אֶת הַתּוֹרָה
Had He brought us out of Egypt . . . but not given us the Torah

R' Yerucham of Mir Had we not received the Torah, what value would there have been in leaving Egypt?

אִלּוּ עָשָׂה בָהֶם שְׁפָטִים,

וְלֹא עָשָׂה בֵאלֹהֵיהֶם, דַּיֵּנוּ.

אִלּוּ עָשָׂה בֵאלֹהֵיהֶם,

וְלֹא הָרַג אֶת בְּכוֹרֵיהֶם, דַּיֵּנוּ.

אִלּוּ הָרַג אֶת בְּכוֹרֵיהֶם,

וְלֹא נָתַן לָנוּ אֶת מָמוֹנָם, דַּיֵּנוּ.

אִלּוּ נָתַן לָנוּ אֶת מָמוֹנָם,

וְלֹא קָרַע לָנוּ אֶת הַיָּם, דַּיֵּנוּ.

אִלּוּ קָרַע לָנוּ אֶת הַיָּם,

וְלֹא הֶעֱבִירָנוּ בְתוֹכוֹ בֶּחָרָבָה, דַּיֵּנוּ.

אִלּוּ הֶעֱבִירָנוּ בְתוֹכוֹ בֶּחָרָבָה,

וְלֹא שִׁקַּע צָרֵינוּ בְּתוֹכוֹ, דַּיֵּנוּ.

אִלּוּ שִׁקַּע צָרֵינוּ בְּתוֹכוֹ,

וְלֹא סִפֵּק צָרְכֵּנוּ בַּמִּדְבָּר אַרְבָּעִים שָׁנָה, דַּיֵּנוּ.

אִלּוּ סִפֵּק צָרְכֵּנוּ בַּמִּדְבָּר אַרְבָּעִים שָׁנָה,

וְלֹא הֶאֱכִילָנוּ אֶת הַמָּן, דַּיֵּנוּ.

אִלּוּ הֶאֱכִילָנוּ אֶת הַמָּן,

וְלֹא נָתַן לָנוּ אֶת הַשַּׁבָּת, דַּיֵּנוּ.

אִלּוּ נָתַן לָנוּ אֶת הַשַּׁבָּת,

וְלֹא קֵרְבָנוּ לִפְנֵי הַר סִינַי, דַּיֵּנוּ.

אִלּוּ קֵרְבָנוּ לִפְנֵי הַר סִינַי,

וְלֹא נָתַן לָנוּ אֶת הַתּוֹרָה, דַּיֵּנוּ.

When we left Egypt we became servants of Hashem, as it is stated: "You saw what I have done to Egypt. And I carried you on eagles' wings and brought you to Me." Onkelos interprets — "I brought you close to My service" (*Shemos* 19:4). It is for the service to Hashem that we say, "It would have sufficed us."

Had He executed judgments against them, but not upon their gods, it would have sufficed us.

Had He executed judgments against their gods, but not slain their firstborn, it would have sufficed us.

Had He slain their firstborn, but not given us their wealth, it would have sufficed us.

Had He given us their wealth, but not split the Sea for us, it would have sufficed us.

Had He split the Sea for us, but not led us through it on dry land, it would have sufficed us.

Had He led us through on dry land, but not drowned our oppressors in it, it would have sufficed us.

Had He drowned our oppressors in it, but not provided for our needs in the desert for forty years, it would have sufficed us.

Had He provided for our needs in the desert for forty years, but not fed us the Manna, it would have sufficed us.

Had He fed us the Manna, but not given us the Shabbos, it would have sufficed us.

Had He given us the Shabbos, but not brought us before Mount Sinai, it would have sufficed us.

Had He brought us before Mount Sinai, but not given us the Torah, it would have sufficed us.

אִלּוּ קֵרְבָנוּ לִפְנֵי הַר סִינַי, וְלֹא נָתַן לָנוּ אֶת הַתּוֹרָה

Had He brought us before Mount Sinai, but not given us the Torah

R' Yerucham of Mir

Does the assembling of Israel at the foot of Sinai mean anything without the Torah?

Yes! We would have been prepared. That preparation implies a special state of exaltation.

With the parting of the Red Sea (קְרִיעַת יַם סוּף), even the least significant in Israel rose to grasp that which was to be beyond the perception of the prophet Yechezkel (*Mechilta, Beshalach*). Subsequently, in the fifty days between *Pesach* and *Shavuos* (סְפִירַת הָעֹמֶר), and, in particular, in the three days preceding the Divine Revelation at Sinai (שְׁלֹשֶׁת יְמֵי הַגְבָּלָה), they rose yet higher; they reached the level at which Hashem spoke to them face to face (*Devarim* 5:4).

אִלּוּ נָתַן לָנוּ אֶת הַתּוֹרָה,

וְלֹא הִכְנִיסָנוּ לְאֶרֶץ יִשְׂרָאֵל, דַּיֵּנוּ.

אִלּוּ הִכְנִיסָנוּ לְאֶרֶץ יִשְׂרָאֵל,

וְלֹא בָנָה לָנוּ אֶת בֵּית הַבְּחִירָה, דַּיֵּנוּ.

עַל אַחַת כַּמָּה, וְכַמָּה טוֹבָה כְפוּלָה וּמְכֻפֶּלֶת לַמָּקוֹם עָלֵינוּ. שֶׁהוֹצִיאָנוּ מִמִּצְרַיִם, וְעָשָׂה בָהֶם שְׁפָטִים, וְעָשָׂה בֵאלֹהֵיהֶם, וְהָרַג אֶת בְּכוֹרֵיהֶם, וְנָתַן לָנוּ אֶת מָמוֹנָם, וְקָרַע לָנוּ אֶת הַיָּם, וְהֶעֱבִירָנוּ בְתוֹכוֹ בֶּחָרָבָה, וְשִׁקַּע צָרֵינוּ בְּתוֹכוֹ, וְסִפֵּק צָרְכֵּנוּ בַּמִּדְבָּר אַרְבָּעִים שָׁנָה,

Animals are led by their instincts (even a day-old calf does not fall into a pit). Man, in general, lets his intelligence rule him. The Torah became Israel's second nature. And, just as man in general, who follows his reason, becomes the lowest of living creatures when his reason is impaired, so, too, Israel when it swerves from the way of the Torah, becomes the worst of nations: "When you twist the Torah, you will be considered mindless fools" (*Rashi* to *Devarim* 4:9). The wicked of Israel can be wicked without limit and even behave against the dictates of reason. They have done away with the guidelines of the Jew, the bounds of the Torah.

It was while we stood at the foot of Sinai that we gained these guidelines. It was at Sinai that we acquired the potential to live by these guidelines. There we became a holy nation (*Shemos* 19:6); there our very bodies became sanctified (*Shabbos* 143). When we fulfill the Torah we become alive through it (*Vayikra* 18:5); it is our wisdom and understanding (*Devarim* 4:6).

עַל אַחַת כַּמָּה, וְכַמָּה טוֹבָה כְפוּלָה . . .
Thus, how much more so, should we be grateful

R' Eliahu Dessler   When man receives a favor from Hashem, he knows that he owes Him thanks. Yet, he is aware that he cannot repay the favor and thus, he sees himself as being somewhat of a thief. *Chazal* have given voice to the similar discomfort that arises in a comparable situation: He who eats another's food is ashamed to look him in the face (*Yerushalmi Kelaim*). The prayer called *Nishmas* (נִשְׁמַת כָּל חַי) reflects the problem: ". . . we cannot praise You enough, not one part of thousands upon thousands and many myriads, for the bounties You have given us and the miracles and wonders which You have done for us and our forefathers."

Had He given us the Torah, but not brought us into the Land of Israel, it would have sufficed us.

Had He brought us into the Land of Israel, but not built the Temple for us, it would have sufficed us.

Thus, how much more so, should we be grateful to the Omnipresent for all the numerous favors He showered upon us: He brought us out of Egypt; executed judgments against the Egyptians; and against their gods; slew their firstborn; gave us their wealth; split the Sea for us; led us through it on dry land; drowned our oppressors in it; provided for our needs in the desert for forty years;

This is what lies behind the "enough" (דַּיֵּנוּ) which we say to Hashem in the *Haggadah* of *Pesach*. We are in effect saying, "How can we receive more? By what merit have we received so much?"

But such questions do not reflect the fullest measure of humility before Hashem. Complete self-belittlement moves a man to say, "Who am I that I should not wish to receive favors, just because I cannot give proper thanks? I am so insignificant that I should not have such a thought. If it is Hashem's will that I receive, how can I say, 'Enough,' because of my small-minded personal feelings? The Ever-present has multiplied His favors upon us; He wishes us to receive the outpouring of good which He grants us, without thoughts of thanks.

The prophet has already indicated such a position: "I (Hashem) will pour down boundless (עַד בְּלִי דָי) blessing" (*Malachi* 3:10), which *Chazal* interpret: until your lips will be worn out from saying דַי — "enough" (*Shabbos* 32). You will receive blessing after blessing and you will no longer feel the discomfort of not being able to give proper thanks; you will no longer say "enough."

וְנָתַן לָנוּ אֶת מָמוֹנָם / *And He gave us their wealth*

The Alter of Kelm

True, the Holy One had promised that Israel would leave with great wealth (*Bereishis* 15:14). But, when Moshe saw that the people were too involved in gathering the riches which the Sea spewed forth (בִּזַּת הַיָּם), he forced them to depart from there (*Shemos* 15:22 and *Rashi* there). He wished to teach them that everything must be done in moderation. *Chazal* express the same idea: If you take pleasure from a meal, draw away from it (*Gittin* 70).

Moshe did not act on his own initiative. For at the first way-camp which Israel made in the desert, at Marah, they were unable to drink the water. This brought home the lesson: Now, look! Of what good are your silver and gold and precious stones? Just try to eat them!

וְהֶאֱכִילָנוּ אֶת הַמָּן, וְנָתַן לָנוּ אֶת הַשַּׁבָּת, וְקֵרְבָנוּ לִפְנֵי הַר סִינַי, וְנָתַן לָנוּ אֶת הַתּוֹרָה, וְהִכְנִיסָנוּ לְאֶרֶץ יִשְׂרָאֵל, וּבָנָה לָנוּ אֶת בֵּית הַבְּחִירָה, לְכַפֵּר עַל כָּל עֲוֹנוֹתֵינוּ.

וְהֶאֱכִילָנוּ אֶת הַמָּן / Fed us the Manna

R' Eliahu Lopian   The *Manna* is called "bread from heaven" (*Shemos* 16:4), because it is spiritual food, "bread which is the fare of the angels" (*Yoma* 75). Since it is such a "higher" form of food, we should examine its characteristics and see what they can teach us.

That which is holy has no waste matter. And when the sun rose, after Israel had collected its portions, the *Manna* would melt into rivers and the stags and does would drink their fill of it. The nations of the world would hunt down the deer and in eating would taste the *Manna*. Then, they understood how excellent Israel was (*Rashi* to *Shemos* 16:21). But if it had no waste element, why did the *Manna* which the Jews left over to the following morning become wormy and smell (*Shemos* 16:20)? How can the spiritual turn rotten?

The *Manna*, in itself, tasted like "wafers in honey" (*Shemos* 16:31), but one could taste in it all the flavors he would wish to imagine; he could, at will, improve on its naturally excellent flavor. And on *Shabbos*, its taste and smell were all the more exceptional.

These descriptions show us that man can spoil the most spiritual essence by sin; he can destroy even a *Gan Eden* (Paradise). But, on the other hand, when he himself rises, spiritually, he can transform even the loftiest matter to something higher and purer; he can improve even the *Manna*.

וְהִכְנִיסָנוּ לְאֶרֶץ יִשְׂרָאֵל / Brought us to the Land of Israel

R' Eliahu Lopian   How terrible familiarity can be! I remember that when I first set foot in *Eretz Yisrael* I could not bring myself to spit on its holy soil. I kept many handkerchiefs in my pockets and, when I felt the need to spit, I would spit into them. At times, my pockets bulged with handkerchiefs. But, with the passage of time, when I became accustomed to living in *Eretz Yisrael,* I would spit on the ground.

❦ ❦ ❦

[Once, while strolling, he noticed a Jew at work repairing the road and made the following remark:] Just look at that! Here is a Jew who is involved in fulfilling a *mitzvah* (commandment) during the entire day, the *mitzvah* of settling the land (יִשּׁוּב הָאָרֶץ). But he does not think in terms of fulfilling a commandment. If one performs the act of a commandment and sees it in the light of making a living, he loses the sense of its value as a *mitzvah*.

fed us the Manna; gave us the Shabbos; brought us before Mount Sinai; gave us the Torah; brought us to the Land of Israel; and built us the Temple, to atone for our sins.

R' Eliahu Dessler — *Chazal* say that the air of *Eretz Yisrael* makes one wise (*Bava Basra* 155); that there is no Torah like the Torah of *Eretz Yisrael* (*Sifri, Ekev*). I, myself, clearly feel that in *Eretz Yisrael* it is easier to learn *mussar* (ethics) and move the heart. We can see that youngsters engaged in learning Torah in the Land succeed in acquiring wide knowledge and achieve much more than do their fellows who study within the framework of Torah education offered in other countries; they develop much more here than elsewhere.

Chazal explain the verse "And HASHEM will give you there (in Babylonia) an angry heart" (*Devarim* 28:65) as follows: In *Eretz Yisrael* murder was not committed because of anger.

People were such in those days that the holiness of the Land had its influence even on murderers. But, even in our own day, we see that the Land imparts to those who inhabit her a sense of security. For, when the Nazi forces were drawing near, a tranquility could be felt here. And, despite the many enemies who ring the country all about, everyone — even those who have not as yet seen the light of faith — has a trust in miracles, a trust which can only be explained as one of the blessings of the Holy Land.

וּבָנָה לָנוּ אֶת בֵּית הַבְּחִירָה / And built us the Temple

R' Yerucham of Mir — How difficult it was to build the *Beis HaMikdash*! Before Adam sinned, the Divine Presence (שְׁכִינָה) was on earth (*Bereishis Rabbah* 9); in other words, creatures were in close contact with their Creator. The sin put a distance between them: "Your sins separated you from HASHEM" (*Yeshayahu* 59:2). And, when sin exists anywhere on earth, the earth is no longer a fit resting place for the Divine Presence and sacrifice is not well received by God.

Of the future it is said: "the offering of Yehudah and Jerusalem will be sweet, as in the days of old and as in ancient years" (*Malachi* 3:2). The offerings of remote antiquity are those of Hevel and Noach who brought their sacrifices when the world was free of idolatry (*Vayikra Rabbah* 7). But, for the present, one cannot easily find a suitable setting for sacrifices which will make them acceptable; not every place is fitting: "Take care that you do not sacrifice your burnt-offerings in every place you see" (*Devarim* 12:13).

Moshe found it extremely difficult to erect the Tabernacle (מִשְׁכָּן). It was completed in Kislev, but lay folded for three months. Then he raised it and dismantled it for each of eight days in succession. When it was finally erected on the eighth day, a special prayer was necessary to have the Divine Presence consent to rest there. So, too, for the first fourteen years after Israel

רַבָּן גַּמְלִיאֵל הָיָה אוֹמֵר. כָּל שֶׁלֹא אָמַר שְׁלשָׁה דְבָרִים אֵלּוּ בַּפֶּסַח, לֹא יָצָא יְדֵי חוֹבָתוֹ, וְאֵלּוּ הֵן,

פֶּסַח. מַצָּה. וּמָרוֹר.

had entered the Land, they sacrificed burnt-offerings (עוֹלוֹת) only, and they were found worthy of establishing the *Beis HaMikdash* only four hundred and eighty years later. All this, because traces of the sin of the Golden Calf made it impossible to build the *Beis HaMikdash*.

לְכַפֵּר עַל כָּל עֲוֹנוֹתֵינוּ / *To atone for all our sins*

The Alter of Slobodka   Just see how important atonement is! In the *Pesach Haggadah* we say: How much more so, should we give our thanks to the Ever-present and we tell over, one after the other, the favors that Hashem has done for us: He took us out of Egypt; He supplied our wants for forty years; He gave us the Torah; He brought us into *Eretz Yisrael,* etc. The apex of this list of benefits is: He built the Home of His Choice (*Beis HaBechirah*) to atone for all our sins. All the others were but preliminaries for this final and highest good.

כָּל שֶׁלֹא אָמַר שְׁלשָׁה דְבָרִים אֵלּוּ
Whoever has not explained the following three things

The Alter of Kelm   "Whoever has not explained the following three things on *Pesach* has not fulfilled his obligation, and they are: *Pesach, Matzah* and *Maror*" (פֶּסַח מַצָּה וּמָרוֹר). The statement could have been condensed: "Whoever does not say *Pesach, Matzah* and *Maror* has not fulfilled his obligation."

There is a purpose for the lengthier version and it can stand as an example of how to arouse curiosity and have an idea penetrate deeply. We are first given a general statement that the entire story of the *Haggadah*, that of the Exodus, turns on three matters. Our curiosity is aroused; we wish to know what they are and we are told, "*Pesach, Matzah* and *Maror.*" We become excited and wish to know why these three elements are so important.

The prophet followed this approach. He opened with a question which arouses curiosity: "With what shall I approach Hashem, submit myself to God of Heaven?" He suggests the obvious and concrete, but rejects them: "Shall I approach Him with burnt-offerings (עוֹלוֹת), with one-year-old calves? Will Hashem be pleased with thousands of rams, with myriads of rivers of oil? Shall I offer my firstborn for my sin, the fruit of my belly for my

Rabban Gamliel used to say: Whoever has not explained the following three things on Passover has not fulfilled his duty, namely; PESACH — the Pesach offering; MATZAH — the unleavened bread; MAROR — the bitter herbs.

---

transgression?" And only then does he give the startling and moving answer: "Man, He has told you what is good and what HASHEM asks of you — to practice justice, to love acting with kindness and to walk modestly in the presence of God" (*Michah* 6).

It is with this in mind that *Chazal* say: If you have found that which you sought without effort, do not believe that you have truly found it (*Megillah* 4). For knowledge that a man acquires which has not had an effect on his inner self does not become part of the personality.

פֶּסַח מַצָּה וּמָרוֹר
Pesach, Matzah, and Marror

R' Yisrael of Salant

The bitter herbs remind us of the servitude, the *matzah* of the Redemption. Were we to follow the order of the events, we would mention the bitter herbs before the *matzah*. But there is another factor which enters into the picture.

When the Divine reckoning is made of sins committed against *mitzvos* fulfilled, the difficulty of the circumstances involved in each act is taken into consideration; in the words of the *Mishnah*: "the reward is in accordance with the pain" (*Avos* 5:27). *Chazal* also have said on a similar note: "the punishment of the white is greater than that of the blue." (*Menachos* 43: Among the woolen threads of each of the fringes — צִיצִית — of a garment, there was a costly blue-dyed strand. The punishment for one who neglected to attach the white, easily obtained, threads is more severe than that for one who did not attach the rare and expensive blue thread.)

The people of Israel were mired in a bog of immorality (מ״ט שַׁעֲרֵי טֻמְאָה) and had fulfilled few *mitzvos*. And yet, they were delivered from bondage, because their sins were committed while they suffered the pressure of slavery and were in contact with the corruption of Egypt. Thus, the few *mitzvos* performed under excruciating conditions weighed down the scale in their favor. The Torah says: "And their cry went up to Elokim, from the labor" (*Shemos* 2:23); their cry was heard because it came as a result of the slavery and its difficulties.

When we make note of the *matzah* and bitter herbs, we are not telling over a piece of history in a chronological order; we are concerned with highlighting the Redemption. Hence, we mention the *matzah*, the symbol of deliverance, first, and then explain the cause — the difficult servitude, symbolized by the bitter herbs. That cause gave the few *mitzvos* fulfilled more worth than the many transgressions.

פֶּסַח שֶׁהָיוּ אֲבוֹתֵינוּ אוֹכְלִים בִּזְמַן שֶׁבֵּית
הַמִּקְדָּשׁ הָיָה קַיָּם, עַל שׁוּם מָה? עַל שׁוּם
שֶׁפָּסַח הַקָּדוֹשׁ בָּרוּךְ הוּא עַל בָּתֵּי אֲבוֹתֵינוּ
בְּמִצְרַיִם. שֶׁנֶּאֱמַר, וַאֲמַרְתֶּם, זֶבַח פֶּסַח הוּא
לַיהוה, אֲשֶׁר פָּסַח עַל בָּתֵּי בְנֵי יִשְׂרָאֵל בְּמִצְרַיִם
בְּנָגְפּוֹ אֶת מִצְרַיִם, וְאֶת בָּתֵּינוּ הִצִּיל, וַיִּקֹּד הָעָם
וַיִּשְׁתַּחֲווּ.[1]

עַל שׁוּם שֶׁפָּסַח / *Because . . . He passed over*

R' Yerucham of Mir It is amazing that Hashem's "passing over" of the houses of Israel supplies the name to both the sacrifice and the festival (פֶּסַח). When we look at all the miraculous events of the ten plagues and the Exodus in their totality, the "passing over" seems to be rather marginal.

This shows us that the most important element of the deliverance from Egypt, that which can be attributed solely to the Holy One Himself and no other, is the act of differentiating, differentiating between firstborn and non-firstborn, between Jew and Egyptian. The act of making such distinctions stands above all the miracles.

שֶׁלֹּא הִסְפִּיק בְּצֵקָם . . . לְהַחֲמִיץ
The dough . . . did not have time to become leavened

R' Eliahu Dessler *Chazal* tell us that, in Egypt, Israel had sunk to all but the ultimate depth of corruption. Had they descended to the ultimate depth, the fiftieth gate, they would have intermingled completely with the Egyptians and it would have been impossible to save them. But Hashem guarded and saved them "before they fermented," before they were permanently trapped.

The leavening, *chametz*, symbolizes the ultimate depth of corruption and we are commanded to remove it completely, just as we are commanded to blot out Amalek, the symbol of the forces of evil.

It is understandable, then, why the punishment for eating leavening on *Pesach* is the uprooting of the soul (*kares*) and death at the hands of Heaven.

The Alter of Kelm Hashem timed the departure of Israel from Egypt, so that there was insufficient time for the dough to rise. The Torah wished to teach us that Hashem did not take us out of bondage to have us pamper ourselves with luxuries, which force us into a never-ending race to seek them. Through them, man becomes a slave to

Pesach — Why did our fathers eat a Pesach offering during the period when the Temple stood? — Because the Holy One, Blessed is He, passed over the houses of our fathers in Egypt, as it is written: You shall say: 'It is a Pesach offering for HASHEM, Who passed over the houses of the Children of Israel in Egypt when He struck the Egyptians and spared our houses; and the people bowed down and prostrated themselves.'[1]

---

1. *Shemos* 12:27.

---

himself. And, in contrast, if a man knows how to limit pleasures — an attitude which is symbolized by the non-rising *matzah* — he can embrace true freedom, freedom of thought and freedom from anxiety. Thus it is that *Chazal* declare: "Such is the way of the Torah. Eat bread dipped in salt and drink water in measured quantity" (*Avos* 6:4). If he follows such a pattern, he will not be a slave to his desires. That is the true free man. For "there is no truly free man other than he who is occupied with the Torah" (*Eruvin* 54).

Our whole purpose in life is to be free from desire, and then we will experience bliss. We will be happy with what we have and not wish for that which we don't possess. But he who suffers from desire is unfortunate. He is preoccupied with trying to obtain that which he does not have and is not free to enjoy that which he does possess.

Each year, the *matzah* reminds us to be happy with our lot. This leads to a fortunate life in accordance with the Torah.

וְלֹא יָכְלוּ לְהִתְמַהְמֵהַּ / *And could not delay*

R' Yehudah Leib Chasman

Chazal say that had another moment gone by, the time of Redemption would have passed and Israel could not have been saved. This should teach us how valuable each moment is, in the life of a man. In a single moment he may move from the depths of the impure (מ״ט שַׁעֲרֵי טֻמְאָה) to the heights of light and holiness, and receive the Torah! We should, therefore, improve ourselves in each present moment, for we do not know what the next will bring: "Do not say, 'I shall study when I have a free moment.' Perhaps you will not have that free moment" (*Avos* 2:4).

Every community has its home for the elderly, where we try to make life for the aged as pleasant as possible. But imagine an institution which rejuvenated the old, made the weak strong and the sick healthy! Who would not race to enter it? That is exactly the kind of thing that repentance (תְּשׁוּבָה) accomplishes. Man does an about-face; he passes from darkness to light, and this, in a single instant: "He who betroths a woman on condition that he is a righteous man (צַדִּיק), is legally betrothed, even though he is wicked. We

The middle matzah is lifted and displayed while the following paragraph is recited.

מַצָּה זוּ שֶׁאָנוּ אוֹכְלִים, עַל שׁוּם מָה? עַל שׁוּם שֶׁלֹּא הִסְפִּיק בְּצֵקָם שֶׁל אֲבוֹתֵינוּ לְהַחֲמִיץ, עַד שֶׁנִּגְלָה עֲלֵיהֶם מֶלֶךְ מַלְכֵי הַמְּלָכִים הַקָּדוֹשׁ בָּרוּךְ הוּא וּגְאָלָם. שֶׁנֶּאֱמַר, וַיֹּאפוּ אֶת הַבָּצֵק אֲשֶׁר הוֹצִיאוּ מִמִּצְרַיִם עֻגֹת מַצּוֹת כִּי לֹא חָמֵץ, כִּי גֹרְשׁוּ מִמִּצְרַיִם, וְלֹא יָכְלוּ לְהִתְמַהְמֵהַּ, וְגַם צֵדָה לֹא עָשׂוּ לָהֶם.[1]

The maror is lifted and displayed while the following paragraph is recited.

מָרוֹר זֶה שֶׁאָנוּ אוֹכְלִים, עַל שׁוּם מָה? עַל שׁוּם שֶׁמֵּרְרוּ הַמִּצְרִים אֶת חַיֵּי אֲבוֹתֵינוּ בְּמִצְרַיִם. שֶׁנֶּאֱמַר, וַיְמָרְרוּ אֶת חַיֵּיהֶם, בַּעֲבֹדָה קָשָׁה, בְּחֹמֶר וּבִלְבֵנִים, וּבְכָל עֲבֹדָה בַּשָּׂדֶה, אֵת כָּל עֲבֹדָתָם אֲשֶׁר עָבְדוּ בָהֶם בְּפָרֶךְ.[2]

---

take into consideration the possibility that he is penitent in his heart" (*Kiddushin* 49). A sinner who has transgressed thousands of times, in both light and weighty matters, even such as deserve the punishment of uprooting of the soul (כָּרֵת) and hellfire (גֵּיהִנֹּם) for generation upon generation, can in a single moment cleanse himself completely, rise to the level of a righteous man, rest in the shadow of the Divine Presence (שְׁכִינָה) and gain eternal life.

We gain a new dimension of understanding of the account of the Exodus: "For you went out of Egypt in haste (בְּחִפָּזוֹן), that you might remember the day on which you left the land of Egypt all the days of your life" (*Devarim* 16:3) — that you might remember for all time the value of a single moment.

R' Yerucham of Mir

The haste and hurry of the departure from Egypt teaches us that we should make use of each fleeting opportunity. Our Sages have said: "And you shall eat it in haste" — this refers to the haste on the part of the Divine Presence — שְׁכִינָה (*Mechilta, Bo*). The Divine Presence is in a hurry — "Behold the voice of my Beloved approaches. He leaps over the mountains and skips over the hills" (*Shir HaShirim* 2:8), like a man who has agreed to come out and accompany his friend, when that friend will tap at his window. The friend comes, taps at the window and continues on his way. And his would-be companion must rush

The middle matzah is lifted and displayed while the following paragraph is recited.

Matzah — Why do we eat this unleavened bread? — Because the dough of our fathers did not have time to become leavened before the King of Kings, the Holy One, Blessed is He, revealed Himself to them and redeemed them, as it is written: They baked the dough which they had brought out of Egypt into unleavened bread, for it had not fermented, because they were driven out of Egypt and could not delay, nor had they prepared any provisions for the way.[1]

The maror is lifted and displayed while the following paragraph is recited.

Maror — Why do we eat this bitter herb? — Because the Egyptians embittered the lives of our fathers in Egypt, as it says: They embittered their lives with hard labor, with mortar and bricks, and with all manner of labor in the field: whatever service they made them perform was with hard labor.[2]

---

1. *Shemos* 12:39.   2. 1:14.

out and overtake him.

"The day is short, there is work in abundance, the laborers are lazy and the master presses" (*Avos* 2:15). The master is in a hurry to be on his way; he cannot wait for the lazy workers.

"There is a time for everything" (*Koheles* 3:1) — there was a time for the Torah to be given (*Koheles Rabbah* 3). Had Israel been late, the world would have reverted to chaos (*Shabbos* 88).

"He who does not have the (*Shemoneh Esrei*) prayer immediately follow the blessing of Redemption (the blessing which follows the *Shema* of the morning prayer) can be compared to the beloved companion of a king who knocked on the royal door and, when the king opened it, he found no one there. His friend had gone on his way" (*Yerushalmi, Berachos* 1). The man will pray in a moment, but, then, he will find a shut door. The Divine Presence does not stand waiting.

There is no room for delay in the world. Eliezer, the servant of Avraham, said: "Do not make me delay, for Hashem has made my journey a success" (*Bereishis* 24:56). Yaakov said: "Bring me my wife, for my days have been completed" (*Bereishis* 29:21). And R' Eliezer said: "In all my days no one came to the house of study (בֵּית מִדְרָשׁ) before me. Once, when I arose, I saw that the garbage collectors had risen before me, and I made it a practice to rise earlier" (*Shir HaShirim Rabbah* 1) — and the Midrash concludes: "R' Pinchas ben Yair said, 'This shows that the study of Torah develops care and

בְּכָל דּוֹר וָדוֹר חַיָּב אָדָם לִרְאוֹת אֶת עַצְמוֹ כְּאִלּוּ הוּא יָצָא מִמִּצְרָיִם. שֶׁנֶּאֱמַר, וְהִגַּדְתָּ לְבִנְךָ בַּיּוֹם הַהוּא לֵאמֹר, בַּעֲבוּר זֶה עָשָׂה יהוה לִי, בְּצֵאתִי מִמִּצְרָיִם.[1] לֹא אֶת אֲבוֹתֵינוּ בִּלְבָד גָּאַל הַקָּדוֹשׁ בָּרוּךְ הוּא, אֶלָּא אַף אֹתָנוּ גָּאַל עִמָּהֶם. שֶׁנֶּאֱמַר, וְאוֹתָנוּ הוֹצִיא מִשָּׁם, לְמַעַן הָבִיא אֹתָנוּ לָתֶת לָנוּ אֶת הָאָרֶץ אֲשֶׁר נִשְׁבַּע לַאֲבוֹתֵינוּ.[2]

The matzos are covered and the cup is lifted and held until it is to be drunk. According to some customs, however, the cup is put down after the following paragraph, in which case the matzos should once more be uncovered.

לְפִיכָךְ אֲנַחְנוּ חַיָּבִים לְהוֹדוֹת, לְהַלֵּל, לְשַׁבֵּחַ, לְפָאֵר, לְרוֹמֵם, לְהַדֵּר, לְבָרֵךְ, לְעַלֵּה,

---

care leads to diligence.' " All the virtues run into and follow one another; there are no slack and pauses between them.

חַיָּב אָדָם לִרְאוֹת אֶת עַצְמוֹ כְּאִלּוּ הוּא יָצָא מִמִּצְרָיִם
It is one's duty to regard himself as though he personally had gone out of Egypt

The Alter of Kelm

Whenever we find the term *must* (חַיָּב), we can sense that this refers to a required obligation. How can a man fulfill such an obligation?

Chazal have said: "Achashverosh, in removing his ring and handing it over to Haman, was more effective than all the exhortations of the prophets" (*Megillah* 14). The prophets addressed the mind; Haman's decree of annihilation shook their senses. And when the Sages enumerate the ways to combat the evil nature within oneself (יֵצֶר הָרָע) they say: "Remind him of the day of death" (*Berachos* 5) — him, the man himself, for himself. He should not think abstractly about death, but picture the pangs of death in all their horrors, as if he is experiencing them now. It is with this in mind that it is written: "It is better to go to a house of mourning than to a house of a banquet . . . and the living should take it to heart" (*Koheles* 7:2). When they tore R' Akiva's flesh with combs of iron, he accepted the yoke of the heavenly kingdom and said: "All my days I was pained, wondering when the opportunity would present itself to me to sacrifice myself for the holiness of the Name" (*Berachos*). "I was pained . . ." He had pained himself by imagining realistic pictures of actually sacrificing himself. And thus the Torah tells us: "If you lend money to the poor man with you" — imagine that you are the poor man and then you will easily lend him the money willingly

In every generation it is one's duty to regard himself as though he personally had gone out of Egypt, as it is written: You shall tell your son on that day: 'It was because of this that HASHEM did for "me" when I went out of Egypt.'[1] It was not only our fathers whom the Holy One redeemed from slavery; we, too, were redeemed with them, as it is written: He brought "us" out from there so that He might take us to the land which He had promised to our fathers.[2]

The matzos are covered and the cup is lifted and held until it is to be drunk. According to some customs, however, the cup is put down after the following paragraph, in which case the matzos should once more be uncovered.

Therefore it is our duty to thank, praise, pay tribute, glorify, exalt, honor, bless, extol,

_____
1. *Shemos* 13:8. 2. *Devarim* 6:23.

_____

(*Rashi* to *Shemos* 22:24). That kind of advice is the best kind of advice. Try to come close to experiencing things with your senses.

In a like manner, one can fulfill the obligation to "regard himself as though he personally had gone out from Egypt." He should picture himself as a slave who has been freed. How he would contemplate the greatness of his Liberator! How he would sacrifice all he possessed — and himself — for Him! By imagining such a picture of the mind, he will be impressed by the miracles and he will see that the world has a Creator and Governor, Whom we should fear and serve.

וְאוֹתָנוּ הוֹצִיא מִשָּׁם
He brought "us" out from there

_____
The Alter of Kelm   *Rambam* explains the *halachah* that one is to see (or
_____   show) oneself as having gone out of Egypt as a demonstration of this verse, but he adds that this is also a fulfillment of the commandment: "And you will remember that you were a slave in the land of Egypt" (*Devarim* 5:15; see *Hilchos Chametz U'matzah* 7:6).

Rambam has, possibly, indicated that there are two levels of awareness suggested in the Exodus.

The Exodus was meant to raise Israel to the highest possible point of service to, and understanding of, Hashem. "He brought us out from there" with signs and miracles and chose us to do service to Him. However, if we have not reached such heights, we should at least be aware that "You were a slave and HASHEM freed you." We are now servants to the Creator and it is better to serve Him than to serve Pharaoh.

These two aspects are reflected in the two parts of the first verse of the

וּלְקַלֵּס, לְמִי שֶׁעָשָׂה לַאֲבוֹתֵינוּ וְלָנוּ אֶת כָּל הַנִּסִּים
הָאֵלּוּ, הוֹצִיאָנוּ מֵעַבְדוּת לְחֵרוּת, מִיָּגוֹן לְשִׂמְחָה,
וּמֵאֵבֶל לְיוֹם טוֹב, וּמֵאֲפֵלָה לְאוֹר גָּדוֹל, וּמִשִּׁעְבּוּד
לִגְאֻלָּה, וְנֹאמַר לְפָנָיו שִׁירָה חֲדָשָׁה, הַלְלוּיָהּ.

Ten Commandments. "I am HASHEM your God" and revealed Myself to you for your eternal good. But until you understand this and accept His royal authority willingly, know that "He took you out of Egypt, out of the house of bondage" and it is better that you serve Me rather than slave at hard labor in Egypt.

לְמִי שֶׁעָשָׂה לַאֲבוֹתֵינוּ וְלָנוּ אֶת כָּל הַנִּסִּים הָאֵלּוּ
And acclaim Him Who performed all these miracles
for our fathers and for us

R' Yerucham of Mir We do not, here, refer to the Holy One by name, but by a roundabout description — He Who performed miracles. This is to show that Hashem is ultimately unknowable.

Miracles — the breaks in the order of things — show that the usual picture of nature is a kind of front, a mask, for the unseen, the hidden. Whatever conception we have of the Creator, no matter how elevated, stands on a lower rung than His true being, which is hidden from us.

Thus all blessings begin in the second person (*You*, the party addressed and seen — נוֹכַח), but end in the third person (*He*, the party spoken about and unseen — נִסְתָּר) — "Blessed are You . . . Who has sanctified us with His *mitzvos*," etc. For Hashem is unseen.

Rosh ruled that we should shut our eyes when we recite the blessings (*Orchos Chaim* 38). By shutting our eyes we close out that which is seen and stand in a state of prayer before the Unseen (נִסְתָּר), Hashem.

כָּל הַנִּסִּים הָאֵלּוּ / All these miracles

R' Eliahu Dessler Nature itself is a miracle. Should someone protest and say that nature is rooted in a cause, we may very well ask him why that particular cause produces such a particular result. Nature *is* a miracle — but we have become accustomed to it.

Were we to be told that a man died, was buried, that his body had rotted in the ground and that the grave had opened and he had come forth, we would exclaim, "A miracle, a revival of the dead (תְּחִיַּת הַמֵּתִים)." Yet, when a seed is planted and grows forth after it has rotted in the ground, is that not, too, a revival of the dead? Bury the lobe of a calf's ear deep in fertilizer. If a full-grown cow were to spring up, that's a miracle. When a full-branched tree grows from the planting of a small shoot, is that any more natural? But

and acclaim Him Who performed all these miracles for our fathers and for us. He brought us forth from slavery to freedom, from grief to joy, from mourning to festivity, from darkness to great light, and from servitude to redemption. Let us, therefore, recite a new song before Ḥim! Halleluyah!

---

to the one we are accustomed and see it as part of nature; to the other we are not and name it a miracle.

Chazal have said that the power of blessing rests only on that which is hidden from the eye (*Bava Metzia* 42). Nature by being visible gives an illusion of fact and gives rise to error. Blessing no longer affects that which can be seen and measured. It is only on that which is as yet unseen and unmeasured that the miraculous works its wonder.

The illusion that things are natural is an obstacle. This was why Yosef felt that he must emphasize to Pharaoh, from the outset, "It is not within me (בִּלְעָדַי)" — I myself can effect nothing; all is God's work (*Bereishis* 41:16). That is why *Chazal* say that the miracle by which man receives his livelihood is greater than that of the dividing of the Red Sea (*Pesachim* 118). "Greater" is not to be understood from the perspective of the Holy One. Nothing is more difficult or less difficult to Him. To man it is a *greater* miracle, in the sense that he has *greater* difficulty in perceiving it as a miracle, he must labor to see that his livelihood is not the fruit of *his* force and power.

There are people who view themselves as having faith. Nevertheless, they imagine that plans prosper because nature runs its course. They only pray to Hashem that He see to it that they will be successful and they will thank Him because He gives them the strength to accomplish their undertakings. In effect, they believe in a shared divinity (שִׁתּוּף); they and nature are partners of Hashem in the governing of the world.

R' Nachum Ze'ev of Kelm offered a parable on the topic: A man may peek through the keyhole and see a pen writing and imagine that it writes on its own. The heretic is like that man. He views nature as a force and imagines that it operates on its own. But, when the man at the keyhole opens the door, he sees the one holding the pen. So, too, the man of faith knows that the Holy One brings all things to be and man does not, truly, control his deeds.

וּמֵאֲפֵלָה לְאוֹר גָּדוֹל / *From darkness to great light*

R' Eliahu Dessler

Psychology is well aware of the force of sudden shock. Sudden joy has been known to cure the dumb; electric shocks have removed depression. That is what lies behind the sudden punishment of the evil. Sodom was overturned in an instant (*Eichah* 4:6). Their habitual behavior led them to forget that there was a future day of judgment. Only sudden retribution could shake them.

הַלְלוּיָהּ הַלְלוּ עַבְדֵי יהוה, הַלְלוּ אֶת שֵׁם יהוה. יְהִי שֵׁם יהוה מְבֹרָךְ, מֵעַתָּה וְעַד עוֹלָם. מִמִּזְרַח שֶׁמֶשׁ עַד מְבוֹאוֹ, מְהֻלָּל שֵׁם יהוה. רָם עַל כָּל גּוֹיִם יהוה, עַל הַשָּׁמַיִם כְּבוֹדוֹ. מִי כַּיהוה אֱלֹהֵינוּ, הַמַּגְבִּיהִי לָשָׁבֶת. הַמַּשְׁפִּילִי לִרְאוֹת, בַּשָּׁמַיִם וּבָאָרֶץ. מְקִימִי מֵעָפָר דָּל, מֵאַשְׁפֹּת יָרִים אֶבְיוֹן. לְהוֹשִׁיבִי עִם נְדִיבִים, עִם נְדִיבֵי עַמּוֹ. מוֹשִׁיבִי עֲקֶרֶת הַבַּיִת, אֵם הַבָּנִים שְׂמֵחָה, הַלְלוּיָהּ.[1]

בְּצֵאת יִשְׂרָאֵל מִמִּצְרָיִם, בֵּית יַעֲקֹב מֵעַם לֹעֵז. הָיְתָה יְהוּדָה לְקָדְשׁוֹ, יִשְׂרָאֵל מַמְשְׁלוֹתָיו. הַיָּם רָאָה וַיָּנֹס, הַיַּרְדֵּן יִסֹּב לְאָחוֹר.

The final redeemer, the *Mashiach*, can only come in a generation which is wholly blameworthy (כּוּלוֹ חַיָּב), which has forgotten that a day of judgment shall come (*Sanhedrin*). "The master (the *Mashiach*) shall come to his palace of a sudden" (*Malachi* 3:1). The suddenness will clarify and sharpen the feeling of Hashem's deliverance. And in the past, too, the deliverance from Egypt was sharp and sudden — from darkness to light.

הַלְלוּ עַבְדֵי ה׳

Praise, you servants of HASHEM

R' Yosef Leib Nenedik

Chazal say: "Servants of HASHEM" — and not slaves of Pharaoh (*Megillah* 14).

What is servitude? It can be defined as a state in which a man limits his aspirations and forgoes his "rights," in order to fulfill the master's bidding. The master need not be another person; a man may be a slave to his desires. He may be so addicted to satisfying his desires that he is willing to pay a dear price in terms of health, honor, or even life. And though this slave to his desires derives a certain pleasure in so doing, the slave of another man also gains a measure of benefit — food, clothing and shelter. But he is a slave, because he has submitted himself to the possibility of cruel treatment for the price of some paltry benefit. And he who is addicted to satisfying his desires is lower than the slave of another man, because, in addition to his loss of freedom, he has been unable to preserve the human aspect of himself.

Service to Hashem is a blessing, for it frees man from servitude to another. "The yoke of the regime is removed from him who accepts the yoke of the Torah" (*Avos* 3:5). And then, too, the yoke of desires falls away,

Halleluyah! Praise, you servants of HASHEM, praise the Name of HASHEM. Blessed be the Name of HASHEM from now and forever. From the rising of the sun to its setting, HASHEM's Name is praised. High above all nations is HASHEM, above the heavens is His glory. Who is like HASHEM, our God, Who is enthroned on high, yet deigns to look, upon the heaven and earth? He raises the destitute from the dust, from the trash heaps He lifts the needy — to seat them with nobles, with nobles of His people. He transforms the barren wife into a glad mother of children. Halleluyah![1]

When Israel went forth from Egypt, Yaakov's household from a people of alien tongue, Yehudah became His sanctuary, Israel His dominion. The Sea saw and fled; the Jordan turned backward.

---

1. *Tehillim* 113.

---

because the Torah is the counter-force to man's evil nature — יֵצֶר הָרָע (*Kiddushin* 30). But whoever throws off the yoke of service to Hashem faces one of two possibilities — he becomes a slave to his desires, or to another man. And of these two choices, it is preferable to be a slave to another. Thus, "the yoke of the regime is placed upon him who throws off the yoke of the Torah" (*Avos* 3:5).

When Moshe wondered why Israel had been found worthy of Redemption (*Shemos Rabbah* 3), he in effect was saying that it seemed preferable to him that they be slaves to Pharaoh rather than to their desires. And the Holy One replied that they were to be delivered from bondage through the Torah which they were to receive; they were to gain the blessing inherent in service to Hashem.

הַיָּם רָאָה וַיָּנֹס / *The Sea saw and fled*

R' Yechezkel Levenstein

Chazal say that when Israel entered the Sea of Reeds, it did not part until the people had reached a depth where the waters were up to their noses. Even then the Sea parted before them only as they proceeded, pace by pace.

Hashem wished to teach them faith. And faith is gained only by trials which follow one after the other, as the prophet says: "He who has walked in darkness and has no light, let him trust in the name of HASHEM and lean on his God" (*Yeshayahu* 50:10). Because he is in a state of utter darkness without a ray of light he should have trust, although there seems to be no way out.

הֶהָרִים רָקְדוּ כְאֵילִים, גְּבָעוֹת כִּבְנֵי צֹאן. מַה לְּךָ
הַיָּם כִּי תָנוּס, הַיַּרְדֵּן תִּסֹּב לְאָחוֹר. הֶהָרִים תִּרְקְדוּ
כְאֵילִים, גְּבָעוֹת כִּבְנֵי צֹאן. מִלִּפְנֵי אָדוֹן חוּלִי
אָרֶץ, מִלִּפְנֵי אֱלוֹהַּ יַעֲקֹב. הַהֹפְכִי הַצּוּר אֲגַם מָיִם,
חַלָּמִישׁ לְמַעְיְנוֹ מָיִם.‎¹

According to all customs the cup is lifted and the matzos covered
during the recitation of this blessing.

בָּרוּךְ אַתָּה יהוה אֱלֹהֵינוּ מֶלֶךְ הָעוֹלָם, אֲשֶׁר
גְּאָלָנוּ וְגָאַל אֶת אֲבוֹתֵינוּ מִמִּצְרַיִם,
וְהִגִּיעָנוּ הַלַּיְלָה הַזֶּה לֶאֱכָל בּוֹ מַצָּה וּמָרוֹר. כֵּן יהוה
אֱלֹהֵינוּ וֵאלֹהֵי אֲבוֹתֵינוּ, יַגִּיעֵנוּ לְמוֹעֲדִים וְלִרְגָלִים
אֲחֵרִים הַבָּאִים לִקְרָאתֵנוּ לְשָׁלוֹם, שְׂמֵחִים בְּבִנְיַן

הַיַּרְדֵּן יִסֹּב לְאָחוֹר / *The Jordan turned backward*

R' Eliahu Dessler — Two miracles occurred when Israel crossed the Jordan into *Eretz Yisrael*. The Ark of the Covenant (אֲרוֹן הַבְּרִית) was carried into the river by the priests, the waters halted and the nation passed over on dry land to the farther shore. The priests retreated with the Ark to the shore they had come from, and the river resumed its flow. And then the priests, together with the Ark, were miraculously carried over the face of the water to the farther shore (*Sotah* 35). They did not cross over together with the rest of Israel but experienced a wondrous act of their own.

These two miracles represent two types of marvels. The laws of nature may be pushed aside; this happened when the river waters were brought to a halt. But an act may take place completely outside the framework of nature (מֵעַל הַטֶּבַע); such was the passing of the Ark over the face of the Jordan.

The Ark was itself not subject to the laws of nature. It did not take up space in the *Beis HaMikdash* (*Bava Basra* 99) and carried those who were assigned to carry it along with itself (*Sotah* 35). They, too, were lifted above the laws of nature. Such activity, beyond the bounds of nature, also embraced the Sages who expressed the name of Hashem and worked miracles (*Yevamos* 49; *Bechoros* 8) — they became one with the spiritual and thereby were elevated above the physical. Such was the foreshortening of the journey (קְפִיצַת הַדֶּרֶךְ) of our forefather Yaakov who clung to Hashem in prayer on the site of the *Beis HaMikdash* (*Rashi* to *Bereishis* 28:17).

Just as there are two types of miracles, so, in a like manner, man can serve Hashem in one of two ways. He can push aside nature. He can engage in the

The mountains skipped like rams, and the hills like young lambs. What ails you, O Sea, that you flee? O Jordan, that you turn backward? O mountains, that you skip like rams? O hills, like young lambs? Before HASHEM's presence — tremble, O earth, before the presence of the God of Yaakov, Who turns the rock into a pond of water, the flint into a flowing fountain.[1]

According to all customs the cup is lifted and the matzos covered during the recitation of this blessing.

Blessed are You, HASHEM, our God, King of the universe, Who redeemed our ancestors from Egypt and enabled us to reach this night that we may eat matzah and maror. So, HASHEM, our God and God of our fathers, bring us also to future Festivals and holidays in peace, gladdened in the

1. *Tehillim* 114.

---

study of the Torah for ulterior motives (שֶׁלֹּא לִשְׁמָהּ) and this will lead to study of the Torah for pure (לִשְׁמָהּ) reasons (*Pesachim* 50). Pushing aside obstacles is a long laborious step-by-step procedure. However, man can gain the world in an instant (*Avodah Zarah* 17) and transcend nature through prayer. As *Chazal* express it: The gateway of tears is never locked (*Berachos* 32). In prayer which rises from the depths of his being, man breaks the fetters which bind his heart and, with a seven-league leap, he soars above the obstacles of nature. Such prayers are described as "matters which stand at the world's summit" (*Berachos* 6) — it is above the laws which govern the world. Through such prayer man is borne aloft in an instant without delay.

יַגִּיעֵנוּ לְמוֹעֲדִים וְלִרְגָלִים אֲחֵרִים

Bring us also to future Festivals

R' Yerucham of Mir

When Yaakov arrived in Aram Naharaim, he found a well stopped up with a huge stone surrounded by three herds of grazing sheep. The shepherds would roll the stone off to water their sheep and then roll it on and stop up the well once again (*Bereishis* 29). The Midrash interprets as follows: Israel gathers about the *Beis HaMikdash* three times a year during the Festivals (שָׁלֹשׁ רְגָלִים) and rolls off the stone which covers the well, so to speak; they remove the physical barrier and draw up the spiritual in full measure. The well of the spirit is then stopped up until the coming Festival (*Bereishis Rabbah* 70). But why stop up the source of the spirit at the end of the Festival? We would gather from this, that there are specific times and places which are designated for an overflow

(On *Motzaei Shabbos* the phrase in parentheses substitutes for the preceding phrase.)

עִירֶךָ וְשָׂשִׂים בַּעֲבוֹדָתֶךָ, וְנֹאכַל שָׁם מִן הַזְּבָחִים
וּמִן הַפְּסָחִים [מִן הַפְּסָחִים וּמִן הַזְּבָחִים] אֲשֶׁר יַגִּיעַ
דָּמָם עַל קִיר מִזְבַּחֲךָ לְרָצוֹן. וְנוֹדֶה לְךָ שִׁיר חָדָשׁ
עַל גְּאֻלָּתֵנוּ וְעַל פְּדוּת נַפְשֵׁנוּ. בָּרוּךְ אַתָּה יהוה,
גָּאַל יִשְׂרָאֵל.

בָּרוּךְ אַתָּה יהוה אֱלֹהֵינוּ מֶלֶךְ הָעוֹלָם, בּוֹרֵא פְּרִי
הַגָּפֶן.

The second cup is drunk while leaning on the left side
— preferably the entire cup, but at least most of it.

רחצה

The hands are washed for matzah and the following blessing is recited. It is
preferable to bring water and a basin to the head of the household at the Seder table.

בָּרוּךְ אַתָּה יהוה אֱלֹהֵינוּ מֶלֶךְ הָעוֹלָם, אֲשֶׁר
קִדְּשָׁנוּ בְּמִצְוֹתָיו, וְצִוָּנוּ עַל נְטִילַת יָדָיִם.

of the spirit. Man must drink his fill at those times — on the Festivals. And
he must drink in sufficient quantity to last him until the coming opportunity.

In our day, the period of the open well is the period of study in the
yeshivah and the student must drink deeply enough of the spirit to have it
last him a lifetime.

וְנוֹדֶה לְךָ שִׁיר חָדָשׁ
We shall then sing a new song of praise to You

R' Yosef Leib Bloch of Telshe The Sages say that, from the day that
Hashem created the world until Israel sang
its song of praise on the shore of the Sea of Reeds, no one had ever sung a
song of praise to the Holy One. He created Adam, and Adam did not sing;
He saved Avraham from the fiery furnace and from the kings, and Avraham
did not sing. But when Israel went into the sea and it parted before them,
they sang in praise (*Shemos Rabbah* 23). Yet, that song at the Sea is only a
prelude to the song of the future, for the Torah says: "then Moshe *will* sing"
(יָשִׁיר; *Shemos* 15:1), in the future tense.

It was song that had not been heard previously, because true song, which
bursts forth from the depths of the soul and is rooted in emotions, faith and
the Divine spirit — רוּחַ הַקֹּדֶשׁ — (*Shemos Rabbah*), requires enthusiasm and
excitement. Adam was created but did not sing out in praise, because,

(On *Motzaei Shabbos* the phrase in parentheses substitutes for the preceding phrase.)

rebuilding of Your city, and joyful at Your service. There we shall eat of the offerings and Pesach sacrifices (of the Pesach sacrifices and offerings) whose blood will gain the sides of Your altar for gracious acceptance. We shall then sing a new song of praise to You for our redemption and for the liberation of our souls. Blessed are You, HASHEM, Who has redeemed Israel.

Blessed are You, HASHEM, our God, King of the universe, Who creates the fruit of vine.

The second cup is drunk while leaning on the left side — preferably the entire cup, but at least most of it.

RACHTZAH

The hands are washed for matzah and the following blessing is recited. It is preferable to bring water and a basin to the head of the household at the Seder table.

Blessed are You, HASHEM, our God, King of the universe, Who has sanctified us with His commandments, and has commanded us concerning the washing of the hands.

---

though he was enthusiastic about Creation, he knew that Hashem had created the world in the way He had planned and the world was following a natural course. When Avraham was saved from the fiery furnace, he did not sing out in praise, because he took it for granted that the righteous man (צַדִּיק) is delivered by a miracle; it was natural: "If you shall go in the midst of fire you shall not be scorched and a flame will not burn you" (*Yeshayahu* 43:2). But Israel in Egypt had been sunken in the depths of corruption (מ״ט שַׁעֲרֵי טֻמְאָה) and was not worthy of being saved, even by a miracle of the sort that could be taken for granted. They could only be saved by a miracle of the highest order, on the order of: "I Hashem and not an agent" — not through any of God's attributes (מִידוֹת). Hence, they were moved to song.

They continued to be treated in an unusual and supernatural never-to-be-repeated manner: "And I carried you on the wings of eagles and brought you to Me" (*Shemos* 19:4), to an exceptionally lofty level, which was not to be seen again. And this was but a reflection of what will be the normal state in the future. Then, Hashem will be one and his Name will be one. Things will be arranged above and beyond the laws of nature. Then, true song of praise will enthusiastically break out. And we shall then sing a new song of praise to You on our (physical) deliverance from the nations and on the redemption of our soul, our spiritual self.

מוציא

The following two blessings are recited over matzah; the first is recited over matzah as food, and the second for the special mitzvah of eating matzah on the night of Pesach. [The latter blessing is to be made with the intention that it also apply to the 'sandwich' and the afikoman.]

The head of the household raises all the matzos on the seder plate and recites the following blessing:

בָּרוּךְ אַתָּה יהוה אֱלֹהֵינוּ מֶלֶךְ הָעוֹלָם, הַמּוֹצִיא לֶחֶם מִן הָאָרֶץ.

The bottom matzah is put down and the following blessing is recited while the top (whole) matzah and the middle (broken) piece are still raised.

מצה

בָּרוּךְ אַתָּה יהוה אֱלֹהֵינוּ מֶלֶךְ הָעוֹלָם, אֲשֶׁר קִדְּשָׁנוּ בְּמִצְוֹתָיו, וְצִוָּנוּ עַל אֲכִילַת מַצָּה.

Each participant is required to eat an amount of matzah equal in volume to an egg. Since it is usually impossible to provide a sufficient amount of matzah from the two matzos for all members of the household, the other matzos should be available at the head of the table from which to complete the required amounts. However, each participant should receive a piece from each of the top two matzos. The matzos are to be eaten while reclining on the left side and without delay; they need not be dipped in salt.

מַצָּה
The matzah

The Alter of Kelm

The *halachah* states that it is preferable to make the blessing for bread over a full loaf, even if it is small and of coarse flour, rather than over a slice, even if it is large and of fine flour. Importance, then, is measured not by size but by completeness (שְׁלֵמוּת). Even a minute lack in the picture of the complete and perfect is a fault which embraces the total whole.

His disciple *R' Yerucham of Mir* found this need for the perfect whole expressed in the Midrash: Avraham had successfully completed nine terrible trials — the first was his being cast by Nimrod into the fiery furnace. And then, the Holy One said: "Please take your only child whom you love . . . and offer him up as a burnt-offering" (*Bereishis* 22:2); "Please take" —

MOTZI

The following two blessings are recited over matzah; the first is recited over matzah as food, and the second for the special mitzvah of eating matzah on the night of Pesach. [The latter blessing is to be made with the intention that it also apply to the 'sandwich' and the afikoman.]

The head of the household raises all the matzos on the seder plate and recites the following blessing:

Blessed are You, HASHEM, our God, King of the universe, Who brings forth bread from the earth.

The bottom matzah is put down and the following blessing is recited while the top (whole) matzah and the middle (broken) piece are still raised.

MATZAH

Blessed are You, HASHEM, our God, King of the universe, Who has sanctified us with His commandments, and has commanded us concerning the eating of the matzah.

Each participant is required to eat an amount of matzah equal in volume to an egg. Since it is usually impossible to provide a sufficient amount of matzah from the two matzos for all members of the household, the other matzos should be available at the head of the table from which to complete the required amounts. However, each participant should receive a piece from each of the top two matzos. The matzos are to be eaten while reclining on the left side and without delay; they need not be dipped in salt.

Hashem said, "I have had you face many trials and you stood up to them all. Now, sustain this trial successfully, lest they say the others were not difficult tests" (*Bereishis Rabbah* 55). If Avraham fails this final trial, he will lose his wholeness (שְׁלֵמוּת) and a fault in his completeness renders the entire structure, the entire series of trials which he had successfully weathered, incomplete.

In prayer (וּבָא לְצִיּוֹן) we make the following escalating request: "May He open our hearts in His Torah, put His love and fear into our hearts to do His will and serve Him." But this is not the final word. We add: "and serve Him with a complete (שָׁלֵם) heart, so that we not work in vain and give birth to confusion." How alarming! One can climb from level to level and only fail to "serve with a complete heart" and all his effort is in vain and he gives birth to confusion.

מרור

The head of the household takes a half-egg volume of maror, dips it into charoses, and gives each participant a like amount. The following blessing is recited with the intention that it also apply to the maror of the 'sandwich'. The maror is eaten without reclining, and without delay.

בָּרוּךְ אַתָּה יהוה אֱלֹהֵינוּ מֶלֶךְ הָעוֹלָם, אֲשֶׁר קִדְּשָׁנוּ בְּמִצְוֹתָיו, וְצִוָּנוּ עַל אֲכִילַת מָרוֹר.

כורך

The bottom (thus far unbroken) matzah is now taken. From it, with the addition of other matzos, each participant receives a half-egg volume of matzah with an equal volume portion of maror (dipped into charoses which is shaken off). The following paragraph is recited and the 'sandwich' is eaten while reclining.

זֵכֶר לְמִקְדָּשׁ כְּהִלֵּל. כֵּן עָשָׂה הִלֵּל בִּזְמַן שֶׁבֵּית הַמִּקְדָּשׁ הָיָה קַיָּם. הָיָה כּוֹרֵךְ (פֶּסַח) מַצָּה וּמָרוֹר וְאוֹכֵל בְּיַחַד. לְקַיֵּם מַה שֶּׁנֶּאֱמַר, עַל מַצּוֹת וּמְרֹרִים יֹאכְלֻהוּ.[1]

מָרוֹר

Bitter herbs dipped into charoses

R' Yitzchak Isaac Sher of Slobodka

The bitter herbs (מָרוֹר), which remind us of the bitter bondage in Egypt, are dipped into the sweet *charoses* made from fruits with which *Eretz Yisrael* is blessed and the fruit of the apple tree beneath which the women of Israel gave birth in Egypt. The *charoses* is an antidote to the poisonous substance of the bitter herbs.

The combination of bitter herbs and *charoses* can teach us about the heights which our ancestors reached in Egypt. "R' Akiva expounded: It was by the merit of righteous women that Israel was delivered out of Egypt" (*Sotah* 11). For they would give birth under the apple tree and the Holy One would send angels to rear them. He would produce milk and honey for them and conceal them from the Egyptians. These righteous women gave birth to children who were subject to Pharaoh's decree that all male newborns were to be cast into the river. Their act in the face of such a decree has the flavor of a mass offering up of Yitzchak (עֲקֵדַת יִצְחָק). And it was even greater than Avraham's offering up of Yitzchak. For the women were not commanded by

MAROR

The head of the household takes a half-egg volume of maror, dips it into charoses, and gives each participant a like amount. The following blessing is recited with the intention that it also apply to the maror of the 'sandwich'. The maror is eaten without reclining, and without delay.

Blessed are You, Hashem, our God, King of the universe, Who has sanctified us with His commandments, and has commanded us concerning the eating of maror.

KORECH

The bottom (thus far unbroken) matzah is now taken. From it, with the addition of other matzos, each participant receives a half-egg volume of matzah with an equal volume portion of maror (dipped into charoses which is shaken off). The following paragraph is recited and the 'sandwich' is eaten while reclining.

In remembrance of the Temple we do as Hillel did in Temple times: he would combine (the Pesach offering,) matzah and maror in a sandwich and eat them together, to fulfill what is written in the Torah: They shall eat it with matzos and bitter herbs.[1]

1. *Bamidbar* 9:11.

Hashem to give birth. But these mothers felt that even if their offspring were to be drowned, the children would have a share in the World-to-Come (*Sotah* 12).

Can we imagine a greater sacrifice? The women were willing to suffer the pains of pregnancy, labor and birth and, above these, the possible pain of having an infant slain, in order to benefit some nameless soul and have it enjoy the World-to-Come.

There is a further side to their greatness of spirit. They were filled with such secure trust that they could give birth to the children and say to the Holy One, "We have done our share; You do Your part." And they gave birth, year after year, six at a time (שִׁשָּׁה בְּכֶרֶס אֶחָד). The children would grow up and come to their homes in their numbers. They would speak of the marvels they had witnessed, of Hashem's Providence (הַשְׁגָּחָה) and their angel tutors — and they were taken immediately to backbreaking labor (עֲבוֹדַת פָּרֶךְ) at bricks and mortar. They performed the work, but in a lofty frame of mind, for they knew that Hashem was with them and they were like Avraham in the fiery furnace, who confidently expected Hashem to come at any moment and save him!

Therefore, we dip the bitter herbs, which symbolize the bitterness of

שולחן עורך

The meal should be eaten in a combination of joy and solemnity, for the meal, too, is a part of the Seder service. While it is desirable that zemiros and discussion of the laws and events of Pesach be part of the meal, extraneous conversation should be avoided. It should be remembered that the afikoman must be eaten while there is still some appetite for it. In fact, if one is so sated that he must literally force himself to eat it, he is not credited with the performance of the mitzvah of afikoman. Therefore, it is unwise to eat more than a moderate amount during the meal.

צפון

From the afikoman matzah (and from additional matzos to make up the required amount) a half-egg volume portion — according to some, a full egg's volume portion — is given to each participant. It should be eaten before midnight, while reclining, without delay, and uninterruptedly. Nothing may be eaten or drunk after the afikoman (with the exception of water and the like) except for the last two Seder cups of wine.

ברך

The third cup is poured and Bircas HaMazon (Grace After Meals) is recited. According to some customs, the Cup of Eliahu is poured at this point.

שִׁיר הַמַּעֲלוֹת, בְּשׁוּב יהוה אֶת שִׁיבַת צִיּוֹן, הָיִינוּ כְּחֹלְמִים. אָז יִמָּלֵא שְׂחוֹק פִּינוּ וּלְשׁוֹנֵנוּ רִנָּה, אָז יֹאמְרוּ בַגּוֹיִם, הִגְדִּיל יהוה לַעֲשׂוֹת עִם אֵלֶּה. הִגְדִּיל יהוה לַעֲשׂוֹת עִמָּנוּ,

---

bondage into the *charoses*, the crushed apple, to remember that the bitterness was softened by the clearly evident miracles and the wondrous trust in Hashem. And in our own exile, despite the bitterness, let us not forget the dipping into *charoses*, the hand of Hashem which sustains us by miracle upon miracle and acts as an antidote to the poison in the bitter herbs.

הָיִינוּ כְּחֹלְמִים
We will have been like dreamers

R' Eliahu Dessler

When the Redemption comes, we will look back over the road we have traveled and understand that all that we experienced was to our benefit. The afflictions only appeared as such in our imagination, in a kind of dream sequence. But in their true essence, they were a blessing and a good. The experience of Yosef's brothers may serve as an example. They were disturbed by the accusations and schemes of the viceroy. But the moment Pharaoh's chief minister said, "I am Yosef," everything became clear in retrospect.

SHULCHAN ORECH

The meal should be eaten in a combination of joy and solemnity, for the meal, too, is a part of the Seder service. While it is desirable that zemiros and discussion of the laws and events of Pesach be part of the meal, extraneous conversation should be avoided. It should be remembered that the afikoman must be eaten while there is still some appetite for it. In fact, if one is so sated that he must literally force himself to eat it, he is not credited with the performance of the mitzvah of afikoman. Therefore, it is unwise to eat more than a moderate amount during the meal.

TZAFUN

From the afikoman matzah (and from additional matzos to make up the required amount) a half-egg volume portion — according to some, a full egg's volume portion — is given to each participant. It should be eaten before midnight, while reclining, without delay, and uninterruptedly. Nothing may be eaten or drunk after the afikoman (with the exception of water and the like) except for the last two Seder cups of wine.

BARECH

The third cup is poured and Bircas HaMazon (Grace After Meals) is recited. According to some customs, the Cup of Eliahu is poured at this point.

A song of Ascents. When HASHEM brings back the exiles to Zion, we will have been like dreamers. Then our mouth will be filled with laughter, and our tongue with glad song. Then will it be said among the nations: HASHEM has done great things for us,

---

While we suffer in exile, we do not understand how the suffering is beneficial, but we can accept this on principle and say, "Whatever Heaven does is for the best" (*Berachos* 60). However, the more a man rises in spirit, the more he can accept sufferings with love and rise above them. Then it is that he is fortunate and experiences the Redemption as an individual. This is what R' Moshe Chaim Luzzatto (*Ramchal*) meant when he said that the fully righteous man (צַדִּיק גָּמוּר) will have the fortune to experience the light of the *Mashiach* before the Redemption.

We, too, can sense the feel of the Redemption when we realize that our principal aspiration should be to rise spiritually. Then, inevitably, the troubles which surround a man, because of lack of honor, or money, or meaning to life, become petty to his eye. And with each step upwards away from the domination of the body and its tendencies, there is a greater revelation of the light of Redemption and an awareness that "we were as in a dream." For that which pressed him but yesterday is now of no importance and only an imagined ill. He is spiritually redeemed and is bound up in a true life, a life of the spirit.

הָיִינוּ שְׂמֵחִים. שׁוּבָה יהוה אֶת שְׁבִיתֵנוּ, כַּאֲפִיקִים בַּנֶּגֶב. הַזֹּרְעִים בְּדִמְעָה בְּרִנָּה יִקְצֹרוּ. הָלוֹךְ יֵלֵךְ וּבָכֹה נֹשֵׂא מֶשֶׁךְ הַזָּרַע, בֹּא יָבֹא בְרִנָּה, נֹשֵׂא אֲלֻמֹּתָיו.[1]

If three or more males, aged thirteen or older, participated in the meal, the leader is required to formally invite the others to join him in the recitation of Grace after Meals. Following is the 'Zimun,' or formal invitation.

The leader begins:

רַבּוֹתַי נְבָרֵךְ.

The group responds:

יְהִי שֵׁם יהוה מְבֹרָךְ מֵעַתָּה וְעַד עוֹלָם.[2]

The leader continues:

יְהִי שֵׁם יהוה מְבֹרָךְ מֵעַתָּה וְעַד עוֹלָם.[2]

If ten men join in the Zimun, the words (in parentheses) are included.

בִּרְשׁוּת מָרָנָן וְרַבָּנָן וְרַבּוֹתַי, נְבָרֵךְ (אֱלֹהֵינוּ) שֶׁאָכַלְנוּ מִשֶּׁלּוֹ.

The group responds:

בָּרוּךְ (אֱלֹהֵינוּ) שֶׁאָכַלְנוּ מִשֶּׁלּוֹ וּבְטוּבוֹ חָיִינוּ.

The leader continues:

בָּרוּךְ (אֱלֹהֵינוּ) שֶׁאָכַלְנוּ מִשֶּׁלּוֹ וּבְטוּבוֹ חָיִינוּ.

The following line is recited if ten men join in the Zimun.

בָּרוּךְ הוּא וּבָרוּךְ שְׁמוֹ.

וּבְטוּבוֹ חָיִינוּ

And through Whose goodness we live

R' Yerucham of Mir

"Whoever says (in the introduction to the blessing after the meal — בִּרְכַּת הַמָּזוֹן) '*from* His goodness (מִטּוּבוֹ) we live' is unlearned, because he limits the benevolence (חֶסֶד) of the Holy One" (*Berachos* 50). The eating of a slice of bread lifts a man up to an awareness of all of Hashem's bounty without limit! We imagined, previously, that eating requires a blessing of thanks. But if we once pronounce the blessing as it should be said, with thoughtful purpose (כַּוָּנָה), we would realize the truth: The blessing is the purpose of the need to eat. The Creator embedded the need to eat within us, so that we would pronounce the blessing and our eyes would be opened to recognize His vast goodness. Otherwise, why should such wondrous recognition be related to the eating of a small slice of bread?

and we rejoiced. Restore our captives, HASHEM, like streams in the dry land. Those who sow in tears shall reap in joy. Though the farmer bears the measure of seed to the field in tears, he shall come home with joy, bearing his sheaves.[1]

If three or more males, aged thirteen or older, participated in the meal, the leader is required to formally invite the others to join him in the recitation of Grace after Meals. Following is the 'Zimun,' or formal invitation.

The leader begins:
Gentlemen, let us bless.

The group responds:
Blessed is the Name of HASHEM from this moment and forever![2]

The leader continues:
Blessed is the Name of HASHEM from this moment and forever![2]

If ten men join in the Zimun, the words (in parentheses) are included.
With the permission of the distinguished people present, let us bless [our God] for we have eaten from what is His.

The group responds:
Blessed is [our God] He of Whose we have eaten and through Whose goodness we live.

The leader continues:
Blessed is [our God] He of Whose we have eaten and through Whose goodness we live.

The following line is recited if ten men join in the Zimun.
Blessed is He and Blessed is His Name.

1. *Tehillim* 126. 2. 113:2.

The view that the blessing is merely an inevitable addendum to eating as against the view that eating was only created to allow for the blessing is a distinction like that which differentiates the wicked from the righteous man. The Midrash defines this difference: The wicked stand on their gods as it is stated: "And Pharaoh dreamt, and, behold he was standing on the river" (*Bereishis* 41:1); the Egyptians worshipped the Nile. But Hashem stands upon the righteous as it is stated: "And, behold, HASHEM was standing above him" (above Yaakov; *Bereishis* 28:13). The wicked man sees himself as central; his needs, his wishes, his desires and even his gods must bow to him. Certainly, to him the act of eating is the important ingredient and the blessing of thanks (בִּרְכַּת הַמָּזוֹן) is only secondary. But to the righteous man, his entire world centers about God, so much so, that the righteous are said to be the chariot of the Divine Presence — שְׁכִינָה — (*Bereishis Rabbah* 87). They are secondary to It and governed by It. Their entire life is devoted to

בָּרוּךְ אַתָּה יהוה אֱלֹהֵינוּ מֶלֶךְ הָעוֹלָם, הַזָּן אֶת הָעוֹלָם כֻּלּוֹ, בְּטוּבוֹ, בְּחֵן בְּחֶסֶד וּבְרַחֲמִים, הוּא נֹתֵן לֶחֶם לְכָל בָּשָׂר, כִּי לְעוֹלָם חַסְדּוֹ.[1] וּבְטוּבוֹ הַגָּדוֹל, תָּמִיד לֹא חָסַר לָנוּ, וְאַל יֶחְסַר לָנוּ מָזוֹן לְעוֹלָם וָעֶד. בַּעֲבוּר שְׁמוֹ הַגָּדוֹל, כִּי הוּא אֵל זָן וּמְפַרְנֵס לַכֹּל, וּמֵטִיב לַכֹּל, וּמֵכִין מָזוֹן לְכָל בְּרִיּוֹתָיו אֲשֶׁר בָּרָא. בָּרוּךְ אַתָּה יהוה, הַזָּן אֶת הַכֹּל.

נוֹדֶה לְּךָ יהוה אֱלֹהֵינוּ, עַל שֶׁהִנְחַלְתָּ לַאֲבוֹתֵינוּ אֶרֶץ חֶמְדָּה טוֹבָה וּרְחָבָה. וְעַל שֶׁהוֹצֵאתָנוּ יהוה אֱלֹהֵינוּ מֵאֶרֶץ מִצְרַיִם, וּפְדִיתָנוּ

---

their Creator: "I shall praise HASHEM with my life" — אֲהַלְלָה ה׳ בְּחַיָּי (the usually understood sense is: "I will praise Hashem while I am alive"; *Tehillim* 146:2 and see *Ramban* to *Devarim* 6:13). From their perspective eating is but a necessary introduction to what follows, the blessing and the recognition of the overwhelming bounty of the Creator of Whom we say "through Whose goodness we live."

הַזָּן אֶת הָעוֹלָם / *Who nourishes the entire world*

The Alter of Kelm

How blind man is that he does not know how to value the basic gifts in life! I have never heard a man say on the eve of Rosh Hashanah, "Thank God, I had enough to eat last year." No one thinks about that at all. He will feel that it has been a successful year, if he has managed to save a sum of money. But our forefather Yaakov praised Hashem as "The God Who gave me food from my first being to this day" (*Bereishis* 48:15 as *Onkelos* interprets).

I was amazed at this uncommon view of our forefather Yaakov. That is, until I pronounced the after-the-meal blessings of thanks (בִּרְכַּת הַמָּזוֹן). And then I was amazed at my own previous imperception. How had I neglected to think about that which I said day after day? The entire set of blessings is praise for the bounty of our sustenance.

בְּחֵן בְּחֶסֶד וּבְרַחֲמִים

With grace, with kindness, and with mercy

R' Eliahu Lopian

" . . . Who nourishes the entire world (הָעוֹלָם כֻּלּוֹ), in His goodness." He gives the righteous their food with grace (חֵן); they find grace in the eyes of Hashem. The average (בֵּינוֹנִים) who

Blessed are You, HASHEM, our God, King of the universe, Who nourishes the entire world, in His goodness — with grace, with kindness, and with mercy. He gives nourishment to all flesh, for His kindness is eternal.[1] And through His great goodness, we have never lacked, and may we never lack, nourishment, for all eternity. For the sake of His Great Name, because He is God Who nourishes and sustains all, and benefits all, and He prepares food for all of His creatures which He has created. Blessed are You, HASHEM, Who nourishes all.

We thank You, HASHEM, our God, because You have given to our forefathers as a heritage a desirable, good and spacious land; because You removed us, HASHEM, our God, from the land of Egypt and You redeemed us from the house of bondage;

---

1. *Tehillim* 136:25.

---

are neither righteous nor wicked are given their sustenance through benevolence (חֶסֶד). And the wicked require Hashem's pity (רַחֲמִים) to receive their food. For they are not worthy of such bounty on their own accord.

עַל שֶׁהִנְחַלְתָּ לַאֲבוֹתֵינוּ אֶרֶץ
Because You have given to our forefathers as a heritage a land . . .

The Alter of Kelm A Jew living in *Eretz Yisrael* must bring the first produce of his fields (בִּכּוּרִים), each year, to the *Beis HaMikdash*, in order to express his thanks to Hashem. And there, when offering his fruits, he relates the story of Israel in brief, starting with Yaakov's stay in the house of Lavan down through the Exodus from Egypt.

It is not sufficient that he give thanks for the last bounty which he personally received. He must go back to the beginning and feel thankful for each step along the way of history.

And we, too, when we give thanks for our food must also give thanks for the whole sequence of kindness shown to our nation by Hashem, from that time when He gave our forefathers a lovely, good and spacious land (אֶרֶץ חֶמְדָּה טוֹבָה וּרְחָבָה) until these, our own days.

שֶׁהוֹצֵאתָנוּ . . . מֵאֶרֶץ מִצְרַיִם, וּפְדִיתָנוּ מִבֵּית עֲבָדִים
You removed us . . . from the land of Egypt
and You redeemed us from the house of bondage

R' Yechezkel Levenstein We express a dual praise. First, that we were taken out of Egypt and secondly, that we were

מִבֵּית עֲבָדִים, וְעַל בְּרִיתְךָ שֶׁחָתַמְתָּ בִּבְשָׂרֵנוּ, וְעַל
תּוֹרָתְךָ שֶׁלִּמַּדְתָּנוּ, וְעַל חֻקֶּיךָ שֶׁהוֹדַעְתָּנוּ, וְעַל
חַיִּים חֵן וָחֶסֶד שֶׁחוֹנַנְתָּנוּ, וְעַל אֲכִילַת מָזוֹן
שָׁאַתָּה זָן וּמְפַרְנֵס אוֹתָנוּ תָּמִיד, בְּכָל יוֹם וּבְכָל עֵת
וּבְכָל שָׁעָה.

וְעַל הַכֹּל יהוה אֱלֹהֵינוּ אֲנַחְנוּ מוֹדִים לָךְ,
וּמְבָרְכִים אוֹתָךְ, יִתְבָּרַךְ שִׁמְךָ בְּפִי
כָּל חַי תָּמִיד לְעוֹלָם וָעֶד. כַּכָּתוּב, וְאָכַלְתָּ
וְשָׂבָעְתָּ, וּבֵרַכְתָּ אֶת יהוה אֱלֹהֶיךָ, עַל הָאָרֶץ
הַטֹּבָה אֲשֶׁר נָתַן לָךְ.[1] בָּרוּךְ אַתָּה יהוה, עַל הָאָרֶץ
וְעַל הַמָּזוֹן.

---

freed from slavery to Pharaoh and became servants of Hashem.

Moshe wondered what made Israel worthy to be taken out of Egypt and Hashem answered that it was in the merit of receiving the Torah. The *Alter* of Kelm explained this answer as follows: Hashem admitted that were they to be released from servitude to Pharaoh and become independent they would need great merit and that they did not have. However, since they were not to be independent, but rather, servants to Hashem, they did not need merit of their own.

וְעַל בְּרִיתְךָ שֶׁחָתַמְתָּ בִּבְשָׂרֵנוּ
Your covenant which You sealed in our flesh

The Alter of Kelm We are directed to make note of circumcision daily in the after-the-meal blessings (בִּרְכַּת הַמָּזוֹן) to instill faith within us. For it is not reasonable to assume that Avraham, a man of ninety-nine years of age would circumcise himself on his own; that is, clearly, a life-threatening action. He must have done so through prophetic instruction from Hashem.

R' Yechezkel Levenstein would add: We also mention inheriting the land in the after-the-meal blessings, because that, too, gives rise to faith. It was promised to Avraham four hundred years before his descendants received it and it was promised to them as a perpetual possession. Who can make promises four hundred years in advance, or promise something to the end of time other than the Omnipotent Creator?

And the promise was fulfilled. The nations of the world did not settle our land. But it is our good fortune to return and live within her borders. See how

for Your covenant which You sealed in our flesh; for Your Torah which You taught us and for Your statutes which You made known to us; for life, grace, and kindness which You granted us; and for the provision of food with which You nourish and sustain us constantly, in every day, in every season, and in every hour.

For all, HASHEM, our God, we thank You and bless You. May Your Name be blessed by the mouth of all the living, continuously for all eternity. As it is written: 'And you shall eat and you shall be satisfied and you shall bless HASHEM, your God, for the good land which He gave you.'[1] Blessed are You, HASHEM, for the land and for the nourishment.

---

1. *Devarim* 8:10.

---

it is possible to strengthen one's faith with each step, if only we take thought!

וְעַל תּוֹרָתְךָ שֶׁלִּמַּדְתָּנוּ
For Your Torah which You taught us

R' Eliahu Lopian　　First we give thanks for "Your Torah which You taught us" and only after that, "for the provision of food with which You nourish and sustain us." For without Torah and *mitzvos*, there would be no value to food and life. Would it be worthwhile to live the life of an animal — to live to eat and eat to live — without further purpose? Would one give praise for such a life? Only the Torah invests life and food, which sustains life, with value.

We end the blessing with the unique praise that "You nourish and sustain us constantly, in every day, in every season, and in every hour." Even during those hours in which we are not occupied in the study of Torah and *mitzvos* and do not, then, deserve the gift of life, we are nevertheless sustained by a particular act of kindness, for which we must, separately, give thanks.

וְאָכַלְתָּ וְשָׂבָעְתָּ
And you shall eat and you shall be satisfied

R' Eliahu Dessler　　Hunger drives one to eat. And man is constantly moved to fill his physical and spiritual needs. Of the wicked it is said: "The belly of the wicked is in want" — וּבֶטֶן רְשָׁעִים תֶּחְסָר — (*Mishlei* 13:25), "and the soul shall not be full" (*Koheles* 6:7). They are never satisfied: "A man does not die even filling the half of his desires; if he has a hundred, he wants two hundred" (*Koheles Rabbah* 3). He is in a constant,

רַחֵם יהוה אֱלֹהֵינוּ עַל יִשְׂרָאֵל עַמֶּךָ, וְעַל יְרוּשָׁלַיִם עִירֶךָ, וְעַל צִיּוֹן מִשְׁכַּן כְּבוֹדֶךָ, וְעַל מַלְכוּת בֵּית דָּוִד מְשִׁיחֶךָ, וְעַל הַבַּיִת הַגָּדוֹל וְהַקָּדוֹשׁ שֶׁנִּקְרָא שִׁמְךָ עָלָיו. אֱלֹהֵינוּ אָבִינוּ רְעֵנוּ זוּנֵנוּ פַּרְנְסֵנוּ וְכַלְכְּלֵנוּ וְהַרְוִיחֵנוּ, וְהַרְוַח לָנוּ יהוה אֱלֹהֵינוּ מְהֵרָה מִכָּל צָרוֹתֵינוּ. וְנָא אַל תַּצְרִיכֵנוּ יהוה אֱלֹהֵינוּ, לֹא לִידֵי מַתְּנַת בָּשָׂר וָדָם, וְלֹא לִידֵי הַלְוָאָתָם, כִּי אִם לְיָדְךָ הַמְּלֵאָה הַפְּתוּחָה הַקְּדוֹשָׁה וְהָרְחָבָה, שֶׁלֹּא נֵבוֹשׁ וְלֹא נִכָּלֵם לְעוֹלָם וָעֶד.

On Shabbos add the following paragraph.

רְצֵה וְהַחֲלִיצֵנוּ יהוה אֱלֹהֵינוּ בְּמִצְוֹתֶיךָ, וּבְמִצְוַת יוֹם הַשְּׁבִיעִי הַשַּׁבָּת הַגָּדוֹל וְהַקָּדוֹשׁ הַזֶּה, כִּי יוֹם זֶה גָּדוֹל וְקָדוֹשׁ הוּא לְפָנֶיךָ, לִשְׁבָּת בּוֹ וְלָנוּחַ בּוֹ בְּאַהֲבָה כְּמִצְוַת רְצוֹנֶךָ, וּבִרְצוֹנְךָ הָנִיחַ לָנוּ יהוה אֱלֹהֵינוּ, שֶׁלֹּא תְהֵא צָרָה וְיָגוֹן וַאֲנָחָה בְּיוֹם מְנוּחָתֵנוּ, וְהַרְאֵנוּ יהוה אֱלֹהֵינוּ בְּנֶחָמַת צִיּוֹן עִירֶךָ, וּבְבִנְיַן יְרוּשָׁלַיִם עִיר קָדְשֶׁךָ, כִּי אַתָּה הוּא בַּעַל הַיְשׁוּעוֹת וּבַעַל הַנֶּחָמוֹת.

unceasing race to satisfy his appetites, always seeking to receive and take.

But the righteous man "bestows and gives" (*Tehillim* 37:21). He does not run after his desires; he is happy with his lot (*Avos* 4:1). He is calm and unwanting (שָׁלֵם); he lacks nothing. His state is the result of the Creator's blessing: "And you shall eat and you shall be satisfied."

לְיָדְךָ הַמְּלֵאָה / *Your Hand that is full*

R' Eliahu Lopian — After reciting the after-the-meal blessings (בִּרְכַּת הַמָּזוֹן) he once remarked: If the Holy One's "Hand" is full, open and spacious (הַמְּלֵאָה הַפְּתוּחָה וְהָרְחָבָה) why do so many people not enjoy its outpouring of blessing? The answer is that there is another attribute given to Hashem's "Hand;" it is also holy (הַקְּדוֹשָׁה). And a man who himself is not holy cannot reach out and come into contact with the holy "Hand."

שֶׁלֹּא נֵבוֹשׁ . . . לְעוֹלָם וָעֶד
That we not feel inner shame . . . for ever and ever

[The Slobodka school of *mussar* (ethics) stressed the view that man is a lofty and noble creature.]

Have mercy HASHEM, our God, on Israel Your people; on Jerusalem, Your city, on Zion, the resting place of Your Glory; on the monarchy of the house of David, Your anointed; and on the great and holy House upon which Your Name is called. Our God, our Father — tend us, nourish us, sustain us, support us, relieve us; HASHEM, our God, grant us speedy relief from all our troubles. Please, make us not needful — HASHEM, our God — of the gifts of human hands nor of their loans, but only of Your Hand that is full, open, holy, and generous, that we not feel inner shame nor be humiliated for ever and ever.

On Shabbos add the following paragraph.

May it please You, HASHEM, our God — give us rest through Your commandments and through the commandment of the seventh day, this great and holy Shabbos. For this day is great and holy before You to rest on it and be content on it in love, as ordained by Your will. May it be Your will, HASHEM, our God, that there be no distress, grief, or lament on this day of our contentment. And show us, HASHEM, our God, the consolation of Zion, Your city, and the rebuilding of Jerusalem, City of Your holiness, for You are the Master of salvations and Master of consolations.

The Alter of Slobodka

Imagine what a *Gan Eden* (Paradise) man is meant to live in! In the after-the-meal blessings (בִּרְכַּת הַמָּזוֹן) we do not ask that we be sustained by a human being or even an angel. We seek our sustenance from no less a source than Hashem's holy and spacious "hand," so that we not feel shame for ever and ever. Should we ever, even once in our lives, receive help from flesh and blood — not as charity, but even as a loan — we are to feel constantly and perpetually shamed and disgraced!

For each human being is a royal prince, an only son to the Holy One, for whose sake alone the world was created (*Sanhedrin* 37) and the slightest discomfort should be felt by him as terrible suffering: "even if he puts his hand into his purse for three coins and draws forth only two" (*Arachin* 16). And *Chazal* expounded the curse of the verse: "And your life shall be suspended before you . . . and you shall have no trust in your life" (*Devarim* 28:66) as referring to a man who does not grow his own grain but must buy baker's bread (*Menachos* 103b). If we are not shot through and through with

אֱלֹהֵינוּ וֵאלֹהֵי אֲבוֹתֵינוּ, יַעֲלֶה, וְיָבֹא, וְיַגִּיעַ, וְיֵרָאֶה, וְיֵרָצֶה, וְיִשָּׁמַע, וְיִפָּקֵד, וְיִזָּכֵר זִכְרוֹנֵנוּ וּפִקְדוֹנֵנוּ, וְזִכְרוֹן אֲבוֹתֵינוּ, וְזִכְרוֹן מָשִׁיחַ בֶּן דָּוִד עַבְדֶּךָ, וְזִכְרוֹן יְרוּשָׁלַיִם עִיר קָדְשֶׁךָ, וְזִכְרוֹן כָּל עַמְּךָ בֵּית יִשְׂרָאֵל לְפָנֶיךָ, לִפְלֵיטָה לְטוֹבָה לְחֵן וּלְחֶסֶד וּלְרַחֲמִים, לְחַיִּים וּלְשָׁלוֹם בְּיוֹם חַג הַמַּצוֹת הַזֶּה. זָכְרֵנוּ יהוה אֱלֹהֵינוּ בּוֹ לְטוֹבָה, וּפָקְדֵנוּ בוֹ לִבְרָכָה, וְהוֹשִׁיעֵנוּ בוֹ לְחַיִּים. וּבִדְבַר יְשׁוּעָה וְרַחֲמִים, חוּס וְחָנֵּנוּ וְרַחֵם עָלֵינוּ וְהוֹשִׁיעֵנוּ, כִּי אֵלֶיךָ עֵינֵינוּ, כִּי אֵל חַנּוּן וְרַחוּם אָתָּה.[1]

the feeling that we are living out our lives in a hell (גֵּיהִנֹּם), then we lack the true perspective of the greatness of man.

אֱלֹהֵינוּ וֵאלֹהֵי אֲבוֹתֵינוּ
Our God and God of our forefathers

The Alter of Kelm — There are two categories of believers. There are those who follow with trusting simplicity (תְּמִימוּת) in the footsteps of their forebears and there are those who come to their faith by their own intellectual efforts.

The two groups differ from one another. A member of the former is strong in his faith and will not be bothered by questions. However, his faith is but superficial and external. The faith of a member of the latter group has intellectual depth, but the man can be disturbed by problematic questions.

Above them both stands the one whose faith rests on the faith of his fathers and, yet, applies thought and plumbs the depths of that faith. He it is who can speak of "our God and God of our fathers." To him, too, we can apply the verse: "Taste and see that Hashem is good" (*Tehillim* 34:9). You, yourselves "taste;" examine it in depth and you will get the taste. "And see." Look at what your fathers do and follow in their ways.

זִכְרוֹנֵנוּ
The remembrance of ourselves

R' Yosef Leib Bloch of Telshe — How can we presume to ask Hashem, Who does not forget, to remember us? How can we understand what the prophet means when he says: "For when I (Hashem) speak of him, I will surely remember him' (*Yirmeyahu* 31:19). Or what does the verse "I (Hashem) will remember My covenant" (*Vayikra*

Our God and God of our forefathers, may there rise, come, reach, be noted, be favored, be heard, be considered, and be remembered – the remembrance and consideration of ourselves; the remembrance of our forefathers; the remembrance of Messiah, son of David, Your servant; the remembrance of Jerusalem, the City of Your Holiness; the remembrance of Your entire people the Family of Israel – before You for deliverance, for goodness, for grace, for kindness, and for compassion, for life, and for peace on this day of the Festival of Matzos. Remember us on it, HASHEM, our God, for goodness; consider us on it for blessing; and help us on it for life. In the matter of salvation and compassion, pity, be gracious and compassionate with us and help us, for our eyes are turned to You, because You are God, the gracious, and compassionate.[1]

1. *Nechemiah* 9:31.

26:42) mean? True, we know that Hashem's "names" and His "actions" relate only to the way He governs Creation and not to His essence, which no one can grasp. And He governs by the principle of: *action calls forth a parallel reaction* (מִדָּה כְּנֶגֶד מִדָּה). When man forgets Hashem, Hashem, as it were, forgets man.

Yet forgetfulness and remembrance are not absolute. There are degrees of remembering and forgetting. For example, a rabbinical court (בֵּית דִּין) cannot pass punishment on a transgressor unless he commits the crime "within speaking time" (תּוֹךְ כְּדֵי דִבּוּר) after he has been given a warning (הַתְרָאָה) not to do so (*Sanhedrin* 40b). The "speaking time" is in the neighborhood of two seconds. And it is eminently clear that he did not forget that the act is forbidden in such a short space of time. *Chazal* assumed that even a tiny block of time can dim a man's perception, if only a little; he has "forgotten," if only in a pale, weak form, that the act is prohibited.

When we approach categories of memory and forgetfulness in the upper worlds, we must not do so in a simplistic manner or assume that only the absolute extremes exist.

With this in mind, we may find the key to understanding a difficult Midrash (*Pesikta D'Rav Kahane* 45): When Israel's sins are weighed on *Yom Kippur* and are found to be equal to the merits, the Satan searches for "forgotten" sins and, while he is off searching, the Holy One removes sins from the scales and hides them under His cloak, as it is stated: "I have covered all their sins" (*Tehillim* 88:3). Satan returns and cannot discover the

וּבְנֵה יְרוּשָׁלַיִם עִיר הַקֹּדֶשׁ בִּמְהֵרָה בְיָמֵינוּ. בָּרוּךְ אַתָּה יהוה, בּוֹנֵה (בְּרַחֲמָיו) יְרוּשָׁלָיִם. אָמֵן.

בָּרוּךְ אַתָּה יהוה אֱלֹהֵינוּ מֶלֶךְ הָעוֹלָם, הָאֵל אָבִינוּ מַלְכֵּנוּ אַדִּירֵנוּ בּוֹרְאֵנוּ גּוֹאֲלֵנוּ יוֹצְרֵנוּ קְדוֹשֵׁנוּ קְדוֹשׁ יַעֲקֹב, רוֹעֵנוּ רוֹעֵה יִשְׂרָאֵל, הַמֶּלֶךְ הַטּוֹב וְהַמֵּטִיב לַכֹּל, שֶׁבְּכָל יוֹם וָיוֹם הוּא הֵטִיב, הוּא מֵטִיב, הוּא יֵיטִיב לָנוּ. הוּא גְמָלָנוּ הוּא גוֹמְלֵנוּ הוּא יִגְמְלֵנוּ לָעַד, לְחֵן וּלְחֶסֶד וּלְרַחֲמִים וּלְרֶוַח הַצָּלָה וְהַצְלָחָה, בְּרָכָה וִישׁוּעָה נֶחָמָה פַּרְנָסָה וְכַלְכָּלָה וְרַחֲמִים

---

sins, as it is stated: "The sin of Israel will be sought and not be found (Yirmeyahu 50:20).

How can the Satan, whose task it is to keep an account of the sins, "forget" and not find them? And what does Hashem's hiding the sins under His cloak mean?

Just as there are layers upon layers and degrees upon degrees of human forgetfulness, so, too, we find layers and layers of "forgetfulness" in the world above. At first, the Satan collects the sins which stand out to the eye, those which are clearly recognizable. When he sees that they do not weigh down the scale, he searches for the "forgotten" sins. He insinuates himself into the depths of a man's soul to find the wayward musings of man performing a *mitzvah*, the faults in thoughtful purpose (כַּוָּנָה). These are sins of forgetfulness, the "forgotten" sins. It is then that the Holy One "sits" wrapped in His cloak; He conceals Himself with the mask of the "natural" workings of Creation (הֶסְתֵּר פָּנִים). When He sees that the Satan has wormed his way into the depths of the soul to make his charges of accusation, He stands in opposition and defends Israel by hiding the sins in His cloak; He blames the presence of sin on His cloak. They sin because they do not sense the Divine Presence (שְׁכִינָה). It is not evident; it is hidden within the Creation.

Hashem is not "forgetful" in a simplistic sense. He has concealed Himself and man must penetrate through the robes of concealment. The closer man approaches to Hashem, the deeper becomes the bond between them. And He removes fold after fold of the concealing robe of Creation and reveals a heightened dimension of "remembrance" and the light of His greatness.

Rebuild Jerusalem, the Holy City, soon in our days. Blessed are You, HASHEM, Who rebuilds Jerusalem (in His mercy). Amen.

Blessed are You, HASHEM, our God, King of the Universe, the Almighty, our Father, our King, our Sovereign, our Creator, our Redeemer, our Maker, our Holy One, Holy One of Yaakov, our Shepherd, the Shepherd of Israel, the King Who is good and Who does good for all. For every single day He did good, He does good, and He will do good to us. He was bountiful with us, He is bountiful with us, and He will forever be bountiful with us — with grace and with kindness and with mercy, with relief, salvation, success, blessing, help, consolation, sustenance, support, mercy,

---

בּוֹנֵה (בְּרַחֲמָיו) יְרוּשָׁלָיִם

Who rebuilds Jerusalem (in His mercy)

The Alter of Slobodka

"Who rebuilds Jerusalem in His mercy" — in the present tense. And the blessings of the *Shemoneh Esrei* prayer are also in the present tense: builds Jerusalem (בּוֹנֵה יְרוּשָׁלָיִם); gathers the dispersed of His people, Israel (מְקַבֵּץ נִדְחֵי עַמּוֹ יִשְׂרָאֵל); restores His Divine Presence to Zion (מַחֲזִיר שְׁכִינָתוֹ לְצִיּוֹן). The rebuilding is an ongoing process which began at the very Destruction itself; the Destruction was a step in the process. It is like a step in a *halachic* argument which leads towards the concluding decisions. For example, rabbinic judges must know how to legally rule that an impure reptile (שֶׁרֶץ) is pure (טָהוֹר), though it is an object of defilement by nature (*Sanhedrin*). Such a step is on the road towards the conclusion that it is impure (טָמֵא).

The universe itself was a culmination of a process of building worlds and destroying them (*Bereishis Rabbah* 9); Noach established the world out of the destruction of the Flood; Avraham came to the fore out of the generation of the Division into nations (דוֹר הַפְּלָגָה); Israel rose out of the depths of depravity (מ״ט שַׁעֲרֵי טֻמְאָה) to receive the Torah and out of the sin of the Golden Calf to be worthy of the Tabernacle (מִשְׁכָּן). And the final Redemption will come to fruition in a generation which is wholly blameworthy, in which government will be in the hands of heretics and knowledge will be held in contempt (*Sotah* 49): "From the midst of your impurities and all of your idols" — particularly from such a beginning — "I will purify you" (*Yechezkel* 36:26).

וְחַיִּים וְשָׁלוֹם וְכָל טוֹב, וּמִכָּל טוּב לְעוֹלָם אַל יְחַסְּרֵנוּ.

הָרַחֲמָן הוּא יִמְלוֹךְ עָלֵינוּ לְעוֹלָם וָעֶד. הָרַחֲמָן הוּא יִתְבָּרַךְ בַּשָּׁמַיִם וּבָאָרֶץ. הָרַחֲמָן הוּא יִשְׁתַּבַּח לְדוֹר דּוֹרִים, וְיִתְפָּאַר בָּנוּ לָעַד וּלְנֵצַח נְצָחִים, וְיִתְהַדַּר בָּנוּ לָעַד וּלְעוֹלְמֵי עוֹלָמִים. הָרַחֲמָן הוּא יְפַרְנְסֵנוּ בְּכָבוֹד. הָרַחֲמָן הוּא יִשְׁבּוֹר עֻלֵּנוּ מֵעַל צַוָּארֵנוּ, וְהוּא יוֹלִיכֵנוּ קוֹמְמִיּוּת לְאַרְצֵנוּ. הָרַחֲמָן הוּא יִשְׁלַח לָנוּ בְּרָכָה מְרֻבָּה בַּבַּיִת הַזֶּה, וְעַל שֻׁלְחָן זֶה שֶׁאָכַלְנוּ עָלָיו. הָרַחֲמָן הוּא יִשְׁלַח לָנוּ אֶת אֵלִיָּהוּ הַנָּבִיא זָכוּר לַטּוֹב, וִיבַשֶּׂר לָנוּ בְּשׂוֹרוֹת טוֹבוֹת יְשׁוּעוֹת וְנֶחָמוֹת.

וּמִכָּל טוּב לְעוֹלָם אַל יְחַסְּרֵנוּ

And of all good things may He never deprive us

R' Yitzchak Blazer

When R' Eliezer fell ill, his students went to visit him. They wept but R' Akiva smiled and said to them, "Whenever I noticed that our teacher's wine never turned sour and his flax never suffered a blight, I thought that perhaps he had received his next world's reward in this world. Now that I witness his suffering, I realize that his reward awaits him intact in the World-to-Come" (*Sanhedrin* 101).

In the after-the-meal blessing, we ask that all the pleasures we experience in the here and now ("all good things") not diminish our reward in the true world, that we not be lacking in the World-to-Come (לְעוֹלָם).

הָרַחֲמָן הוּא יְפַרְנְסֵנוּ בְּכָבוֹד

The compassionate One! May He sustain us in honor

The Alter of Kelm

We ask that our sustenance come from Hashem. R' Yisrael of Salant would say that nothing is given to us free of charge. Our world is like a hotel, an expensive hotel.

The Holy One does not owe anyone anything and yet He gives everything with a liberal hand. But payment shall be demanded for it all. R' Yisrael would say that a man could "eat away" the reward of his *mitzvos* in a single dish of turnips.

How can one manage to eat in the hotel without paying? He can join the

life, peace, and all good; and of all good things may He never deprive us.

The compassionate One! May He reign over us forever. The compassionate One! May He be blessed in heaven and on earth. The compassionate One! May He be praised throughout all generations, may He be glorified through us forever to the ultimate ends, and be honored through us forever and for all eternity. The compassionate One! May He sustain us in honor. The compassionate One! May He break the yoke of oppression from our necks and guide us erect to our Land. The compassionate One! May He send us abundant blessing to this house and upon this table at which we have eaten. The compassionate One! May He send us Eliahu, the Prophet — he is remembered for good — to proclaim to us good tidings, salvations, and consolations.

---

hotel staff; he can dedicate his life to serve all, as the Creator wishes. That is what is meant by the prayer which we add to the *Shemoneh Esrei* during the Days of Penitence (עֲשֶׂרֶת יְמֵי תְּשׁוּבָה): "and record us in the book of life, for Your sake, O living God." To be written in the book of life, one should live for the sake of the Creator and in His service.

הָרַחֲמָן הוּא יִשְׁלַח לָנוּ אֶת אֵלִיָּהוּ הַנָּבִיא

The compassionate One! May He send us Eliahu the Prophet

R' Eliahu Dessler

The Midrash tells us, "When the *shofar* of the *Mashiach* is heard there will be decrees of slaughter and fire" — and we have had no lack of fiery ovens and slaughter — "The door of Redemption shall not be opened all at once. Eliahu will come to a particular city and pass by another; he will speak to one individual and be invisible to his companion" (*Shir HaShirim Rabbah* 2). *Maharal* wrote that at times Eliahu reveals things to a man and that man believes that they are his own thoughts (*Netzach Yisrael* 28).

How is it possible that one should not see or know? The *shofar* has been blasting forth worldwide these last decades, in sharp staccatos of war and destruction; the foundations of society are being uprooted! What, if not that, is Communism; the sick and faltering state of economy; the awful Holocaust? Have we not already heard the *shofar* of Eliahu in our midst? Do we not yet see that the final hour approaches?

Shall we persist in playing with children's toys and hugging our little idols,

הָרַחֲמָן הוּא יְבָרֵךְ

Guests recite the following.
Children at their parents' table add words in parentheses.

אֶת (אָבִי מוֹרִי) בַּעַל הַבַּיִת הַזֶּה,
וְאֶת (אִמִּי מוֹרָתִי) בַּעֲלַת הַבַּיִת הַזֶּה,

Those eating at their own table recite the following,
adding the appropriate parenthesized phrases:

אוֹתִי (וְאֶת אִשְׁתִּי/בַּעְלִי. וְאֶת זַרְעִי)
וְאֶת כָּל אֲשֶׁר לִי.

All guests recite the following:

אוֹתָם וְאֶת בֵּיתָם וְאֶת זַרְעָם
וְאֶת כָּל אֲשֶׁר לָהֶם.

All continue here:

אוֹתָנוּ וְאֶת כָּל אֲשֶׁר לָנוּ, כְּמוֹ שֶׁנִּתְבָּרְכוּ אֲבוֹתֵינוּ אַבְרָהָם יִצְחָק וְיַעֲקֹב בַּכֹּל מִכֹּל כֹּל, כֵּן יְבָרֵךְ אוֹתָנוּ כֻּלָּנוּ יַחַד בִּבְרָכָה שְׁלֵמָה, וְנֹאמַר, אָמֵן.

בַּמָּרוֹם יְלַמְּדוּ עֲלֵיהֶם וְעָלֵינוּ זְכוּת, שֶׁתְּהֵא לְמִשְׁמֶרֶת שָׁלוֹם. וְנִשָּׂא בְרָכָה מֵאֵת יהוה, וּצְדָקָה מֵאֱלֹהֵי יִשְׁעֵנוּ, וְנִמְצָא חֵן וְשֵׂכֶל טוֹב בְּעֵינֵי אֱלֹהִים וְאָדָם.[1]

On Shabbos add the following sentence:

הָרַחֲמָן הוּא יַנְחִילֵנוּ יוֹם שֶׁכֻּלּוֹ שַׁבָּת וּמְנוּחָה לְחַיֵּי הָעוֹלָמִים.

---

and not abandon these vain and empty things: Shall we be like the child in the time of the Destruction who expired while embracing his heathen image (*Sanhedrin* 64)? All the signs which *Chazal* have enumerated as signs of the generation of *Mashiach* have come to pass. Decrees, burnings, slaughter, famine and want; these have come to pass. The rule of the wicked shall spread; that has come to pass. All the nations of the world shall be ranged against us; that has come to pass. Can we still stop up our ears to the voice of Eliahu? The month of Nisan possesses a special quality. It is the once and future month of Redemption in which we can be fortunate to hear the sound of the great *shofar* and the voice of Eliahu. And, if not now, when?

The compassionate One! May He bless

Guests recite the following.
Children at their parents' table add words in parentheses.

**(my father, my teacher) the master of this house,
and (my mother, my teacher) lady of this house,**

Those eating at their own table recite the following,
adding the appropriate parenthesized phrases:

**me (my wife/husband and family)
and all that is mine,**

All guests recite the following:

them, their house, their family, and all that is theirs,

All continue here:

ours and all that is ours — just as our forefathers Avraham, Yitzchak, and Yaakov were blessed in everything, from everything, with everything. So may He bless us all together with a perfect blessing. And let us say: Amen!

On high, may merit be pleaded upon them and upon us, for a safeguard of peace. May we receive a blessing from HASHEM and just kindness from the God of our salvation, and find favor and good understanding in the eyes of God and man.[1]

> On Shabbos add the following sentence:
>
> The compassionate One! May He cause us to inherit the day which will be completely a Shabbos and rest day for eternal life.

---

1. *Mishlei* 3:4.

יוֹם שֶׁכֻּלוֹ שַׁבָּת וּמְנוּחָה
The day which will be completely a Shabbos and rest

R' Eliahu Dessler   The *Shabbos* gives us a foretaste of the World-to-Come (*Berachos* 57). It is an entrance test to that world. For *Shabbos* brings with it revelation of the spirit. Whoever does not keep it properly and take joy in it will not find pleasure when the *Mashiach* comes. To such a man the World-to-Come will be an eternity of pain. He has shown that he has no aspirations towards spiritual discovery; he tends towards the concrete and prefers that the Divine remain hidden.

The Torah reflects this, for it says: "Those who keep guard over the *Shabbos* and proclaim its joy" — in this world — "shall rejoice in Your

The words in parentheses are added on the two Seder nights in some communities.

הָרַחֲמָן הוּא יַנְחִילֵנוּ יוֹם שֶׁכֻּלּוֹ טוֹב. (יוֹם שֶׁכֻּלּוֹ אָרוּךְ. יוֹם שֶׁצַּדִּיקִים יוֹשְׁבִים וְעַטְרוֹתֵיהֶם בְּרָאשֵׁיהֶם וְנֶהֱנִים מִזִּיו הַשְּׁכִינָה וִיהִי חֶלְקֵנוּ עִמָּהֶם).

הָרַחֲמָן הוּא יְזַכֵּנוּ לִימוֹת הַמָּשִׁיחַ וּלְחַיֵּי הָעוֹלָם הַבָּא. מִגְדּוֹל יְשׁוּעוֹת מַלְכּוֹ וְעֹשֶׂה חֶסֶד לִמְשִׁיחוֹ לְדָוִד וּלְזַרְעוֹ עַד עוֹלָם.[1] עֹשֶׂה שָׁלוֹם בִּמְרוֹמָיו, הוּא יַעֲשֶׂה שָׁלוֹם עָלֵינוּ וְעַל כָּל יִשְׂרָאֵל. וְאִמְרוּ, אָמֵן.

יְראוּ אֶת יהוה קְדֹשָׁיו, כִּי אֵין מַחְסוֹר לִירֵאָיו. כְּפִירִים רָשׁוּ וְרָעֵבוּ, וְדֹרְשֵׁי יהוה

---

majesty" — in the World-to-Come (יִשְׂמְחוּ בְמַלְכוּתְךָ שׁוֹמְרֵי שַׁבָּת וְקוֹרְאֵי עֹנֶג). This positive side of the coin indicates the reverse.

יוֹם שֶׁכֻּלּוֹ טוֹב יוֹם שֶׁכֻּלּוֹ אָרוּךְ

That day which is altogether good, that everlasting day

The Alter of Kelm

Altogether good (שֶׁכֻּלּוֹ טוֹב) without an admixture of the bad. This world is filled with concern. The wealthy man worries about guarding his wealth; the man who indulges in food worries about his health. But in the World-to-Come, the good will be pure; it will be unadulterated, everlasting (שֶׁכֻּלּוֹ אָרוּךְ). In this world the pleasure of this moment is gone with the next; the present moment has streamed away. But the World-to-Come is not bound by the limits of time. Each moment is of unending length; all of eternity is included and compressed within it.

The pleasure in the radiance of the Divine Presence is the height of spiritual attainment. Man will be able to reach this lofty height, if he provisions himself for the journey with Torah and *mitzvos*. How foolish he is, if he indolently fails to gather up *mitzvos* for which he would receive boundless pleasure forever!

וּלְחַיֵּי הָעוֹלָם הַבָּא / ***And the life of the World-to-Come***

R' Zvi Hirsch Broide

Chazal have said: "An hour of contentment (קוֹרַת רוּחַ) in the World-to-Come brings more happiness

The words in parentheses are added on the two Seder nights in some communities.

The compassionate One! May He cause us to inherit that day which is altogether good (that everlasting day, the day when the just will sit with crowns on their heads, enjoying the reflection of God's majesty — and may our portion be with them!).

The compassionate One! May He make us worthy of the days of Messiah and the life of the World-to-Come. He Who is a tower of salvations to His king and does kindness for His anointed, to David and to his descendants forever.[1] He Who makes peace in His heights, may He make peace upon us and upon all Israel. Now respond: Amen!

Fear HASHEM, you — His holy ones — for there is no deprivation for His reverent ones. Young lions may want and hunger, but those who seek HASHEM

1. *II Shmuel* 22:51.

---

than the totality of life in this world" (*Avos* 4:17). Were we to take all the moments of happiness of a man, in his entire lifetime, plus all those of his acquaintances, townsmen, countrymen and the entire generation to boot, concentrate the contents of the entire sum of happiness into the space of sixty seconds, and let the man experience this joy, he would be overwhelmed by its potency. Yet, even this would not constitute the "totality of life." To arrive at the sum total in order to produce such a concentrate, we would be required to add up the happy experiences of all of humanity — whoever lived in times gone by and whoever shall live in the future, until the end of days. And, even so, a single hour of contentment-to-come has the greater weight.

"Nor do we speak of the full contentment of the World-to-Come," said R' Nachum Ze'ev of Kelm. "Imagine a man passing a pastry shop and smelling the aroma wafted out from within. He will have some idea, but a very weak one, of how delicious the confections are. Even this pale intimation of the full happiness in the World-to-Come is more significant than all the concentrated joy of all the combined generations of humanity."

And a man is rewarded by such pale contentment for the fulfillment of even the slightest of *mitzvos*. And still, the joy of the entire world cannot match the contentment gained through that very minor *mitzvah*. And because this world does not contain enough to reward a man for even the

לֹא יַחְסְרוּ כָל טוֹב.¹ הוֹדוּ לַיהוה כִּי טוֹב, כִּי לְעוֹלָם חַסְדּוֹ.² פּוֹתֵחַ אֶת יָדֶךָ, וּמַשְׂבִּיעַ לְכָל חַי רָצוֹן.³ בָּרוּךְ הַגֶּבֶר אֲשֶׁר יִבְטַח בַּיהוה, וְהָיָה יהוה מִבְטַחוֹ.⁴ נַעַר הָיִיתִי גַּם זָקַנְתִּי, וְלֹא רָאִיתִי צַדִּיק נֶעֱזָב, וְזַרְעוֹ מְבַקֶּשׁ לָחֶם.⁵ יהוה עֹז לְעַמּוֹ יִתֵּן, יהוה יְבָרֵךְ אֶת עַמּוֹ בַשָּׁלוֹם.⁶

Upon completion of Bircas HaMazon the blessing over wine is recited and the third cup is drunk while reclining on the left side. It is preferable to drink the entire cup, but at the very least, most of the cup should be drained.

בָּרוּךְ אַתָּה יהוה אֱלֹהֵינוּ מֶלֶךְ הָעוֹלָם, בּוֹרֵא פְּרִי הַגָּפֶן.

---

slightest of *mitzvos*, Hashem cannot possibly give a man his due in this world of the here and now for *mitzvos* he has performed.

וְדֹרְשֵׁי ה' לֹא יַחְסְרוּ כָל טוֹב
But those who seek HASHEM will not lack any good

R' Eliahu Lopian They are not promised all that is good, but that they shall not lack it. The following parable will clarify the matter: A sickly man entered the home of an acquaintance. He looked roundabout and commented, "What a pity that you don't have a complete medicine chest." His friend laughed and replied, "We are healthy and don't need the medicines. It is you, who are sick and need them, who deserves our pity."

David HaMelech says as much: "Lions grew poor and went hungry" — those who do not turn to Hashem, like lions, grow poor spending their wealth following the dictates of envy and desire and pursuing honor; "but those who seek Hashem will not lack any good" (*Tehillim* 34:11) — they are healthy in spirit and lack nothing.

The *Mishnah*, too, looks in the same direction: "Such is the way of Torah: Eat bread dipped in salt; drink water in small measure; sleep on the ground and live a severe life. If you do so, you will be fortunate in this life and enjoy the good in the life-to-come" (*Avos* 4:6). Whoever has gone through the experience finds that if he lives a life of simplicity, he is indeed fortunate in this world, for he is free from the mad pursuit of fulfilling his desires.

ה' יְבָרֵךְ אֶת עַמּוֹ בַשָּׁלוֹם
HASHEM will bless His people with peace

R' Zvi Hirsch Broide *Chazal* say: The Holy One could not find a more fitting vessel to contain His outpouring of blessing

will not lack any good.[1] Give thanks to God for He is good; His kindness endures forever.[2] You open Your hand and satisfy the desire of every living thing.[3] Blessed is the man who trusts in HASHEM, then HASHEM will be his security.[4] I was a youth and also have aged, and I have not seen a righteous man forsaken, with his children begging for bread.[5] HASHEM will give might to His people; HASHEM will bless His people with peace.[6]

Upon completion of Bircas HaMazon the blessing over wine is recited and the third cup is drunk while reclining on the left side. It is preferable to drink the entire cup, but at the very least, most of the cup should be drained.

Blessed are You, HASHEM, our God, King of the universe, Who creates the fruit of the vine.

1. *Tehillim* 34:10-11. 2. 136:1. 3. 145:16.
4. *Yirmeyahu* 17:7. 5. *Tehillim* 37:25. 6. 29:11.

than peace (*Ukzain* 3:12). Man is the end purpose of Creation and, when he ascends to a lofty plane, he stands higher than the angels (*Pirkei D'R' Eliezer* 6). But when he descends, he is lower than an animal. For man is a composite of body and soul. They, the material body and the spiritual soul, are contradictory elements. And from them man must fashion harmony. Those who succeed in creating a harmony ascend to the heavens in their physical form (Chanoch, Eliahu, Moshe). David has given expression to this harmony of body and soul: "My *soul* thirsts for You; my *flesh* yearns for You" (*Tehillim* 63:2).

How can we achieve this peace between body and soul? The body will not make overtures to the soul; it does not feel that it is wanting in anything. It has food and drink sufficient for its needs and its other desires are also satisfied. But the soul knows that she must persuade the body to work together with her in harmony; she was breathed into the body for just that purpose. She is meant to educate the body, at the rate which is appropriate to it.

Yet peace is a result of compromise. What compromise may the soul make to the body? Only the Holy One has an answer to that question. The answer lies within the totality of Torah and *mitzvos*. Through them the soul knows what concessions she can make and on what issues she cannot wave the flag of surrender, lest they, the body and soul, be damaged beyond repair. When all is said and done, the positive *mitzvos* and the prohibitions give the guidelines; the soul must operate within the framework which they set. Bit by bit, she accustoms the body to adapt itself to a life of harmony and holiness. And the body arrives at the stage where it is embarrassed to demand that the soul grant compromises. It realizes that every concession which it wrings from the soul creates a veil which separates man from his Creator. Such recognition is the highest of levels. But the main obligation of man in

The fourth cup is poured. According to most customs, the cup of Eliahu is poured at this point, after which the door is opened in accordance with the verse, 'It is a guarded night.' Then the following paragraph is recited.

שְׁפֹךְ חֲמָתְךָ אֶל הַגּוֹיִם אֲשֶׁר לֹא יְדָעוּךָ וְעַל מַמְלָכוֹת אֲשֶׁר בְּשִׁמְךָ לֹא קָרָאוּ. כִּי אָכַל אֶת יַעֲקֹב וְאֶת נָוֵהוּ הֵשַׁמּוּ.[1] שְׁפָךְ עֲלֵיהֶם זַעְמֶךָ וַחֲרוֹן אַפְּךָ יַשִּׂיגֵם.[2] תִּרְדֹּף בְּאַף וְתַשְׁמִידֵם מִתַּחַת שְׁמֵי יהוה.[3]

הלל

The door is closed and the recitation of the Haggadah is continued.

לֹא לָנוּ יהוה לֹא לָנוּ, כִּי לְשִׁמְךָ תֵּן כָּבוֹד, עַל חַסְדְּךָ עַל אֲמִתֶּךָ. לָמָּה יֹאמְרוּ הַגּוֹיִם,

this world is to wage the constant war to reach final peace and harmony.

לְשִׁמְךָ תֵּן כָּבוֹד
For Your Name's sake give glory

R' Eliahu Dessler   To be worthy to receive the first set of Tablets of the Covenant (לוּחוֹת הַבְּרִית), Israel had to go through fifty days of spiritual ascent which culminated in three days of preparation before the event. Thereby, they rid themselves of the foulness of their evil nature — יֵצֶר הָרָע (*Shabbos* 146). After receiving the Tablets, they committed the sin of the Golden Calf and descended from their lofty state; the Tablets were shattered.

When they received the second set of Tablets, they did not first undergo, once more, fifty days of ascent and preparation: This second set was the fruit of Moshe's prayer: ''Do not destroy Your people . . . lest the inhabitants of the land from which You took us out will say that, because Hashem was unable to bring them into the land which He had promised to them and because He hated them, He took them out to slay them in the desert'' (*Devarim* 9:26-28). Strange! Was Israel saved and did it gain the second set of Tablets only to prevent the Egyptians from falling into error?

It would, indeed, seem so. The prayer *For Your Name's sake give glory* does not mean that there is a possibility that the Holy One, as it were, would be deficient in some aspect, if our request is turned down; He, inasmuch as He Himself is concerned, lacks nothing. The prayer has reference to us; we ask that our plea not be rejected, that we should not suffer and should be allowed to see the revelation of this perfect benevolence (חֶסֶד). If someone is hungry and asks food of Hashem with which to still his pangs of hunger,

The fourth cup is poured. According to most customs, the cup of Eliahu is poured at this point, after which the door is opened in accordance with the verse, 'It is a guarded night.' Then the following paragraph is recited.

Pour Your wrath upon the nations that do not recognize You and upon the kingdoms that do not invoke Your Name. For they have devoured Yaakov and destroyed His habitation.[1] Pour Your anger upon them and let Your fiery wrath overtake them.[2] Pursue them with wrath and annihilate them from beneath the heavens of HASHEM.[3]

HALLEL

The door is closed and the recitation of the Haggadah is continued.

Not for our sake, HASHEM, not for our sake, but for Your Name's sake give glory, for Your kindness and for Your truth! Why should the nations say,

---

1. *Tehillim* 79:6-7.   2. 69:25.   3. *Eichah* 3:66.

---

and says in so asking, *For Your Name's sake give glory,* he but fools himself. However, should he rise above the immediate needs of his belly and truly aspire, in the main, to experience the revelation of Hashem's majesty and benevolence, through His act of granting food, the prayer will be answered — R' Yisrael of Salant would emphasize the point that prayer of hope to experience the revelation of the Divine is never returned unanswered.

This spirit fills us on Rosh Hashanah when we put forth the request, "And, too, let Your dread fall upon all that You have fashioned, Your awe upon all that You have created and let all that You have made feel fear and all that You have created bow down before You." This prayer brought forth R' Yerucham of Mir's question, "Why should we be concerned if, say, some stray, drunken peasant of a non-Jew does not prostrate himself to Hashem?" And his answer was that we must be concerned. For he who wishes that the Name of Hashem be sanctified cannot come to terms with the possibility that there should be even one, solitary, common fool, anywhere in the world, who does not partake of service to Hashem when all assemble into one body to fulfill His bidding with a complete heart.

It was with such a view in mind, as it were that, when Avraham talked about, and prayed for, the inhabitants of Sodom, the Holy One answered him as follows: "They accuse Me of not judging properly. Examine the case and, if I am mistaken, teach Me" (*Bereishis Rabbah* 16). Hashem certainly does not err; by no stretch of the imagination can that happen. The Midrash, however, wishes to tell us that it is as if Hashem says, "If, as your limited understanding sees it, I have ruled too harshly against Sodom and this disturbs you in your service to Me and you cannot see My

אַיֵּה נָא אֱלֹהֵיהֶם. וֵאלֹהֵינוּ בַשָּׁמָיִם, כֹּל אֲשֶׁר חָפֵץ עָשָׂה. עֲצַבֵּיהֶם כֶּסֶף וְזָהָב, מַעֲשֵׂה יְדֵי אָדָם. פֶּה לָהֶם וְלֹא יְדַבֵּרוּ, עֵינַיִם לָהֶם וְלֹא יִרְאוּ. אָזְנַיִם לָהֶם וְלֹא יִשְׁמָעוּ, אַף לָהֶם וְלֹא יְרִיחוּן. יְדֵיהֶם וְלֹא יְמִישׁוּן, רַגְלֵיהֶם וְלֹא יְהַלֵּכוּ, לֹא יֶהְגּוּ בִּגְרוֹנָם. כְּמוֹהֶם יִהְיוּ עֹשֵׂיהֶם, כֹּל אֲשֶׁר בֹּטֵחַ בָּהֶם. יִשְׂרָאֵל בְּטַח בַּיהוה, עֶזְרָם וּמָגִנָּם הוּא. בֵּית אַהֲרֹן בִּטְחוּ בַיהוה, עֶזְרָם וּמָגִנָּם הוּא. יִרְאֵי יהוה בִּטְחוּ בַיהוה, עֶזְרָם וּמָגִנָּם הוּא.

---

benevolence to My creations, pray and you shall be answered."

The same approach underlies the dictum: "The righteous man decrees and the Holy One carries out his wish" (*Shabbos* 59). For the righteous man experiences the ways of Hashem through all the phenomena that occur — "the benevolence of HASHEM fills the world" (*Tehillim* 33:5). And when he sees that Hashem in donning His judge's robe has someone singled out for punishment and thereby caused His majesty and benevolence to be concealed, he is permitted to ask that the punishment be removed. That is, provided that he does not fool himself as to what he is praying for.

The Midrash discusses the proper attitude in prayer: "So that My children will not say, 'We, too, as did Avraham, shall speak (sharply) to Hashem and He will remain silent' . . . I will not remain silent. I held My peace for Avraham only. Why? Because he remained silent when I commanded him to bring his son as a burnt offering" (*Yalkut Iyov* 927). Avraham in his dialogue with Hashem, about the fate of Sodom, was truly concerned only about the glory of Hashem's Name and he was pained that His benevolence would become concealed within creation. Proof can be seen by the fact that when a decree touched him, personally, he chose to remain silent. And so, his prayer that the glory of Heaven be revealed was answered. Moshe's prayer, too, had no tinge of a personal request; he said, "And if not, erase me from Your book." His pain and concern are the result of the fear lest the heavenly glory would become concealed and not be seen in creation. He begged, "Give glory to Your Name." Such prayer is answered.

יִשְׂרָאֵל בְּטַח בַּה', עֶזְרָם וּמָגִנָּם הוּא

O Israel, trust in HASHEM; their help and their shield is He!

The Alter of Kelm

Their help and shield, not *our* help and shield. *Our* trust in Hashem receives support when we see that He helps and shields *them*, the non-Jews.

'Where is their God now?' Our God is in the heavens; whatever He pleases, He does! Their idols are silver and gold, the handiwork of man. They have a mouth, but cannot speak; they have eyes, but cannot see. They have ears, but cannot hear; they have a nose, but cannot smell. Their hands — they cannot feel; their feet — they cannot walk; they cannot utter a sound from their throat. Those who make them should become like them, whoever trusts in them! O Israel, trust in HASHEM; — their help and their shield is He! House of Aaron, trust in HASHEM; their help and their shield is He! You who fear HASHEM, trust in HASHEM; their help and their shield is He!

When a man sees that the wicked prosper in this world, he realizes that they are receiving their reward in the here and now for their meager store of *mitzvos*, so that they may be destroyed in the eternal World-to-Come. He trembles, because he knows that there is not enough good in this world to serve as a reward for even a single *mitzvah*. But the wicked wish to enjoy the life of this world — and they will. The righteous man lives with restraint in this world and suffers pain and punishment, over and above what he deserves for his transgressions. This, so that he may receive the just and full reward, to which he looks forward, in the eternal world of the future.

Why should the nations say, "Where is their God?" Why do they wonder why Israel is oppressed by suffering? It is for Israel's future eternal good. Because Hashem is their help and their shield, the help and shield of the other nations of the world, therefore we, Israel, trust in Hashem and rejoice that He will safeguard our reward for the World-to-Come.

The awareness of such a sense of trust must have prompted the repeated phrase in the following: "The right hand of HASHEM acts heroically, the right hand of HASHEM is exalted" (*Shemos* 15:6). When a wise man capably answers each and every query that is put to him and balks at replying to one particular question, we assume that he knows the answer but, for reasons of his own, refuses to divulge it. So, too, we see the greatness of the Creator and His strength in governing nature: "The right hand of HASHEM acts heroically, the right hand of HASHEM is exalted." We can assume that "the right hand of HASHEM acts heroically" even when we are not given the details and the reasons and do not understand what is happening. That is the implication of the repeated phrase.

The verse states: "HASHEM is exalted above all the nations" (*Tehillim* 113:4). The non-Jews (the nations) think that it is impossible to understand how Hashem conducts His world, but those who try to see things from

יהוה זְכָרָנוּ יְבָרֵךְ, יְבָרֵךְ אֶת בֵּית יִשְׂרָאֵל, יְבָרֵךְ אֶת בֵּית אַהֲרֹן. יְבָרֵךְ יִרְאֵי יהוה, הַקְּטַנִּים עִם הַגְּדֹלִים. יֹסֵף יהוה עֲלֵיכֶם, עֲלֵיכֶם וְעַל בְּנֵיכֶם. בְּרוּכִים אַתֶּם לַיהוה, עֹשֵׂה שָׁמַיִם וָאָרֶץ. הַשָּׁמַיִם שָׁמַיִם לַיהוה, וְהָאָרֶץ נָתַן לִבְנֵי אָדָם. לֹא הַמֵּתִים יְהַלְלוּ יָהּ, וְלֹא כָּל יֹרְדֵי דוּמָה. וַאֲנַחְנוּ נְבָרֵךְ יָהּ, מֵעַתָּה וְעַד עוֹלָם, הַלְלוּיָהּ.

אָהַבְתִּי כִּי יִשְׁמַע יהוה, אֶת קוֹלִי תַּחֲנוּנָי. כִּי הִטָּה אָזְנוֹ לִי, וּבְיָמַי אֶקְרָא. אֲפָפוּנִי חֶבְלֵי מָוֶת, וּמְצָרֵי שְׁאוֹל מְצָאוּנִי, צָרָה וְיָגוֹן

Heaven's perspective "above the heavens" do sense His glory: "Above the heavens is His glory" (ibid.) To them this seemingly inexplicable way in which the world is governed is the proper and true one.

הַשָּׁמַיִם שָׁמַיִם לַה'

As for the heavens — the heavens are Hashem's

R' Eliahu Lopian

The heavens, of their own accord, declare that they belong to Hashem. "But the earth He has given to mankind" (וְהָאָרֶץ נָתַן לִבְנֵי אָדָם), so that man might declare that it belongs to Hashem.

Thus, although Hashem "descended" upon Sinai and gave the Torah there, the holiness which rested upon it with the Divine Presence departed from the mountain with His "departure" (*Shemos* 19:13). Man was not the initiator in that act of sanctification. In contrast, Mount Moriah, the site of the *Beis HaMikdash,* retains its holiness even after the Destruction (*Megillah* 10). Man labored to sanctify Mount Moriah. It was there that Avraham was to offer up Yitzchak; there, Yaakov prayed; it was there that Israel built the *Beis HaMikdash*. By that act they sanctified it forever.

לֹא הַמֵּתִים יְהַלְלוּ יָהּ

Neither the dead can praise God

The Alter of Kelm

The dead differ from the living in that they no longer experience feeling. The wicked are referred to as dead, for they, too, have lost the sense of feeling. David committed but one solitary sin and said: "My sin is constantly before me" (*Tehillim* 51:5). And whenever he gained a further insight in Torah he felt as if he "had come

HASHEM Who has remembered us will bless — He will bless the House of Israel; He will bless the House of Aharon; He will bless those who fear HASHEM, the small as well as the great. May HASHEM increase upon you, upon you and upon your children! You are blessed of HASHEM, maker of heaven and earth. As for the heavens — the heavens are HASHEM'S, but the earth He has given to mankind. Neither the dead can praise God, nor any who descend into silence; but we will bless God from this time and forever. Halleluyah!

I love Him, for HASHEM hears my voice, my supplications. As He has inclined His ear to me, so in my days shall I call. The pains of death encircled me; the confines of the grave have found me; trouble

---

upon great booty" (*Tehillim* 119:162). The more a man sins, the more he loses his sensitivity: "the soul of the wicked desires evil; his friend does not find favor in his eyes" (*Mishlei* 21:10). Nothing perturbs him; he has no twinges of conscience. All feeling has died. His soul has departed from him while he is yet alive; it has died by inches.

"Neither the dead can praise God;" "And to the wicked man God says, 'What business do you have speaking of My laws?' " (*Tehillim* 50:16). By praise of Hashem and recounting His wonders one arouses the soul and has it come closer to its Creator and walk in His ways. But the heart of the evildoer is dead within him. His prayer is but lip service and will be to no avail.

In contrast, the man oppressed by suffering, whose sensitivity is not dulled, is alive. The suffering arouses his heart to return to its Maker; he is happy. "God chastened me exceedingly, but he did not let me die," and through the pain he says, "Open for me the gates of righteousness; I will enter them and thank God."

וּמְצָרֵי שְׁאוֹל מְצָאוּנִי

The confines of the grave have found me

R' Yerucham of Mir

To what grave and *Gehinnom* in this world could David be referring?

The essence of *Gehinnom* is that it is incomplete. It is called "destruction" (אֲבַדּוֹן), "the well of the grave" (בְּאֵר שָׁחַת), "the land of the bottom" (אֶרֶץ תַּחְתִּית), "the deep mire" (טִיט הַיָּוֵן). It conjures up entirely the incomplete and an abyss (*Bava Basra* 79). *Chazal* indeed speak of "falling into" *Gehinnom*. And the evil nature (יֵצֶר הָרָע) and desire are related to the

אֶמְצָא. וּבְשֵׁם יהוה אֶקְרָא, אָנָּה יהוה מַלְּטָה נַפְשִׁי. חַנּוּן יהוה וְצַדִּיק, וֵאלֹהֵינוּ מְרַחֵם. שֹׁמֵר פְּתָאִים יהוה, דַּלּוֹתִי וְלִי יְהוֹשִׁיעַ. שׁוּבִי נַפְשִׁי לִמְנוּחָיְכִי, כִּי יהוה גָּמַל עָלָיְכִי. כִּי חִלַּצְתָּ נַפְשִׁי מִמָּוֶת, אֶת עֵינִי מִן דִּמְעָה, אֶת רַגְלִי מִדֶּחִי. אֶתְהַלֵּךְ לִפְנֵי יהוה, בְּאַרְצוֹת הַחַיִּים. הֶאֱמַנְתִּי כִּי אֲדַבֵּר, אֲנִי עָנִיתִי מְאֹד. אֲנִי אָמַרְתִּי בְחָפְזִי, כָּל הָאָדָם כֹּזֵב.

מָה אָשִׁיב לַיהוה, כָּל תַּגְמוּלוֹהִי עָלָי. כּוֹס יְשׁוּעוֹת אֶשָּׂא, וּבְשֵׁם יהוה אֶקְרָא.

---

deficient: "He who sanctifies his desires — goes starving" (*Sukkah* 52). "He who has a hundred strives for two hundred" (*Koheles Rabbah* 3). "The belly of the wicked suffers want" (*Mishlei* 13:25). Surely, this reflects a *Gehinnom*.

David HaMelech cried out, "The confines of the grave have found me" — I am in *Gehinnom*. "You have drawn my soul up out of the grave, you have revived me from among those who have descended into the pit!" (*Tehillim* 30:4). We don't feel the *Gehinnom*, because our senses are dulled. But it is a true *Gehinnom*. I once saw men cleaning latrines. The stench was awful; it was impossible to come close. I thought that if someone were to be bound there, he would choke to death — a veritable *Gehinnom*. And, yet, the workers — they tossed off a drink of whiskey and danced there. Is not our dance, too, that we dance out here in this world a dance within *Gehinnom*? We are so intoxicated that we dance. But the thinking man, if he were to examine his *Gehinnom*, the abyss of the incomplete, a bottomless emptiness, he too would cry out, "Save my soul from the Underworld" (שְׁאוֹל).

It disturbs one to realize that man, who was in *Gan Eden* (Paradise), whom the angels wished to proclaim as "holy" in his presence, fell so greatly, bringing ruin to himself and all creation. From the *Gan Eden* on earth, he sank to the abyss of *Gehinnom*.

וּמְצָרֵי שְׁאוֹל מְצָאוּנִי

The confines of the grave have found me

R' Yerucham of Mir

With each step that he took David HaMelech envisioned *Gehinnom*. In all that occurred to him, he feared sin and the hell that would follow in its wake. When Esav and his four hundred men drew near to give battle, Yaakov, too, "was exceedingly afraid" (*Bereishis* 32:8); he thought that he might have "dirtied" himself with sin (*Rashi* to *Bereishis* 32:11). *Chazal* say that the plague of darkness in Egypt rose

and sorrow I would find. Then I would invoke the Name of HASHEM: 'Please HASHEM, save my soul.' Gracious is HASHEM and righteous, our God is merciful. HASHEM protects the simple; I was brought low, but He saved me. Return, my soul, to your rest; for HASHEM has been kind to you. For You have delivered my soul from death, my eyes from tears, my feet from stumbling. I shall walk before HASHEM in the lands of the living. I have kept faith although I say: 'I suffer exceedingly.' I said in my haste: 'All mankind is deceitful.'

How can I repay HASHEM for all His kindness to me? I will raise the cup of salvations and the Name of

---

up from *Gehinnom* (*Shemos Rabbah* 14). There is no evil and darkness without sin and *Gehinnom*. The *gemara* tells of a poisonous reptile that was killing people. R' Chanina ben Dosa put his heel over its hole; the creature bit him and died. He declared: "It is not the monster which kills; it is the sin that slays" (*Berachos* 33a).

מָה אָשִׁיב לַה'
How can I repay HASHEM

The Alter of Slobodka R' Saadia Gaon lodged in an inn one evening. The following morning the innkeeper approached him to apologize. Although he had treated R' Saadia well, he said, he had not realized who his guest was until now and had not served him as befitted his station. From that day on R' Saadia would mortify himself by rolling in the snow, not as penance for past sins, but because when he performed a *mitzvah*, he had not been previously as aware of the measure of Hashem's greatness as he was at present.

This verse "How can I repay HASHEM?" reflects this attitude. The more I am able to comprehend what Hashem is, the more I see the worthlessness of my service to Him and that I cannot begin to repay Him.

Chazal say that if a man, in a gesture of friendliness, gives another a dish of lentils to eat, his friend should return the favor with a dish of beans (which are higher in price). The man who gave the lentils has performed an unsolicited act of kindness (חֶסֶד), said the *Gaon* of Vilna. And, if the man who ate the lentils were to give lentils in return, he is repaying his friend, as it were, but has not performed a similar act of kindness; he has, in a sense, given what he owes. To perform a parallel act of kindness, he must give more than he got. Hashem acts with undiluted kindness. Man cannot even return what he receives, let alone more than he receives.

נְדָרַי לַיהוה אֲשַׁלֵּם, נֶגְדָה נָּא לְכָל עַמּוֹ. יָקָר בְּעֵינֵי
יהוה, הַמָּוְתָה לַחֲסִידָיו. אָנָּה יהוה כִּי אֲנִי עַבְדֶּךָ,
אֲנִי עַבְדְּךָ, בֶּן אֲמָתֶךָ, פִּתַּחְתָּ לְמוֹסֵרָי. לְךָ אֶזְבַּח
זֶבַח תּוֹדָה, וּבְשֵׁם יהוה אֶקְרָא. נְדָרַי לַיהוה
אֲשַׁלֵּם, נֶגְדָה נָּא לְכָל עַמּוֹ. בְּחַצְרוֹת בֵּית יהוה,
בְּתוֹכֵכִי יְרוּשָׁלָיִם הַלְלוּיָהּ.

הַלְלוּ אֶת יהוה, כָּל גּוֹיִם, שַׁבְּחוּהוּ כָּל הָאֻמִּים.
כִּי גָבַר עָלֵינוּ חַסְדּוֹ, וֶאֱמֶת יהוה לְעוֹלָם,
הַלְלוּיָהּ.

הוֹדוּ לַיהוה כִּי טוֹב,   כִּי לְעוֹלָם חַסְדּוֹ.
יֹאמַר נָא יִשְׂרָאֵל,   כִּי לְעוֹלָם חַסְדּוֹ.
יֹאמְרוּ נָא בֵית אַהֲרֹן,   כִּי לְעוֹלָם חַסְדּוֹ.
יֹאמְרוּ נָא יִרְאֵי יהוה,   כִּי לְעוֹלָם חַסְדּוֹ.

כָּל תַּגְמוּלוֹהִי עָלָי
All His kindness to me

R' Yerucham of Mir   Man is mistaken, if he thinks that he receives benefits from Heaven free of charge. He must repay heavily for whatever he gets. If only a single grain of wheat flourished in an entire field, the owner had to bring that single grain to the *Beis HaMikdash* (when it was still standing) and recite the entire passage relevant to the bringing of first fruits and, in so doing, remind himself of all the kindness which Hashem has shown to us from the time of our forefather Yaakov. The Creator gave him a single grain of wheat and, in return, He received the recitation of the entire passage.

The prophet has stated this quite expressly: "Whatever is called, by My Name and for My glory I have created" (*Yeshayahu* 43:7). Everything was created and given only that the Creator's Name should rest upon it for His glory. "Give thanks to HASHEM, for He is good. His kindness endures forever." Man must think deeply and see how Hashem's kindness (חֶסֶד) fills the entire world. "I shall not die! I shall live — and relate the deeds of HASHEM": I will see the blessings of Hashem in each detail of nature, in all that happens in the world. "Blessed is the glory of HASHEM, wherever He is" — מִמְּקוֹמוֹ — (*Yechezkel* 3:12); Hashem's glory is revealed from nature, from

HASHEM I will invoke. My vows to HASHEM I will pay, in the presence, now, of His entire people. Difficult in the eyes of HASHEM is the death of His devout ones. Please, HASHEM — for I am Your servant, I am Your servant, son of Your handmaid — You have released my bonds. To You I will sacrifice thanksgiving offerings, and the name of HASHEM I will invoke. My vows to HASHEM I will pay, in the presence, now, of His entire people. In the courtyards of the House of HASHEM, in your midst, O Jerusalem, Halleluyah!

Praise HASHEM, all nations; praise Him, all the states! For His kindness has overwhelmed us, and the truth of HASHEM is eternal, Halleluyah!

Give thanks to HASHEM for He is good;
> His kindness endures forever!
Let Israel say: His kindness endures forever!
Let the House of Aharon say:
> His kindness endures forever!
Let those who fear HASHEM say:
> His kindness endures forever!

---

everywhere. And man is to serve Hashem and repay His kindness with praise: "I will raise the cup of salvations, and invoke the name of HASHEM" (*Tehillim* 116:13).

הַלְלוּ אֶת ה', כָּל גּוֹיִם . . . כִּי גָבַר עָלֵינוּ חַסְדּוֹ

Praise HASHEM, all nations . . .
For His kindness has overwhelmed us

The Alter of Kelm   Why should the nations praise Hashem for kindness done to us?

The nations have made a soul-searching self-examination (חֶשְׁבּוֹן הַנֶּפֶשׁ). *They* are in a state of security and tranquility; *they* should have reached the pinnacle of culture and ethical behavior. And yet they see that "His kindness has overwhelmed *us*." And the true measure of His kindness is the ability to understand the outpouring of His kindness; to know that He is wholly good; that *we* are to walk in His ways, be good and do good. The nations see that *we* and not *they*, possess these traits, despite all their tranquility and security — we, the people of wandering and oppression. We have gained these traits through the laws and *mitzvos* which they mocked; these laws have uplifted us.

מִן הַמֵּצַר קָרָאתִי יָּהּ, עָנָנִי בַמֶּרְחָב יָהּ. יהוה לִי לֹא אִירָא, מַה יַּעֲשֶׂה לִי אָדָם.

יהוה לִי בְּעֹזְרָי, וַאֲנִי אֶרְאֶה בְשֹׂנְאָי. טוֹב לַחֲסוֹת בַּיהוה, מִבְּטֹחַ בָּאָדָם. טוֹב לַחֲסוֹת בַּיהוה, מִבְּטֹחַ בִּנְדִיבִים. כָּל גּוֹיִם סְבָבוּנִי, בְּשֵׁם יהוה כִּי אֲמִילַם. סַבּוּנִי גַם סְבָבוּנִי, בְּשֵׁם יהוה כִּי אֲמִילַם. סַבּוּנִי כִדְבֹרִים דֹּעֲכוּ כְּאֵשׁ קוֹצִים, בְּשֵׁם יהוה כִּי אֲמִילַם. דָּחֹה דְחִיתַנִי לִנְפֹּל, וַיהוה עֲזָרָנִי. עָזִּי וְזִמְרָת יָהּ, וַיְהִי לִי לִישׁוּעָה. קוֹל רִנָּה וִישׁוּעָה, בְּאָהֳלֵי צַדִּיקִים, יְמִין יהוה עֹשָׂה חָיִל. יְמִין יהוה רוֹמֵמָה, יְמִין יהוה עֹשָׂה חָיִל. לֹא אָמוּת כִּי אֶחְיֶה, וַאֲסַפֵּר מַעֲשֵׂי יָהּ. יַסֹּר יִסְּרַנִּי יָּהּ, וְלַמָּוֶת לֹא נְתָנָנִי.

ה׳ לִי לֹא אִירָא / *Hashem is with me, I have no fear*

The Alter of Kelm

When Hashem is with me then I have no fear of what a man might do to me. Even if he should attempt to harm me, Hashem will turn it to the good. For example, his brothers sold Yosef in order to frustrate his dreams. But, by that very act, he became chief minister to Pharaoh and the dreams were fulfilled. "You thought (to do) evil against me, God meant it for the good" (*Bereishis* 50:20).

טוֹב לַחֲסוֹת בַּה׳ מִבְּטֹחַ בִּנְדִיבִים
It is better to take refuge in Hashem than to rely on man

R' Yerucham of Mir

There are two extremes and innumerable stages lie between them. There is absolute trust in Hashem at one end and trust in man at the other. But what lies between these two extremes cannot be considered empty space. To the degree that a man puts his trust in mortals, in like measure he fails in his trust in Hashem: "Cursed be the man who puts his trust in mortals . . . and turns his heart away from Hashem" (*Yirmeyahu* 17:5).

Yisro was excited by the dividing of the waters of the Red Sea. That made him realize that "Hashem is greater than all the gods" (*Shemos* 18:11). Yet *Chazal* saw him as only a "partial believer" (*Yalkut Shemos* 269). He still spoke of *other* gods and powers, as if they existed, even though he recognized that Hashem was greater than them all. His faith was not yet perfect. Our Sages classified Adam as a heretic, because he was won over by

From the straits did I call upon God; God answered me with expansiveness. HASHEM is with me, I have no fear; how can man affect me? HASHEM is with me through my helpers; therefore I can face my foes. It is better to take refuge in HASHEM than to rely on man. It is better to take refuge in HASHEM than to rely on nobles. All the nations surround me; in the Name of HASHEM I cut them down! They encircle me, they also surround me; in the Name of HASHEM I cut them down! They encircle me like bees, but they are extinguished as a fire does thorns; in the Name of HASHEM I cut them down! You pushed me hard that I might fall, but HASHEM assisted me. God is my might and my praise, and He was a salvation for me. The sound of rejoicing and salvation is in the tents of the righteous: 'HASHEM's right hand does valiantly. HASHEM's right hand is raised triumphantly; HASHEM's right hand does valiantly!' I shall not die! But I shall live and relate the deeds of God. God has chastened me exceedingly, but He did not let me die.

---

the persuasive tongue of the serpent (*Sanhedrin* 38). Indeed, anyone who really knows himself and is willing to see things honestly is aware that he is not even a "partial believer." He puts his trust in mortals and the forces of nature; he sees his own hand as performing acts of valor. Would that he might, at least, see the power of the Holy One as equal to any of these!

Before the final Redemption (הַגְּאֻלָּה הַשְּׁלֵמָה) when "HASHEM will be one" (*Zechariah* 14:9), all those who trust in mortals will be thrown into confusion and there will be a shattering of all the idols. "The heavens will be destroyed (and vanish) like smoke" (*Yeshayahu* 51:6); nature will be overturned. Straight thinking will become distorted; "truth will be absent." The social order of things will be upended; "youth will shame age." Even spiritual values will totter: the Torah — "the wisdom of the scribes will be despised"; the righteous — "those who fear sin will be held in contempt." All this, that we might realize that "we have no one to lean upon other than our Father in heaven" (*Sotah* 49). "Look, for I, I am He and no one can save from My grasp" (*Devarim* 32:39).

לֹא אָמוּת כִּי אֶחְיֶה וַאֲסַפֵּר מַעֲשֵׂי יָהּ

I shall not die! But I shall live and relate the deeds of God

The *Alter* of Novharodok was extreme in his approach to life. At first, he lived in a very solitary manner, cutting himself off from the world about him.

פִּתְחוּ לִי שַׁעֲרֵי צֶדֶק, אָבֹא בָם אוֹדֶה יָהּ. זֶה
הַשַּׁעַר לַיהוה, צַדִּיקִים יָבֹאוּ בוֹ. אוֹדְךָ כִּי עֲנִיתָנִי,
וַתְּהִי לִי לִישׁוּעָה. אוֹדְךָ כִּי עֲנִיתָנִי, וַתְּהִי לִי
לִישׁוּעָה. אֶבֶן מָאֲסוּ הַבּוֹנִים, הָיְתָה לְרֹאשׁ פִּנָּה.
אֶבֶן מָאֲסוּ הַבּוֹנִים, הָיְתָה לְרֹאשׁ פִּנָּה. מֵאֵת יהוה
הָיְתָה זֹּאת, הִיא נִפְלָאת בְּעֵינֵינוּ. מֵאֵת יהוה הָיְתָה
זֹּאת, הִיא נִפְלָאת בְּעֵינֵינוּ. זֶה הַיּוֹם עָשָׂה יהוה,
נָגִילָה וְנִשְׂמְחָה בוֹ. זֶה הַיּוֹם עָשָׂה יהוה, נָגִילָה
וְנִשְׂמְחָה בוֹ.

But after the *Alter* of Kelm persuaded him to be active, he began to organize what later became a many-branched network of *yeshivos* and discussion groups, a comprehensive program beyond comparison.

However, the first beginnings were disappointing. *Yeshivos* which he founded fell apart, groups which he organized dispersed and those who opposed his views condemned him. In the midst of this crisis, depressed in spirit, he went to spend a *Shabbos* in Kelm.

The *Alter* of Kelm would regularly speak for many hours of the post-*Shabbos* evening (מוֹצָאֵי שַׁבָּת). That week he stood in his usual position at the rostrum — mute. The lengthy silence brought on tension and fear in the expectant audience. Suddenly, he struck the rostrum and cried out loudly and movingly, "It is enough for a man that he be alive! It is enough for a man that he be alive! He repeated himself many times, again and again, with ever-increasing emotion. And, then, had them pray *ma'ariv* (the evening prayer).

The *Alter* of Novharodok said that the single, repeated sentence of the *Alter* of Kelm shook him out of his depression. He decided to continue to spread his views with full force, and not pay attention to any obstacle. It was sufficient that he was alive and "if I but live, I will relate the deeds of Hashem!" He succeeded and his network of *yeshivos* grew by leaps and bounds into a magnificent organization.

פִּתְחוּ לִי שַׁעֲרֵי צֶדֶק
Open for me the gates of righteousness

For seven hours the *Alter* of Kelm pored over the verse "Open for me the gates of righteousness. I will enter them and thank God." Suddenly, he leaped up, as if bitten by a snake and cried out, "Lo, the gates are open! Why do I hesitate to enter?"

An important rabbi was a guest at the home of R' Yitzchak Blazer of

Open for me the gates of righteousness, I will enter them and thank God. This is the gate of HASHEM; the righteous shall enter through it. I thank You for You have answered me and become my salvation. I thank You for You have answered me and become my salvation. The stone the builders despised has become the cornerstone. The stone the builders despised has become the cornerstone. This emanated from HASHEM; it is wondrous in our eyes. This emanated from HASHEM; it is wondrous in our eyes. This is the day HASHEM has made; let us rejoice and be glad on it. This is the day HASHEM has made; let us rejoice and be glad on it.

Kovno. At midnight, when all were asleep, he saw R' Yitzchak rise and repeat again and again as if speaking directly to another party, "I beg of you, open the gates of righteousness for me. I beg of you, I wish to enter and praise Hashem. And what answer am I given? This is the gateway to Hashem; only the righteous shall enter it. But not you, not you."

R' Eliahu Dessler gave vivid life to the verse with then-current imagery: Unseaworthy vessels, packed with survivors of the Holocaust, saved from the crematoria of Europe, made their way to the shores of *Eretz Yisrael*. And the gates were shut. The British seized the ships and rerouted them to the detention camps on Cyprus. What terrible frustration!

What would we feel if, after a successive string of disappointments and afflictions in this world, our ship would reach the gates of the World-to-Come, only to find them shut in our faces? For it is the gateway to Hashem, yet only the righteousness shall enter it. But we are fortunate. We can acquire an entry certificate through our efforts in studying the Torah and performing *mitzvos*. These will open the gates before us.

אוֹדְךָ כִּי עֲנִיתָנִי
I thank You for You have answered me

[*Midrash Tehillim* renders כִּי עֲנִיתָנִי as *"You caused me suffering."*]

The Alter of Kelm   Open the gates of righteousness for me. Man in reality asks the question, "What gates must I pass through to understand the greatness of Hashem?" And he is told that suffering and pain is the gateway to Hashem. I thank You for You caused me pain (אוֹדְךָ כִּי עֲנִיתָנִי) and that was my salvation (וַתְּהִי לִי לִישׁוּעָה).

In order to reach the pleasure of the mind one must do away with the desires of the body, just as we must first melt down the ugly to cast the liquid metal into something beautiful. And just as we apply heat to a wound

אָנָּא יהוה הוֹשִׁיעָה נָּא.

אָנָּא יהוה הוֹשִׁיעָה נָּא.

אָנָּא יהוה הַצְלִיחָה נָא.

אָנָּא יהוה הַצְלִיחָה נָא.

בָּרוּךְ הַבָּא בְּשֵׁם יהוה, בֵּרַכְנוּכֶם מִבֵּית יהוה.
בָּרוּךְ הַבָּא בְּשֵׁם יהוה, בֵּרַכְנוּכֶם מִבֵּית
יהוה. אֵל יהוה וַיָּאֶר לָנוּ, אִסְרוּ חַג בַּעֲבֹתִים, עַד
קַרְנוֹת הַמִּזְבֵּחַ. אֵל יהוה וַיָּאֶר לָנוּ, אִסְרוּ חַג
בַּעֲבֹתִים, עַד קַרְנוֹת הַמִּזְבֵּחַ. אֵלִי אַתָּה וְאוֹדֶךָּ,
אֱלֹהַי אֲרוֹמְמֶךָּ. אֵלִי אַתָּה וְאוֹדֶךָּ, אֱלֹהַי אֲרוֹמְמֶךָּ.
הוֹדוּ לַיהוה כִּי טוֹב, כִּי לְעוֹלָם חַסְדּוֹ. הוֹדוּ לַיהוה
כִּי טוֹב, כִּי לְעוֹלָם חַסְדּוֹ.

יְהַלְלוּךָ יהוה אֱלֹהֵינוּ כָּל מַעֲשֶׂיךָ, וַחֲסִידֶיךָ
צַדִּיקִים עוֹשֵׂי רְצוֹנֶךָ, וְכָל עַמְּךָ בֵּית
יִשְׂרָאֵל בְּרִנָּה יוֹדוּ וִיבָרְכוּ וִישַׁבְּחוּ וִיפָאֲרוּ וִירוֹמְמוּ
וְיַעֲרִיצוּ וְיַקְדִּישׁוּ וְיַמְלִיכוּ אֶת שִׁמְךָ מַלְכֵּנוּ, כִּי לְךָ
טוֹב לְהוֹדוֹת וּלְשִׁמְךָ נָאֶה לְזַמֵּר, כִּי מֵעוֹלָם וְעַד
עוֹלָם אַתָּה אֵל.

---

to draw out pus, painful though the process is, so we inflict pain upon a man
to purify him.

Koheles begins with: "Vanity of vanities, all is vanity." This is the
necessary introduction to its finale: "Fear God and keep His commandments, that is man in his entirety."

בָּרוּךְ הַבָּא בְּשֵׁם ה׳
Blessed is he who comes in the Name of HASHEM

The Alter of Kelm   He who already made his commitment to the Name
of Hashem before entering the *Beis HaMikdash* is
blessed. He doesn't wait for some sudden revelation in the midst of his
prayers. He prepares himself beforehand. Then it is that he is blessed by the

Please, HASHEM, save now!
Please, HASHEM, save now!
Please, HASHEM, bring success now!
Please, HASHEM, bring success now!

Blessed is he who comes in the Name of HASHEM; we bless you from the House of HASHEM. Blessed is he who comes in the Name of HASHEM; we bless you from the House of HASHEM. HASHEM is God, He illuminated for us; bind the festival offering with cords until the corners of the Altar. HASHEM is God, He illuminated for us; bind the festival offering with cords until the corners of the Altar. You are my God, and I will thank You; my God, I will exalt You. You are my God, and I will thank You; my God, I will exalt You. Give thanks to HASHEM, for He is good; His kindness endures forever. Give thanks to HASHEM, for He is good; His kindness endures forever.

All Your works shall praise You, HASHEM our God. And Your devout ones, the righteous, who do Your will, and Your entire people, the House of Israel, with glad song will thank, bless, praise, glorify, exalt, extol, sanctify, and proclaim the sovereignty of Your Name, our King. For to You it is fitting to give thanks, and unto Your Name it is proper to sing praises, for from This World to the World-to-Come You are God.

---

house of Hashem. The very act of service will then have a more powerful effect.

So, too, in the following passage we say: "HASHEM is God, He illuminated for us." At the acquisition of the sacrifice, when we "bind it with cords" for safekeeping (אִסְרוּ חַג בַּעֲבֹתִים), we should do it in the same frame of mind which we will have at the sacrifice on the altar (עַד קַרְנוֹת הַמִּזְבֵּחַ). Then with such previous thoughtful purpose (כַּוָּנָה) the sacrifice is truly to Hashem and the result is that He will give us light. Preparation is an integral part of the performance of the *mitzvah*.

R' Chiya, too, had the importance of preparation (הֲכָנָה) in mind. He said that he had the power to ensure that the Torah not be forgotten. He could plant flax, harvest it, spin threads and wind them into rope. From the rope he would fashion a net to snare deer. He would slaughter the deer and give the

הוֹדוּ לַיהוה כִּי טוֹב כִּי לְעוֹלָם חַסְדּוֹ.
הוֹדוּ לֵאלֹהֵי הָאֱלֹהִים כִּי לְעוֹלָם חַסְדּוֹ.
הוֹדוּ לַאֲדֹנֵי הָאֲדֹנִים כִּי לְעוֹלָם חַסְדּוֹ.
לְעֹשֵׂה נִפְלָאוֹת גְּדֹלוֹת לְבַדּוֹ כִּי לְעוֹלָם חַסְדּוֹ.
לְעֹשֵׂה הַשָּׁמַיִם בִּתְבוּנָה כִּי לְעוֹלָם חַסְדּוֹ.
לְרֹקַע הָאָרֶץ עַל הַמָּיִם כִּי לְעוֹלָם חַסְדּוֹ.
לְעֹשֵׂה אוֹרִים גְּדֹלִים כִּי לְעוֹלָם חַסְדּוֹ.
אֶת הַשֶּׁמֶשׁ לְמֶמְשֶׁלֶת בַּיּוֹם כִּי לְעוֹלָם חַסְדּוֹ.

---

meat to the poor and write the Torah on the hides. From these Torah scrolls, he would teach the youngsters of Israel (*Kesubos* 103). Why should he go to all that trouble? Why not buy completed Torah scrolls? This shows us that preparation (הֲכָנָה) adds to the sanctity of the deed. The greater the preparation, the more successful is the act.

לְעֹשֵׂה נִפְלָאוֹת גְּדֹלוֹת לְבַדּוֹ
To Him Who alone performs great wonders

R' Eliahu Lopian

Is it only the *great* wonders which Hashem does alone? What about the *lesser* wonders?

When men see the "minor wonders," they attribute them to nature. But when they see "major wonders," they clearly recognize the hand of Hashem behind His works. In truth, *we* cannot grasp how miraculous even these major wonders are. Only Hashem, Himself — alone (לְבַדּוֹ) knows to what extent His kindness is everlasting.

לְעֹשֵׂה אוֹרִים גְּדֹלִים
To Him Who made great lights

The Alter of Kelm

Chazal have noted that the present tense — *makes* (עֹשֵׂה) — is used. This shows us that Creation is renewed with each instant. We, on our part, should express our thanks anew, and with increased vigor, at each moment. For a momentary, unrepeated kindness is far different from benevolence exercised over a long period of time, and that cannot be compared to kindness renewed with each moment.

R' Eliahu Dessler

Although the whole of Creation is constantly renewed, there is a particular reason for singling out the heavenly luminaries. With the daily renewal of Creation, new forces of emanation reach man; he gains heavenly aid in his renewed daily service to

Give thanks to HASHEM for He is good,
for His kindness endures forever.
Give thanks to the God of the heavenly powers,
for His kindness endures forever.
Give thanks to the Lord of the lords,
for His kindness endures forever.
To Him Who alone performs great wonders,
for His kindness endures forever.
To Him Who made the heavens with understanding,
for His kindness endures forever.
To Him Who spread out the earth upon the waters,
for His kindness endures forever.
To Him Who made great lights,
for His kindness endures forever.
The sun for the reign of the day,
for His kindness endures forever.

Hashem. That aid should be seen as akin, in its nature, to the light shed on earth. More specifically, we speak of "great luminaries," because we wish the light of the moon to be like that of the sun — to receive a light like that of the Redemption of which the prophet speaks (Yeshayahu 30:26). This Redemption-like radiance should be poured forth upon each and every one, day by day, to reveal the fullness of light in Creation.

אֶת הַשֶּׁמֶשׁ לְמֶמְשֶׁלֶת בַּיּוֹם
The sun for the reign of the day

The Alter of Slobodka   Man is constantly called upon to differentiate between one thing and another. After we have praised Hashem for the kindness of creating the great heavenly luminaries, we are asked to distinguish between His kindness in setting the sun to rule by day and the kindness that is shown by having lights to rule the night. And we make an even finer distinction between moon and stars.

Such differentiation is demanded in the area of deeds, too. The acts of the righteous are compared to light, those of the wicked to darkness (Bereishis Rabbah 3). And after making that division, we find that we must create sub-categories. The more wicked should not be buried with the less wicked (Sanhedrin 46). And on the other side of the coin — Reish Lakish did not carry on a conversation in public unless the other party was a man of exceptionally lofty character. He did not even speak to R' Elazar (Yoma 9b). In another area we also distinguish between lesser holiness and greater holiness and take care not to put a volume of Prophets on a volume of the Chumash.

אֶת הַיָּרֵחַ וְכוֹכָבִים לְמֶמְשְׁלוֹת בַּלָּיְלָה

	כִּי לְעוֹלָם חַסְדּוֹ.
לְמַכֵּה מִצְרַיִם בִּבְכוֹרֵיהֶם	כִּי לְעוֹלָם חַסְדּוֹ.
וַיּוֹצֵא יִשְׂרָאֵל מִתּוֹכָם	כִּי לְעוֹלָם חַסְדּוֹ.
בְּיָד חֲזָקָה וּבִזְרוֹעַ נְטוּיָה	כִּי לְעוֹלָם חַסְדּוֹ.
לְגֹזֵר יַם סוּף לִגְזָרִים	כִּי לְעוֹלָם חַסְדּוֹ.
וְהֶעֱבִיר יִשְׂרָאֵל בְּתוֹכוֹ	כִּי לְעוֹלָם חַסְדּוֹ.
וְנִעֵר פַּרְעֹה וְחֵילוֹ בְיַם סוּף	כִּי לְעוֹלָם חַסְדּוֹ.
לְמוֹלִיךְ עַמּוֹ בַּמִּדְבָּר	כִּי לְעוֹלָם חַסְדּוֹ.
לְמַכֵּה מְלָכִים גְּדֹלִים	כִּי לְעוֹלָם חַסְדּוֹ.
וַיַּהֲרֹג מְלָכִים אַדִּירִים	כִּי לְעוֹלָם חַסְדּוֹ.
לְסִיחוֹן מֶלֶךְ הָאֱמֹרִי	כִּי לְעוֹלָם חַסְדּוֹ.
וּלְעוֹג מֶלֶךְ הַבָּשָׁן	כִּי לְעוֹלָם חַסְדּוֹ.

לְמוֹלִיךְ עַמּוֹ בַּמִּדְבָּר
To Him Who led His people through the wilderness

The Alter of Slobodka   Because Avraham, himself, escorted the angels who had been his guests, Hashem, Himself, went before Israel in the desert (*Bava Metzia* 86). And there is a vast difference whether it is Hashem Who goes before them, or an angel Whom He sends. For after Israel had sinned with the Golden Calf, Hashem wished to send an angel to conduct them. But Moshe said: "If Your Presence (פָּנֶיךָ) does not go, do not take us up from here" (*Shemos* 33:15). Without Hashem Himself to lead them, it is preferable to have the entire nation remain forever "in the vast and awesome desert, place of the serpent, reptile, scorpion and thirst" (*Devarim* 8:15) and forgo entry into the Promised Land and all the promises which accompany it.

Now, picture the scene. One-hundred-year-old Avraham, three days after his circumcision, has brought strangers into his home out of the heat of day. He has fed them of the best that there is, gratis. Had he requested a member of his household to escort them, at the most, this would have reduced his act of being the complete host by some small fraction. Yet, see how tremendous is the reward for that small fraction of the full act of the *mitzvah*.

The moon and the stars for the reign of the night,
for His kindness endures forever.
To Him Who smote Egypt through their firstborn,
for His kindness endures forever.
And brought Israel forth from their midst,
for His kindness endures forever.
With strong hand and outstretched arm,
for His kindness endures forever.
To Him Who divided the Sea of Reeds into parts,
for His kindness endures forever.
And caused Israel to pass through it,
for His kindness endures forever.
And threw Pharaoh and his army into the Sea of
Reeds,   for His kindness endures forever.
To Him Who led His people through the wilderness,
for His kindness endures forever.
To Him Who smote great kings,
for His kindness endures forever.
And slew mighty kings,
for His kindness endures forever.
Sichon, king of the Emorites,
for His kindness endures forever.
And Og, king of Bashan,
for His kindness endures forever.

וּלְעוֹג מֶלֶךְ הַבָּשָׁן / *And Og, king of Bashan*

R' Eliahu Lopian   We are grateful to Hashem for the kindness which He showed towards us in granting us victory over Og. That kindness was not a passing matter; it has an enduring quality about it. We were given that victory, despite Og's act of kindness (חֶסֶד) and the reward due him. He was the fugitive who had fled from the battle and came to Avraham with the bad news that his nephew Lot had been taken captive. He hoped that Avraham would take to the field and be slain in the fighting, leaving him, Og, free to marry Sarah (*Niddah* 61).

See how great is the reward for the *mitzvah* done for ulterior motives; he lived more than five hundred years and was a powerful king. Yet, Moshe feared that enough of his reward was still due, to enable him to crush Israel. Hashem had to assure him; "Do not fear him" (*Bamidbar* 21:35). How much more so does one deserve credit who acts kindly with a pure intent. His due cannot be measured and it stands for an eternity.

וְנָתַן אַרְצָם לְנַחֲלָה כִּי לְעוֹלָם חַסְדּוֹ.
נַחֲלָה לְיִשְׂרָאֵל עַבְדּוֹ כִּי לְעוֹלָם חַסְדּוֹ.
שֶׁבְּשִׁפְלֵנוּ זָכַר לָנוּ כִּי לְעוֹלָם חַסְדּוֹ.
וַיִּפְרְקֵנוּ מִצָּרֵינוּ כִּי לְעוֹלָם חַסְדּוֹ.
נֹתֵן לֶחֶם לְכָל בָּשָׂר כִּי לְעוֹלָם חַסְדּוֹ.
הוֹדוּ לְאֵל הַשָּׁמָיִם כִּי לְעוֹלָם חַסְדּוֹ.

נִשְׁמַת כָּל חַי תְּבָרֵךְ אֶת שִׁמְךָ יהוה אֱלֹהֵינוּ וְרוּחַ כָּל בָּשָׂר תְּפָאֵר וּתְרוֹמֵם זִכְרְךָ מַלְכֵּנוּ תָּמִיד. מִן הָעוֹלָם וְעַד הָעוֹלָם אַתָּה אֵל

The Alter of Kelm Og's great reward was not the result of his act of kindness. Others do far greater deeds and with purer intentions, yet their heavenly credit does not stand so high that there need be fear, lest they be allowed to overcome Israel. Og's reward was multiplied ten times over, because the one who received his kindness was Avraham. Not only the deed but the recipient of the deed is a factor which determines its heavenly worth. Thus, Yirmeyahu, when he was angry at the people of Anasos, prayed that they give their charity to people who were unworthy of it (*Bava Kamma* 16). If such was the reward of Og who acted kindly to Avraham, but with tainted thoughts, what an unimaginable reward would be due one who acted with good intentions. Furthermore, this would be but a pale reflection of Avraham's own heavenly reward.

And yet, despite his high standing, were he together with Yitzchak and Yaakov to stand in judgment before the Holy One, with His kindness (חֶסֶד) turned aside, all three as a group would be found wanting. How little we understand the concept of unrelieved justice!

תְּבָרֵךְ אֶת שִׁמְךָ
Shall bless Your Name

R' Yerucham of Mir We give a name to a permanent phenomenon, but a flash-in-the-pan occurrence is not deemed worthy of a name.

Of our forefather Avraham it is said: "And he called in the Name of HASHEM" (*Bereishis* 12:8). When Hashem was about to deliver Israel from out of Egypt, Moshe wished to know what His Name was (*Shemos* 3:13) — under what permanent guise would Hashem effect the Redemption. And the

And presented their land as a heritage,
> for His kindness endures forever.

A heritage for Israel, His servant,
> for His kindness endures forever.

In our lowliness He remembered us,
> for His kindness endures forever.

And released us from our tormentors,
> for His kindness endures forever.

He gives nourishment to all flesh,
> for His kindness endures forever.

Give thanks to God of the heavens,
> for His kindness endures forever.

The soul of every living being shall bless Your Name, HASHEM our God; the spirit of all flesh shall always glorify and exalt Your remembrance, our King. From This World to the World-to-Come, You are

---

Holy One replied that He would be available to them in all their troubles and answer when they called upon Him. This would be the proof that there was a God in Israel (*Ramban* to *Shemos* 3:13). In a later period, Israel was saved by the *Chanukah* victories of the *Chashmonaim*, when the few overcame the many and the pure defeated the impure. And in our prayers we say: "and for Yourself, You made a great and holy Name in Your world."

When man was created the Holy One asked him, "What is My Name?" (*Bereishis Rabbah* 17). The intent of the question is: Will you, and how will you, reveal My majesty in the world? And when man does see Hashem's majesty in the Creation and its phenomena then: "the soul of every living being shall bless Your Name."

מִן הָעוֹלָם וְעַד הָעוֹלָם אַתָּה אֵל
From This World to the World-to-Come, You are God

The Alter of Kelm   Everywhere in the world, in every period, at each and every point, You are God. The entire force of Your greatness is recognizable, as it is said: "The earth is full of HASHEM's kindness" (*Tehillim* 33:5) — each and every spot is full of Hashem's kindness (חֶסֶד). Even when a man is afflicted with suffering, when Hashem metes out man's desert in judgment, there too His kindness is to be found, for he gives the measure of pain which is proper and needed for man's own good. Through that suffering man learns not to become only a pauper receiving a charitable handout of kindness; with the affliction he also receives a measure of independence.

וּמִבַּלְעָדֶיךָ אֵין לָנוּ מֶלֶךְ גּוֹאֵל וּמוֹשִׁיעַ פּוֹדֶה וּמַצִּיל וּמְפַרְנֵס וּמְרַחֵם בְּכָל עֵת צָרָה וְצוּקָה. אֵין לָנוּ מֶלֶךְ אֶלָּא אָתָּה. אֱלֹהֵי הָרִאשׁוֹנִים וְהָאַחֲרוֹנִים אֱלוֹהַּ כָּל בְּרִיּוֹת אֲדוֹן כָּל תּוֹלָדוֹת הַמְהֻלָּל בְּרֹב הַתִּשְׁבָּחוֹת הַמְנַהֵג עוֹלָמוֹ בְּחֶסֶד וּבְרִיּוֹתָיו בְּרַחֲמִים וַיהוה לֹא יָנוּם וְלֹא יִישָׁן הַמְעוֹרֵר יְשֵׁנִים וְהַמֵּקִיץ נִרְדָּמִים וְהַמֵּשִׂיחַ אִלְּמִים וְהַמַּתִּיר אֲסוּרִים וְהַסּוֹמֵךְ נוֹפְלִים וְהַזּוֹקֵף כְּפוּפִים לְךָ לְבַדְּךָ אֲנַחְנוּ מוֹדִים. אִלּוּ פִינוּ מָלֵא שִׁירָה כַּיָּם וּלְשׁוֹנֵנוּ רִנָּה כַּהֲמוֹן גַּלָּיו וְשִׂפְתוֹתֵינוּ שֶׁבַח כְּמֶרְחֲבֵי רָקִיעַ וְעֵינֵינוּ מְאִירוֹת כַּשֶּׁמֶשׁ וְכַיָּרֵחַ וְיָדֵינוּ פְרוּשׂוֹת כְּנִשְׁרֵי שָׁמָיִם וְרַגְלֵינוּ קַלּוֹת כָּאַיָּלוֹת אֵין אֲנַחְנוּ מַסְפִּיקִים לְהוֹדוֹת לְךָ יהוה אֱלֹהֵינוּ וֵאלֹהֵי אֲבוֹתֵינוּ וּלְבָרֵךְ אֶת שְׁמֶךָ עַל אַחַת מֵאֶלֶף אֶלֶף אַלְפֵי אֲלָפִים וְרִבֵּי רְבָבוֹת פְּעָמִים הַטּוֹבוֹת

וּמִבַּלְעָדֶיךָ אֵין לָנוּ מֶלֶךְ
And other than You we have no king

The Alter of Novharodok

The sons of *Ches* (בְּנֵי חֵת) referred to Avraham as "master" (אֲדֹנִי) several times, but Avraham never once addressed them thus. He bowed before them, but did not crown them with this title of honor. Avraham had only one master — the Holy One.

וְיָדֵינוּ פְרוּשׂוֹת כְּנִשְׁרֵי שָׁמָיִם וְרַגְלֵינוּ קַלּוֹת כָּאַיָּלוֹת
And our hands as outspread as eagles of the sky and our feet as swift as hinds

The Alter of Slobodka

Man is the elect of Creation. How then is he "less" than any other creature in any way that he should use them as examples of excellence (the eagle, the deer)?

Truth to tell, man surpasses *all* creatures in *all* respects. The eagle flies to great heights, but Chanoch went up to the heavens, Moshe Rabbeinu tarried there and Eliahu ascended to the heavens in a whirlwind. The deer is swift of foot, but Naphtali is no less so (*Bereishis* 49:21) and his brothers sent him running from Chevron to Egypt to fetch the bill of sale of the Cave of

God, and other than You we have no king, redeemer or savior. Liberator, Rescuer, Sustainer and Merciful One in every time of distress and anguish, we have no king but You! — God of the first and of the last, God of all creatures, Master of all generations, Who is extolled through a multitude of praises, Who guides His world with kindness and His creatures with mercy. HASHEM neither slumbers nor sleeps. He Who rouses the sleepers and awakens the slumberers, Who makes the mute speak and releases the bound; Who supports the fallen and straightens the bent. To You alone we give thanks. Were our mouth as full of song as the sea, and our tongue as full of joyous song as its multitude of waves, and our lips as full of praise as the breadth of the heavens, and our eyes as brilliant as the sun and the moon, and our hands as outspread as eagles of the sky and our feet as swift as hinds — we still could not thank You sufficiently, HASHEM our God and God of our forefathers, and to bless Your Name for even one of the thousand thousand, thousands of thousands and myriad myriads of favors that You performed for

---

Machpelah so that they might refute Esav's claim to the cave and bury their father Yaakov (*Sotah* 13a). And Asa'el is as fleet as a deer (*II Shmuel* 2:18); he could race over the tops of ears of grain so swiftly that they would not bend beneath his weight as he ran (*Koheles Rabbah* 9). Yehudah is likened to a lion; Dan to a serpent. Our forefather, Yaakov, plucked up the massive rock which covered the face of the well, as one would pull the stopper out of a bottle, though that rock was a load which would weigh down forty other men (*Bereishis Rabbah* 70).

Vast powers are hidden within man and through them he does, indeed, surpass all creatures. His task is to reveal those powers. It is not in a mere metaphorical sense that the *Mishnah* demands: "Be fierce like the leopard, swoop like the eagle, fly like the deer, be brave like the lion to do the bidding of Your Father in heaven" (*Avos* 5:20).

אֵין אֲנַחְנוּ מַסְפִּיקִים לְהוֹדוֹת . . . מִמִּצְרַיִם גְּאַלְתָּנוּ
We still could not thank You sufficiently . . . You redeemed us from Egypt

The Alter of Kelm We say that even were our lips as full of song as the sea we could not give sufficient thanks even for one of

שֶׁעָשִׂיתָ עִם אֲבוֹתֵינוּ וְעִמָּנוּ. מִמִּצְרַיִם גְּאַלְתָּנוּ
יהוה אֱלֹהֵינוּ וּמִבֵּית עֲבָדִים פְּדִיתָנוּ בְּרָעָב זַנְתָּנוּ
וּבְשָׂבָע כִּלְכַּלְתָּנוּ מֵחֶרֶב הִצַּלְתָּנוּ וּמִדֶּבֶר מִלַּטְתָּנוּ
וּמֵחֳלָיִם רָעִים וְנֶאֱמָנִים דִּלִּיתָנוּ. עַד הֵנָּה עֲזָרוּנוּ
רַחֲמֶיךָ וְלֹא עֲזָבוּנוּ חֲסָדֶיךָ וְאַל תִּטְּשֵׁנוּ יהוה
אֱלֹהֵינוּ לָנֶצַח. עַל כֵּן אֵבָרִים שֶׁפִּלַּגְתָּ בָּנוּ וְרוּחַ
וּנְשָׁמָה שֶׁנָּפַחְתָּ בְּאַפֵּינוּ וְלָשׁוֹן אֲשֶׁר שַׂמְתָּ בְּפִינוּ הֵן
הֵם יוֹדוּ וִיבָרְכוּ וִישַׁבְּחוּ וִיפָאֲרוּ וִירוֹמְמוּ וְיַעֲרִיצוּ
וְיַקְדִּישׁוּ וְיַמְלִיכוּ אֶת שִׁמְךָ מַלְכֵּנוּ. כִּי כָל פֶּה
לְךָ יוֹדֶה וְכָל לָשׁוֹן לְךָ תִשָּׁבַע וְכָל בֶּרֶךְ לְךָ תִכְרַע

---

the manifold miracles. And yet, immediately thereafter, we do give praise for the miracle of our liberation from Egypt.

When one witnesses an obvious miracle, a departure from the general patterns of nature, he recognizes that all of nature is a chain of unending miracles. When we realize that *You redeemed us from Egypt*, we come to realize that *until now Your kindness has not forsaken us* and, thus it is, that even *were our mouth as full of song as the sea*, we could *not thank You sufficiently* for the smallest part of the many miracles which are hidden and unseen.

עַד הֵנָּה עֲזָרוּנוּ רַחֲמֶיךָ
Until now Your mercy has helped us

The Alter of Kelm The tale is told of the city in the tribe of Binyamin which acted immorally and shamefully (*Shoftim* 20). All of Israel rose up to do battle against them and wipe out the shame — certainly, a creditable act. They approached the *Urim V'Tumim* and received heavenly permission for the war. And yet, many were felled by the offending tribe in the ensuing battle.

Imagine that situation today! What would people say? "It's not worthwhile serving HASHEM" (*Malachi* 3:14). Why, anyone who performs even the slightest *mitzvah* expects to be handed a bowl overflowing with blessing from Heaven, straightaway!

But they did not, then, question Hashem, but went up and wept before Him and asked once more whether they should go up to do battle. And Hashem answered them, "Go!" And they went off to war in trust and faith. Once more, the tribe of Binyamin overcame them and slew eighteen thousand. Were that to happen today, God alone, Who searches out the

our ancestors and for us. You redeemed us from Egypt, HASHEM our God, and liberated us from the house of bondage. In famine You nourished us and in plenty You sustained us. From sword You saved us; from plague You let us escape; and from severe and enduring diseases You spared us. Until now Your mercy has helped us, and Your kindness has not forsaken us. Do not abandon us, HASHEM our God, forever. Therefore, the organs that You set within us, and the spirit and soul that You breathed into our nostrils, and the tongue that You placed in our mouth — all of them shall thank and bless, praise and glorify, exalt and revere, sanctify and declare the sovereignty of Your Name, our King. For every mouth shall offer thanks to You; every tongue shall vow allegiance to You; every knee shall bend to You;

---

inner recesses of the heart, knows what would happen. But they did not question Hashem's judgment, and saw themselves as the guilty ones. They wept; they fasted; they offered up sacrifices. And, once more, they asked whether they should go to do battle or retreat. They were commanded to fight; they fought and were victorious.

The *Ramban* explains that they were initially defeated, because they trusted in the great numbers of the army of the combined tribes which was ten times that of the tribe of Binyamin.

If one has an establishment in which he offers goods to which he has exclusive rights and there is a great demand for them, would he pray for Hashem's help? And here was the entire people of Israel coming to do battle against a single lone tribe. Should the idea have crossed their minds that Binyamin might overcome them? They were righteous and fought for a just cause. And despite the dual disaster, they fasted and prayed and did not question Providence. Yet, because they did not look forward to Hashem's aid, they suffered one defeat and then another.

"Keep watch, lest you forget HASHEM, your God — and say in your heart, 'My strength and the power of my arm have given me this wealth'; — and you shall remember HASHEM, your God, for He has given you the power to gather wealth" (*Devarim* 8:11-18).

וְכָל בֶּרֶךְ לְךָ תִכְרַע / *Every knee shall bend to You*

R' Yitzchak Blazer

Chazal tell us that when the prophet says: "and every knee shall bend (תִּכְרַע) to You" (*Yeshayahu* 45:23), this refers to the day of death, as it is said: "all who descend to the

וְכָל קוֹמָה לְפָנֶיךָ תִשְׁתַּחֲוֶה וְכָל לְבָבוֹת יִירָאוּךָ וְכָל קֶרֶב וּכְלָיוֹת יְזַמְּרוּ לִשְׁמֶךָ. כַּדָּבָר שֶׁכָּתוּב כָּל עַצְמֹתַי תֹּאמַרְנָה יהוה מִי כָמוֹךָ מַצִּיל עָנִי מֵחָזָק מִמֶּנּוּ וְעָנִי וְאֶבְיוֹן מִגֹּזְלוֹ. מִי יִדְמֶה לָּךְ וּמִי יִשְׁוֶה לָּךְ וּמִי יַעֲרָךְ לָךְ הָאֵל הַגָּדוֹל הַגִּבּוֹר וְהַנּוֹרָא אֵל עֶלְיוֹן קֹנֵה שָׁמַיִם וָאָרֶץ. נְהַלֶּלְךָ וּנְשַׁבֵּחֲךָ וּנְפָאֶרְךָ וּנְבָרֵךְ אֶת שֵׁם קָדְשֶׁךָ כָּאָמוּר לְדָוִד בָּרְכִי נַפְשִׁי אֶת יהוה וְכָל קְרָבַי אֶת שֵׁם קָדְשׁוֹ:

הָאֵל בְּתַעֲצֻמוֹת עֻזֶּךָ הַגָּדוֹל בִּכְבוֹד שְׁמֶךָ הַגִּבּוֹר לָנֶצַח וְהַנּוֹרָא בְּנוֹרְאוֹתֶיךָ הַמֶּלֶךְ הַיּוֹשֵׁב עַל כִּסֵּא רָם וְנִשָּׂא:

---

dust will bow (יִכְרְעוּ) before Him" (*Tehillim* 22:30; see *Nedarim* 30).

What is the nature of this *bowing* that all will bow?

There are two categories of bowing — that which accompanies a plea for mercy, and the bowing of praise and thanks. Both are exemplified by Bas Sheva when she came before David and requested that he crown her son Shlomo (*Melachim* I:1).

At first she bowed to plead for mercy and at the end of the meeting she did so in thanks for his promise.

On the day of death, all will bow before Him — the righteous, to thank Him for the great reward which will be revealed to them; the wicked, to ask mercy in the face of the punishment which awaits them.

כָּל עַצְמֹתַי תֹּאמַרְנָה
All my bones shall say

The Alter of Kelm

Even when a man follows a blueprint in building a house, there are bound to be slight deviations here and there from the plans. But the Holy One created the world with perfect balance and with exceptional accuracy. There are, for example, tens of bones in a man's body, each with its own task and purpose. They are like an orchestra in which each member plays his own instrument and all together create a harmonious symphony. "All my bones shall say," each one individually, "HASHEM, who is like You?" Each knows itself and is aware that no substitute can be found for it; each recognizes the power of its Creator.

every erect spine shall prostrate itself before You; all hearts shall fear You, and all innermost feelings and thoughts shall sing praises to Your name, as it is written: "All my bones shall say: 'HASHEM, who is like You?' You save the poor man from one stronger than he, the poor and destitute from one who would rob him." Who is like unto You? Who is equal to You? Who can be compared to You? O great, mighty, and awesome God, the supreme God, Creator of heaven and earth. We shall laud, praise, and glorify You and bless Your holy Name, as it is said 'Of David: Bless HASHEM, O my soul, and let all my innermost being bless His holy Name!'

O God, in the omnipotence of Your strength, great in the glory of Your Name, mighty forever and awesome through Your awesome deeds, O King enthroned upon a high and lofty throne!

הַגָּדוֹל הַגִּבּוֹר וְהַנּוֹרָא
O Great, Mighty and Awesome

The Alter of Kelm   Moshe Rabbeinu said, "The great, the mighty and the awesome God" (*Devarim* 10:17). Yirmeyahu said, "Gentiles are destroying His Temple. Where is the awe which He inspires?" and in describing Hashem, he omitted *the awesome* (see *Yirmeyahu* 32:18). Daniel said, "Gentiles are enslaving His children. Where is His might?" and he omitted *the mighty* (see *Daniel* 9:4). To which the Men of the Great Synod (אַנְשֵׁי כְּנֶסֶת הַגְּדוֹלָה) answered: To the contrary, this indeed shows His might. He suppresses His anger and is forbearing to the wicked. And this shows His awe. For were it not for the fear of God, how would it be possible for a nation (Israel) to survive among the nations! Yet, how did Yirmeyahu and Daniel allow themselves the right to delete praises which Moshe had given? They (Yirmeyahu and Daniel) knew that Hashem is truth itself and they did not wish to tell falsehoods about Him (see *Yoma* 69b and *Rashi's* comments there).

Certainly, the Holy One is great, mighty and awesome and renews Creation with every passing moment. But the praises uttered in prayer are not just oratorical tags, not even oratorical tags which happen to be true. They must flow from an honest perception. If a man is not shot through with an awareness of what he is saying, he is telling lies before Hashem, because Hashem Himself is truth and knows the workings of man's mind.

The Men of the Great Synod, alone, were able to understand and instill

שׁוֹכֵן עַד מָרוֹם וְקָדוֹשׁ שְׁמוֹ. וְכָתוּב רַנְּנוּ צַדִּיקִים בַּיהוה לַיְשָׁרִים נָאוָה תְהִלָּה: בְּפִי יְשָׁרִים תִּתְהַלָּל וּבְדִבְרֵי צַדִּיקִים תִּתְבָּרַךְ וּבִלְשׁוֹן חֲסִידִים תִּתְרוֹמָם וּבְקֶרֶב קְדוֹשִׁים תִּתְקַדָּשׁ:

וּבְמַקְהֲלוֹת רִבְבוֹת עַמְּךָ בֵּית יִשְׂרָאֵל בְּרִנָּה יִתְפָּאַר שִׁמְךָ מַלְכֵּנוּ בְּכָל דּוֹר וָדוֹר שֶׁכֵּן חוֹבַת כָּל הַיְצוּרִים לְפָנֶיךָ יהוה אֱלֹהֵינוּ וֵאלֹהֵי אֲבוֹתֵינוּ לְהוֹדוֹת לְהַלֵּל לְשַׁבֵּחַ לְפָאֵר לְרוֹמֵם לְהַדֵּר לְבָרֵךְ לְעַלֵּה וּלְקַלֵּס עַל כָּל דִּבְרֵי שִׁירוֹת וְתִשְׁבְּחוֹת דָּוִד בֶּן יִשַׁי עַבְדְּךָ מְשִׁיחֶךָ:

יִשְׁתַּבַּח שִׁמְךָ לָעַד מַלְכֵּנוּ הָאֵל הַמֶּלֶךְ הַגָּדוֹל וְהַקָּדוֹשׁ בַּשָּׁמַיִם וּבָאָרֶץ כִּי לְךָ נָאֶה יהוה אֱלֹהֵינוּ וֵאלֹהֵי אֲבוֹתֵינוּ שִׁיר וּשְׁבָחָה הַלֵּל וְזִמְרָה עֹז וּמֶמְשָׁלָה נֶצַח גְּדֻלָּה וּגְבוּרָה תְּהִלָּה

---

into their hearts the awareness of God's might and awe, even in the time of the Destruction and Exile, by contemplating the miracle of Israel's continued existence and God's suppression of His anger towards the gentiles. They were able to incorporate those expressions into their prayer.

This shows us that prayer involves an awareness of the Creator and His wonders. If a man does not have this inner awareness of the praises which he pronounces, even if he understands them to be correct from an intellectual perspective, his prayer is false!

בְּפִי יְשָׁרִים תִּתְהַלָּל
By the mouth of the upright shall You be lauded

R' Abba Grossbard of Ponoviez

Is it only "by the mouth of the *upright* shall You be lauded" and "by the words of the *righteous* shall You be blessed?" Why, shortly thereafter we say that "such is the duty of *all* creatures" to praise and bless Hashem!

True! All are obligated, but not all can do so. The *Gemara* notes that even the prophets sense the Creator through concealing veils and dividers

He Who abides forever, exalted and holy is His Name. And it is written: 'Sing joyfully, O righteous, before HASHEM; for the upright, praise is fitting.' By the mouth of the upright shall You be lauded; by the words of the righteous shall You be blessed; by the tongue of the devout shall You be exalted; and amid the holy shall You be sanctified.

And in the assemblies of the myriads of Your people, the House of Israel, with joyous song shall Your Name be glorified, our King, throughout every generation. For such is the duty of all creatures – before You, HASHEM, our God, God of our forefathers, to thank, laud, praise, glorify, exalt, adore, bless, raise high, and sing praises – even beyond all expressions of the songs and praises of David the son of Yishai, Your servant, Your anointed.

May Your Name be praised forever – our King, the God, the great and holy King – in heaven and on earth. Because for You is fitting – O HASHEM, our God, and the God of our forefathers – song and praise, lauding and hymns, power and dominion, triumph, greatness and strength, praise

---

(*Yevamos* 49). The *Rambam* explains that these dividers are the personal inclinations and desires of the individual soul which have, as yet, not been thoroughly cleansed. The more distant a man is from the state of being *upright* and *righteous*, the further away he is from, and the blinder he is to, a true perception of the light of Hashem. And, naturally, the less he is able to give praise and blessing. It is only the upright and righteous who can truly do so.

וּבְמַקְהֲלוֹת רִבְבוֹת . . . יִתְפָּאַר שִׁמְךָ

And in the assemblies of the myriads . . .
shall Your Name be glorified

R' Yerucham of Mir

We are meant to pray in congregation (בְּצִיבּוּר) and not privately (בְּיְחִידוּת), and it is even more preferable to do so in huge gatherings, "in the assemblies of the myriads." But,

וְתִפְאֶרֶת קְדֻשָּׁה וּמַלְכוּת בְּרָכוֹת וְהוֹדָאוֹת מֵעַתָּה וְעַד עוֹלָם: בָּרוּךְ אַתָּה יהוה אֵל מֶלֶךְ גָּדוֹל בַּתִּשְׁבָּחוֹת אֵל הַהוֹדָאוֹת אֲדוֹן הַנִּפְלָאוֹת הַבּוֹחֵר בְּשִׁירֵי זִמְרָה מֶלֶךְ אֵל חֵי הָעוֹלָמִים.

The blessing over wine is recited and the fourth cup is drunk while reclining to the left side. It is preferable that the entire cup be drunk.

בָּרוּךְ אַתָּה יהוה אֱלֹהֵנוּ מֶלֶךְ הָעוֹלָם בּוֹרֵא פְּרִי הַגָּפֶן:

After drinking the fourth cup, the concluding blessing is recited. On Shabbos include the passage in parentheses.

בָּרוּךְ אַתָּה יהוה אֱלֹהֵינוּ מֶלֶךְ הָעוֹלָם עַל הַגֶּפֶן וְעַל פְּרִי הַגֶּפֶן וְעַל תְּנוּבַת הַשָּׂדֶה וְעַל אֶרֶץ חֶמְדָּה טוֹבָה וּרְחָבָה שֶׁרָצִיתָ וְהִנְחַלְתָּ לַאֲבוֹתֵינוּ לֶאֱכוֹל מִפִּרְיָהּ וְלִשְׂבּוֹעַ מִטּוּבָהּ. רַחֵם נָא יהוה אֱלֹהֵינוּ עַל יִשְׂרָאֵל עַמֶּךָ וְעַל יְרוּשָׁלַיִם עִירֶךָ וְעַל צִיּוֹן מִשְׁכַּן כְּבוֹדֶךָ וְעַל מִזְבְּחֶךָ וְעַל הֵיכָלֶךָ. וּבְנֵה יְרוּשָׁלַיִם עִיר הַקֹּדֶשׁ בִּמְהֵרָה בְיָמֵינוּ וְהַעֲלֵנוּ לְתוֹכָהּ וְשַׂמְּחֵנוּ בְּבִנְיָנָהּ וְנֹאכַל מִפִּרְיָהּ וְנִשְׂבַּע מִטּוּבָהּ וּנְבָרֶכְךָ עָלֶיהָ בִּקְדֻשָּׁה וּבְטָהֳרָה. [וּרְצֵה וְהַחֲלִיצֵנוּ בְּיוֹם הַשַּׁבָּת הַזֶּה] וְשַׂמְּחֵנוּ בְּיוֹם חַג הַמַּצּוֹת הַזֶּה. כִּי אַתָּה יהוה טוֹב וּמֵטִיב לַכֹּל וְנוֹדֶה לְּךָ עַל הָאָרֶץ וְעַל פְּרִי הַגֶּפֶן: בָּרוּךְ אַתָּה יהוה עַל הָאָרֶץ וְעַל פְּרִי הַגֶּפֶן:

---

although huge crowds generate great excitement (הִתְפַּעֲלוּת), isn't this, seemingly, only an emotional excitement? Would it not be more desirable to

and splendor, holiness and sovereignty, blessings and thanksgivings from this time and forever. Blessed are You, HASHEM, God, King exalted through praises, God of thanksgivings, Master of wonders, Who chooses musical songs of praise — King, God, Life-giver of the world.

The blessing over wine is recited and the fourth cup is drunk while reclining to the left side. It is preferable that the entire cup be drunk.

Blessed are You, HASHEM, our God, King of the universe, Who creates the fruit of the vine.

After drinking the fourth cup, the concluding blessing is recited. On Shabbos include the passage in parentheses.

Blessed are You, HASHEM, our God, King of the universe, for the vine and the fruit of the vine, and for the produce of the field. For the desirable, good, and spacious land that You were pleased to give our forefathers as a heritage, to eat of its fruit and to be satisfied with its goodness. Have mercy, we beg You, HASHEM, our God, on Israel Your people; on Jerusalem, Your city; on Zion, resting place of Your glory; Your Altar, and Your Temple. Rebuild Jerusalem the city of holiness, speedily in our days. Bring us up into it and gladden us in its rebuilding and let us eat from its fruit and be satisfied with its goodness and bless You upon it in holiness and purity. (Favor us and strengthen us on this Shabbos day) and grant us happiness on this Festival of Matzos; for You, HASHEM, are good and do good to all, and we thank You for the land and for the fruit of the vine. Blessed are You, HASHEM, for the land and for the fruit of the vine.

---

pray with greater depth of intellect?

That is just the point. The soul does not awaken to excitement through thought and intellectual introspection, but through action and emotion.

נרצה

חֲסַל סִדּוּר פֶּסַח כְּהִלְכָתוֹ. כְּכָל מִשְׁפָּטוֹ וְחֻקָּתוֹ. כַּאֲשֶׁר זָכִינוּ לְסַדֵּר אוֹתוֹ. כֵּן נִזְכֶּה לַעֲשׂוֹתוֹ: זָךְ שׁוֹכֵן מְעוֹנָה. קוֹמֵם קְהַל עֲדַת מִי מָנָה. בְּקָרוֹב נַהֵל נִטְעֵי כַנָּה. פְּדוּיִם לְצִיּוֹן בְּרִנָּה:

לְשָׁנָה הַבָּאָה בִּירוּשָׁלָיִם:

On the first night recite the following.
On the second night continue on page 174.

וּבְכֵן וַיְהִי בַּחֲצִי הַלַּיְלָה:

אָז רוֹב נִסִּים הִפְלֵאתָ בַּלַּיְלָה.
בְּרֹאשׁ אַשְׁמוֹרֶת זֶה הַלַּיְלָה.
גֵּר צֶדֶק נִצַּחְתּוֹ כְּנֶחֱלַק לוֹ לַיְלָה.
וַיְהִי בַּחֲצִי הַלַּיְלָה.

דַּנְתָּ מֶלֶךְ גְּרָר בַּחֲלוֹם הַלַּיְלָה.
הִפְחַדְתָּ אֲרַמִּי בְּאֶמֶשׁ לַיְלָה.
וַיָּשַׂר יִשְׂרָאֵל לְמַלְאָךְ וַיּוּכַל לוֹ לַיְלָה.
וַיְהִי בַּחֲצִי הַלַּיְלָה.

וַיָּשַׂר יִשְׂרָאֵל לְמַלְאָךְ
Israel (Yaakov) fought with an angel

The Alter of Novharodok

When the *Zohar* says that the angel who pushed Yaakov's hip out of joint gave a blow to those in the community of Israel who uphold the Torah, it refers to the *bnei Torah*, the *yeshivah* students. They do not have the support of their society at large. They do not brook compromise and in this they stand against public opinion.

The *Gemara* presents a difference of opinion as to the physical appearance of the angel who fought with Yaakov. Did he take on the guise of a wise sage

NIRTZAH

The Seder is now concluded in accordance with its laws, with all its ordinances and statutes. Just as we were privileged to arrange it, so may we merit to perform it. O Pure One, Who dwells on high, raise up the countless congregation, soon — guide the offshoots of Your plants, redeemed, to Zion with glad song.

NEXT YEAR IN JERUSALEM

On the first night recite the following.
On the second night continue on page 175.

It came to pass at midnight.

You have, of old, performed many wonders
             by night.
At the head of the watches of   this night.
To the righteous convert (Avraham),
    You gave triumph by dividing for him   the night.
       It came to pass at midnight.

You judged the king of Gerar (Avimelech),
    in a dream   by night.
You frightened the Aramean (Lavan), in the dark
               of night.
Israel (Yaakov) fought with an angel
    and overcame him   by night.
       It came to pass at midnight.

(תַּלְמִיד חָכָם) or a non-Jew (Chullin 91)?

The evil nature (יֵצֶר הָרָע) assumes these two roles when he wrestles with the ben Torah. The non-Jew face represents the popular point of view: Your way does not lead to a livelihood (פַּרְנָסָה). It is an attack on putting one's trust in Hashem.

The wise-sage costume symbolizes the marshaling of seemingly legitimate Torah proofs against extremism, for example: "the study of Torah is a lovely thing when it is accompanied by the way of the world" — socially acceptable behavior (Avos 2:2); "study of Torah which is divorced from

זֶרַע בְּכוֹרֵי פַתְרוֹס מָחַצְתָּ בַּחֲצִי הַלַּיְלָה.
חֵילָם לֹא מָצְאוּ בְּקוּמָם בַּלַּיְלָה.
טִיסַת נְגִיד חֲרוֹשֶׁת סִלִּיתָ בְּכוֹכְבֵי לַיְלָה.

וַיְהִי בַּחֲצִי הַלַּיְלָה.

יָעַץ מְחָרֵף לְנוֹפֵף אִוּי הוֹבַשְׁתָּ פְּגָרָיו בַּלַּיְלָה.
כָּרַע בֵּל וּמַצָּבוֹ בְּאִישׁוֹן לַיְלָה.
לְאִישׁ חֲמוּדוֹת נִגְלָה רָז חֲזוֹת לַיְלָה.

וַיְהִי בַּחֲצִי הַלַּיְלָה.

מִשְׁתַּכֵּר בִּכְלֵי קֹדֶשׁ נֶהֱרַג בּוֹ בַּלַּיְלָה.
נוֹשַׁע מִבּוֹר אֲרָיוֹת פּוֹתֵר בִּעֲתוּתֵי לַיְלָה.
שִׂנְאָה נָטַר אֲגָגִי וְכָתַב סְפָרִים בַּלַּיְלָה.

וַיְהִי בַּחֲצִי הַלַּיְלָה.

עוֹרַרְתָּ נִצְחֲךָ עָלָיו בְּנֶדֶד שְׁנַת לַיְלָה.
פּוּרָה תִדְרוֹךְ לְשׁוֹמֵר מַה מִּלַּיְלָה.
צָרַח כַּשּׁוֹמֵר וְשָׂח אָתָא בֹקֶר וְגַם לַיְלָה.

וַיְהִי בַּחֲצִי הַלַּיְלָה.

קָרֵב יוֹם אֲשֶׁר הוּא לֹא יוֹם וְלֹא לַיְלָה.
רָם הוֹדַע כִּי לְךָ הַיּוֹם אַף לְךָ הַלַּיְלָה.
שׁוֹמְרִים הַפְקֵד לְעִירְךָ כָּל הַיּוֹם וְכָל הַלַּיְלָה.
תָּאִיר כְּאוֹר יוֹם חֶשְׁכַת לַיְלָה.

וַיְהִי בַּחֲצִי הַלַּיְלָה.

---

working (for a livelihood) comes to naught" (*Avos* 4:4). The extreme is censured, because "whoever does not find favor in the eyes of society does not find favor with God" (*Avos* 3:10), and "a wise sage (תַּלְמִיד חָכָם) who has a stain on his clothing deserves the death penalty" (*Shabbos* 114).

The *ben Torah* must know how to fight against this "scholar" and his "proofs." If the evil nature points out that the wise man's external appearance must be proper, he should be reminded that a wise man is defined as one who is expert in the *entire* Torah (*Shabbos* 114). If he speaks

Egypt's first-born You crushed   at midnight.
Their host they found not upon arising   at night.
The army of the prince of Charoshes (Sisera)
        You swept away with stars of   the night.
            It came to pass at midnight.

The blasphemer (Sennacherib) planned to raise his
        hand against Jerusalem —
        but You withered his corpses   by night.
Bel was overturned with its pedestal,
        in the darkness of night.
To the man of Your delights (Daniel),
        was revealed the mystery of the visions of night.
            It came to pass at midnight.

He (Belshazzar) who caroused from the holy vessels
        was killed that very   night.
From the lion's den was rescued he (Daniel)
        who interpreted the 'terrors' of   the night.
The Aggagite (Haman) nursed hatred
        and wrote decrees   at night.
            It came to pass at midnight.

You began Your triumph over him
        when You disturbed (Ahaseurus') sleep   at night.
Trample the wine-press to help those who ask the
        watchman, 'What of the long   night?'
He will shout, like a watchman, and say:
'Morning shall come   after night.'
            It came to pass at midnight.

Hasten the day (of Messiah),
        that is neither day nor   night.
Most High — make known that Yours
        are day and   night.
Appoint guards for Your city,
        all the day and all the   night.
Brighten like the light of day the darkness of night.
            It came to pass at midnight.

───

of the need to find favor with society, he should be reminded of the
Rambam's view; it is better to flee to the desert rather than live among those

On the second night recite the following.
On the first night continue on page 178.

וּבְכֵן וַאֲמַרְתֶּם זֶבַח פֶּסַח:

אֹמֶץ גְּבוּרוֹתֶיךָ הִפְלֵאתָ בַּפֶּסַח.
בְּרֹאשׁ כָּל מוֹעֲדוֹת נִשֵּׂאתָ פֶּסַח.
גִּלִּיתָ לְאֶזְרָחִי חֲצוֹת לֵיל פֶּסַח.

וַאֲמַרְתֶּם זֶבַח פֶּסַח.

דְּלָתָיו דָּפַקְתָּ כְּחֹם הַיּוֹם בַּפֶּסַח.
הִסְעִיד נוֹצְצִים עֻגוֹת מַצּוֹת בַּפֶּסַח.
וְאֶל הַבָּקָר רָץ זֵכֶר לְשׁוֹר עֵרֶךְ פֶּסַח.

וַאֲמַרְתֶּם זֶבַח פֶּסַח.

זוֹעֲמוּ סְדוֹמִים וְלוֹהֲטוּ בָּאֵשׁ בַּפֶּסַח.
חֻלַּץ לוֹט מֵהֶם וּמַצּוֹת אָפָה בְּקֵץ פֶּסַח.
טִאטֵאתָ אַדְמַת מוֹף וְנוֹף בְּעָבְרְךָ בַּפֶּסַח.

וַאֲמַרְתֶּם זֶבַח פֶּסַח.

יָהּ רֹאשׁ כָּל אוֹן מָחַצְתָּ בְּלֵיל שִׁמּוּר פֶּסַח.
כַּבִּיר עַל בֵּן בְּכוֹר פָּסַחְתָּ בְּדַם פֶּסַח.
לְבִלְתִּי תֵּת מַשְׁחִית לָבֹא בִּפְתָחַי בַּפֶּסַח.

וַאֲמַרְתֶּם זֶבַח פֶּסַח.

---

who do not walk in an upright path (*De'ot* 6:1). Let him argue against his evil nature! Let him say, "How can I be concerned about a stain on my clothing and neglect the stains on my inner self? How can I not be fearful when *Chazal* have said: When the evil nature sees a man who is overly careful in his gait, is scrupulous about his dress and puts waves in his hair he says, 'I've got him; he's mine!' (*Bereishis Rabbah, Vayeshev*)?"

Experience shows that compromise leads one to the opposite extreme.

הגדה של פסח [174]

On the second night recite the following.
On the first night continue on page 179.

And you shall say: This is the feast of Passover.

You displayed wondrously Your mighty powers on Passover.
Above all festival You elevated Passover.
To the Oriental (Avraham) You revealed the future midnight of Passover.
And you shall say: This is the feast of Passover.

At his door You knocked in the heat of the day on Passover;
He satiated the angels with matzah-cakes on Passover.
And he ran to the herd — symbolic of the sacrificial beast of Passover.
And you shall say: This is the feast of Passover.

The Sodomites provoked (God) and were devoured by fire on Passover;
Lot was withdrawn from them — he had baked matzos at the time of Passover.
You swept clean the soil of Moph and Noph (in Egypt) when You passed through on Passover.
And you shall say: This is the feast of Passover.

God, You crushed every firstborn of On (in Egypt) on the watchful night of Passover.
But Master — Your own firstborn, You skipped by merit of the blood of Passover,
Not to allow the Destroyer to enter my doors on Passover.
And you shall say: This is the feast of Passover.

הִשְׂעִיד נוֹצְצִים / *He satiated the angels*

The Alter of Kelm

Our forefather Avraham established a lodging house with openings to all the four winds and thus drew masses to come to the recognition of Hashem. Yet of this entire page of hospitality the only incident which the Torah records in detail is the visit of

מְסֻגֶּרֶת סֻגָּרָה בְּעִתּוֹתֵי פֶּסַח.
נִשְׁמְדָה מִדְיָן בִּצְלִיל שְׂעוֹרֵי עֹמֶר פֶּסַח.
שׂוֹרְפוּ מִשְׁמַנֵּי פּוּל וְלוּד בִּיקַד יְקוֹד פֶּסַח.

וַאֲמַרְתֶּם זֶבַח פֶּסַח.

עוֹד הַיּוֹם בְּנֹב לַעֲמוֹד עַד גָּעָה עוֹנַת פֶּסַח.
פַּס יַד כָּתְבָה לְקַעֲקֵעַ צוּל בַּפֶּסַח.
צָפֹה הַצָּפִית עָרוֹךְ הַשֻּׁלְחָן בַּפֶּסַח.

וַאֲמַרְתֶּם זֶבַח פֶּסַח.

קָהָל כִּנְּסָה הֲדַסָּה צוֹם לְשַׁלֵּשׁ בַּפֶּסַח.
רֹאשׁ מִבֵּית רָשָׁע מָחַצְתָּ בְּעֵץ חֲמִשִּׁים בַּפֶּסַח.
שְׁתֵּי אֵלֶּה רֶגַע תָּבִיא לְעוּצִית בַּפֶּסַח.
תָּעֹז יָדְךָ וְתָרוּם יְמִינְךָ כְּלֵיל הִתְקַדֵּשׁ חַג פֶּסַח.

וַאֲמַרְתֶּם זֶבַח פֶּסַח.

---

angels who did not truly eat and were in no need of such an act of kindness.

The Torah wishes to show that the intent (כַּוָּנָה) with which an act is done is its most important ingredient, as *Chazal* have said: God desires the heart — רַחֲמָנָא לִבָּא בָּעֵי (*Sanhedrin* 106b, *Rashi's* variant). Thus the visit of the angels which does not have meaningful effects as an act of hospitality was highlighted even though the angels only pretended to eat. This, because Avraham's intentions were the right ones. All of the "tests" (נִסְיוֹנוֹת) which were imposed upon Avraham were, indeed, meant to make certain of his inner thoughts — "And You found his *heart* true before You" (*Nechemiah* 9:8).

In performing a deed of kindness, the meal that you give the poor man cannot be compared to the full meal of a good heart with which you feed your heart.

And in contrast.

The *Alter* of Slobodka: "Whoever says that the angels did not eat when visiting Avraham is mistaken. But, because of his righteousness and as a

[176] הגדה של פסח

The beleaguered (Jericho) was besieged
on Passover.
Midian was destroyed with a barley cake,
from the Omer of Passover.
The mighty nobles of Pul and Lud (Assyria) were
consumed in a great conflagration on Passover.
And you shall say: This is the feast of Passover.

He (Sennacherib) would have stood that day at Nob,
but for the advent of Passover.
A hand inscribed the destruction of Zul (Babylon)
on Passover.
As the watch was set, and the royal table decked
on Passover.
And you shall say: This is the feast of Passover.

Hadassah (Esther) gathered a congregation
for a three-day fast on Passover.
You caused the head of the evil clan (Haman) to be
hanged on a fifty-cubit gallows on Passover.
Doubly, will You bring in an instant
upon Utsis (Edom) on Passover.
Let Your hand be strong, and Your right arm exalted,
as on that night when You hallowed the festival
of Passover.
And you shall say: This is the feast of Passover.

---

reward for the trouble which he took upon himself, the Holy One opened their mouths and they ate" (*Yalkut Shimoni*).

But why was it necessary (in the light of this Midrash) to create a gullet and innards for the angels? What would be lacking, if they only *appeared* to eat?

Avraham reached the level that he did in terms of bestowing kindness by contemplating Hashem's kindness in Creation. But there was a high point in Hashem's act of kindness which was applicable only to the Holy One — He *created a world* in order to benefit it. Because Avraham longed to imitate his Creator in kindness, the Holy One allowed him to reach even this high point and *created* a digestive tract for the angels, in order to allow Avraham to feed them.

On both nights continue here:

כִּי לוֹ נָאֶה, כִּי לוֹ יָאֶה:

אַדִּיר בִּמְלוּכָה, בָּחוּר כַּהֲלָכָה, גְּדוּדָיו יֹאמְרוּ לוֹ, לְךָ וּלְךָ, לְךָ כִּי לְךָ, לְךָ אַף לְךָ, לְךָ יהוה הַמַּמְלָכָה, כִּי לוֹ נָאֶה, כִּי לוֹ יָאֶה.

דָּגוּל בִּמְלוּכָה, הָדוּר כַּהֲלָכָה, וָתִיקָיו יֹאמְרוּ לוֹ, לְךָ וּלְךָ, לְךָ כִּי לְךָ, לְךָ אַף לְךָ, לְךָ יהוה הַמַּמְלָכָה, כִּי לוֹ נָאֶה, כִּי לוֹ יָאֶה.

זַכַּאי בִּמְלוּכָה, חָסִין כַּהֲלָכָה, טַפְסְרָיו יֹאמְרוּ לוֹ, לְךָ וּלְךָ, לְךָ כִּי לְךָ, לְךָ אַף לְךָ, לְךָ יהוה הַמַּמְלָכָה, כִּי לוֹ נָאֶה, כִּי לוֹ יָאֶה.

יָחִיד בִּמְלוּכָה, כַּבִּיר כַּהֲלָכָה, לִמּוּדָיו יֹאמְרוּ לוֹ, לְךָ וּלְךָ, לְךָ כִּי לְךָ, לְךָ אַף לְךָ, לְךָ יהוה הַמַּמְלָכָה, כִּי לוֹ נָאֶה, כִּי לוֹ יָאֶה.

מוֹשֵׁל בִּמְלוּכָה, נוֹרָא כַּהֲלָכָה, סְבִיבָיו יֹאמְרוּ לוֹ, לְךָ וּלְךָ, לְךָ כִּי לְךָ, לְךָ אַף לְךָ, לְךָ יהוה הַמַּמְלָכָה, כִּי לוֹ נָאֶה, כִּי לוֹ יָאֶה.

עָנָיו בִּמְלוּכָה, פּוֹדֶה כַּהֲלָכָה, צַדִּיקָיו יֹאמְרוּ לוֹ, לְךָ וּלְךָ, לְךָ כִּי לְךָ, לְךָ אַף לְךָ, לְךָ יהוה הַמַּמְלָכָה, כִּי לוֹ נָאֶה, כִּי לוֹ יָאֶה.

כִּי לוֹ נָאֶה / **To Him praise is due!**

R' Eliahu Lopian   A simple man stood before a king and began to sing. They tried to shush him up. But he persisted. "The king is my king," he said. "If he finds it fit to be *my* king, it is fitting that he hear *my* song."

So, too, we say, "For to You, Hashem, our God and God of our father's, it is fitting to be called our King. Therefore, it is only fitting for You to hear our song and praise, *hallel* and hymns."

On both nights continue here:

To Him praise is due! To Him praise is fitting!

Powerful in majesty, perfectly distinguished, His companies of angels say to Him: Yours and only Yours; Yours, yes Yours; Yours, surely Yours; Yours, HASHEM, is the sovereignty. To Him praise is due! To Him praise is fitting!

Supreme in kingship, perfectly glorious, His faithful say to Him: Yours and only Yours; Yours, yes Yours; Yours, surely Yours; Yours, HASHEM, is the sovereignty. To Him praise is due! To Him praise is fitting!

Pure in kingship, perfectly mighty, His angels say to Him: Yours and only Yours; Yours, yes Yours; Yours, surely Yours; Yours, HASHEM, is the sovereignty. To Him praise is due! To Him praise is fitting!

Alone in kingship, perfectly omnipotent, His scholars say to Him: Yours and only Yours; Yours, yes Yours; Yours, surely Yours; Yours, HASHEM, is the sovereignty. To Him praise is due! To Him praise is fitting!

Commanding in kingship, perfectly wondrous, His surrounding (angels) say to Him: Yours and only Yours; Yours, yes Yours; Yours, surely Yours; Yours, HASHEM, is the sovereignty. To Him praise is due! To Him praise is fitting!

Gentle in Kingship, perfectly the Redeemer, His righteous say to Him: Yours and only Yours; Yours, yes Yours; Yours, surely Yours; Yours, HASHEM, is the sovereignty. To Him praise is due! To Him praise is fitting!

גְּדוּדָיו יֹאמְרוּ לוֹ / *His companies of angels say to Him*

R' Yerucham of Mir In prayer (יוֹצֵר אוֹר, the first of the two blessings preceding the *Shema*), we relate in detail that the angels stand on high and call out to one another in awe and say, "Holy, Holy, Holy is HASHEM ..." and "Blessed is the glory of HASHEM." In this

[179]   THE PESACH HAGGADAH

קָדוֹשׁ בִּמְלוּכָה, רַחוּם כַּהֲלָכָה, שִׁנְאַנָּיו יֹאמְרוּ
לוֹ, לְךָ וּלְךָ, לְךָ כִּי לְךָ, לְךָ אַף לְךָ, לְךָ יהוה
הַמַּמְלָכָה, כִּי לוֹ נָאֶה, כִּי לוֹ יָאֶה.

תַּקִּיף בִּמְלוּכָה, תּוֹמֵךְ כַּהֲלָכָה, תְּמִימָיו יֹאמְרוּ
לוֹ, לְךָ וּלְךָ, לְךָ כִּי לְךָ, לְךָ אַף לְךָ, לְךָ יהוה
הַמַּמְלָכָה, כִּי לוֹ נָאֶה, כִּי לוֹ יָאֶה.

אַדִּיר הוּא יִבְנֶה בֵיתוֹ בְּקָרוֹב, בִּמְהֵרָה,
בִּמְהֵרָה, בְּיָמֵינוּ בְּקָרוֹב. אֵל בְּנֵה,
אֵל בְּנֵה, בְּנֵה בֵיתְךָ בְּקָרוֹב.

בָּחוּר הוּא. **גָּדוֹל** הוּא. **דָּגוּל** הוּא. יִבְנֶה בֵיתוֹ
בְּקָרוֹב, בִּמְהֵרָה, בִּמְהֵרָה, בְּיָמֵינוּ בְּקָרוֹב. אֵל
בְּנֵה, אֵל בְּנֵה, בְּנֵה בֵיתְךָ בְּקָרוֹב.

הָדוּר הוּא. **וָתִיק** הוּא. **זַכַּאי** הוּא. **חָסִיד** הוּא.
יִבְנֶה בֵיתוֹ בְּקָרוֹב, בִּמְהֵרָה, בִּמְהֵרָה, בְּיָמֵינוּ
בְּקָרוֹב. אֵל בְּנֵה, אֵל בְּנֵה, בְּנֵה בֵיתְךָ בְּקָרוֹב.

טָהוֹר הוּא. **יָחִיד** הוּא. **כַּבִּיר** הוּא. **לָמוּד** הוּא.
מֶלֶךְ הוּא. **נוֹרָא** הוּא. **סַגִּיב** הוּא. **עִזּוּז** הוּא. **פּוֹדֶה**
הוּא. **צַדִּיק** הוּא. יִבְנֶה בֵיתוֹ בְּקָרוֹב, בִּמְהֵרָה,
בִּמְהֵרָה, בְּיָמֵינוּ בְּקָרוֹב. אֵל בְּנֵה, אֵל בְּנֵה, בְּנֵה
בֵיתְךָ בְּקָרוֹב.

---

recitation of the *kedushah* we sanctify Hashem just as He is sanctified by the angels on high. What is this concern that we have with angels and their songs of praise?

We perforce must say that there is no difference between our service and that of the angels. The palace of the heavenly King is filled with the awe of His majesty and it expresses itself in every motion, in even the slightest

Holy in kingship, perfectly merciful, His troops of angels say to Him: Yours and only Yours; Yours, yes Yours; Yours, surely Yours; Yours, HASHEM, is the sovereignty. To Him praise is due! To Him praise is fitting.

Almighty in kingship, perfectly sustaining, His perfect ones say to Him: Yours and only Yours; Yours, yes Yours; Yours, surely Yours; Yours, HASHEM, is the sovereignty. To Him praise is due! To Him praise is fitting!

He is most mighty. May He soon rebuild His House, speedily, yes speedily, in our days, soon. God, rebuild, God, rebuild, rebuild Your House soon!

He is distinguished, He is great, He is exalted. May He soon rebuild His House, speedily, yes speedily, in our days, soon. God, rebuild, God, rebuild, rebuild Your House soon!

He is all glorious, He is faithful, He is faultless, He is righteous. May He soon rebuild His House, speedily, yes speedily, in our days, soon. God, rebuild, God, rebuild, rebuild Your House soon!

He is pure, He is unique, He is powerful, He is all-wise, He is King, He is awesome, He is sublime, He is all-powerful, He is the Redeemer, He is the all-righteous. May He soon rebuild His House, speedily, yes speedily, in our days, soon. God, rebuild, God, rebuild, rebuild Your House soon!

---

move, from that of the chief minister down to that of the least significant of servants. We, too, are warned to take equal heed of a minor *mitzvah* and a major one (*Avos* 2:1), "for all are dear and through them man praises Hashem at all times" (*Ramban* to *Shemos* 13:16); there is no distinction between a sweeping motion and a slight move.

There is a single goal both in Heaven and on earth. All of creation embroiders the curtain of "there is nothing other than He" — אֵין עוֹד מִלְּבַדּוֹ (*Devarim* 4:35). The entire Creation sings His praises.

קָדוֹשׁ הוּא. רַחוּם הוּא. שַׁדַּי הוּא. תַּקִּיף הוּא.
יִבְנֶה בֵיתוֹ בְּקָרוֹב, בִּמְהֵרָה, בִּמְהֵרָה, בְּיָמֵינוּ
בְּקָרוֹב. אֵל בְּנֵה, אֵל בְּנֵה, בְּנֵה בֵיתְךָ בְּקָרוֹב.

אֶחָד מִי יוֹדֵעַ? אֶחָד אֲנִי יוֹדֵעַ. אֶחָד
אֱלֹהֵינוּ שֶׁבַּשָּׁמַיִם וּבָאָרֶץ.

שְׁנַיִם מִי יוֹדֵעַ? שְׁנַיִם אֲנִי יוֹדֵעַ. שְׁנֵי לֻחוֹת
הַבְּרִית, אֶחָד אֱלֹהֵינוּ שֶׁבַּשָּׁמַיִם וּבָאָרֶץ.

קָדוֹשׁ הוּא / He is holy

R' Eliahu Dessler — *Chazal* chose to call Hashem "The Holy One, Blessed is He" (הקב׳׳ה) rather than use His other bynames, such as The Merciful (הָרַחוּם), The Bountiful (הֶחָנוּן). This choice needs explanation.

Chazal compare the Holy One's workings in the world to that of man's soul in the body (*Berachos* 10). But there is a meaningful difference. For when all is said and done, the soul is influenced by the body and there is a tie between body and soul. The Holy One, however, is not influenced by the world in any degree, as it is written: "And if you are righteous, what do you give Him?" (*Iyov* 35:7). *Holy* (קָדוֹשׁ) expresses this state of independence; it means *separate*.

Thus, all the other names, like Merciful and Bountiful which represent God's conduct vis-a-vis the world, ought to be prefaced by the *Holy One* (הקב׳׳ה), because it clearly denotes that all His actions in the world are only seen from our perspective, as He reveals Himself to us. But as far as His essential Self, as far as He Himself is concerned, we cannot grasp a thing. Even the angels with their infinitely greater understanding praise Him by calling him "Holy" (*Yeshayahu* 6:3). They know that He is beyond comprehension.

And lo! We are told "to walk in His ways" (*Devarim* 28:9) and imitate Him (*Shabbos* 133), not only as far as traits of mercy (רַחֲמִים) and kindness (חֶסֶד) but with regard to holiness also: "Be holy, because I, Hashem, am holy" (*Vayikra* 19:1). Yet, how can a demand be made on us, material man, who are minute in our spiritual dimension, to sanctify ourselves in the sense of Hashem's holiness?

God's holiness tells us that He stands alone and is uninfluenced by Creation. Man, too, is meant to strive to stand above the concrete physical aspects of nature, inasmuch as he can. His actions should be for the sake of

He is holy, He is compassionate, He is Almighty, He is omnipotent. May He soon rebuild His House, speedily, yes speedily, in our days, soon. God, rebuild, God, rebuild, rebuild Your House soon!

Who knows one? I know one: One is our God, in heaven and on earth.

Who knows two? I know two: two are the Tablets of the Covenant; One is our God, in heaven and on earth.

Heaven and he should not allow the desires which are bound to the body to influence him and turn him off the path of the spiritual.

There is an even higher level of holiness. Not only should he not be influenced by the physical side of Creation, but he should war constantly with his evil nature (יֵצֶר הָרָע). By overcoming it, when he receives his reward in the Afterlife, he will not feel that it is a free gift; he will have earned that reward by defeating his will and dedicating himself to the Holy One's service in this world. This sense of spiritual independence, of not receiving spiritual "charity," through his own efforts in Torah and *mitzvos* will grant him the highest level of holiness.

אֶחָד אֱלֹהֵינוּ / One is our God

R' Yosef Leib Bloch of Telshe

When I was in my youth, I met [R' Avraham Azulai] the author of the [kabbalistic work,] Leshem, Shvo V'Achlamah, and during our conversation, I mentioned that, as I understood him, R' Moshe Chaim Luzzatto, the *Ramchal,* said that nothing exists other than God, and those things that are visible to us do not really exist; their existence is imaginary. He told me that I was mistaken; that Creation in all its myriad worlds did exist. Yet nevertheless this does not detract from God's Oneness. He did not elaborate and I did not ask him to explain himself.

But once, something happened which allowed me to understand that in one sense, all the worlds might exist and yet, at the same time, in another sense, they melt away. I noticed two lit candles, but when I stretched out my hand, I realized that there was but one; its reflection appeared in a polished mirror. Were we to have only the sense of sight, to us the appearance of two candles would, indeed, be two candles. But because we also have a sense of touch, we know that there is only one. Perhaps, if we had senses other than those we possess, we would view reality differently and what we think of as

שְׁלֹשָׁה מִי יוֹדֵעַ? שְׁלֹשָׁה אֲנִי יוֹדֵעַ. שְׁלֹשָׁה אָבוֹת, שְׁנֵי לֻחוֹת הַבְּרִית, אֶחָד אֱלֹהֵינוּ שֶׁבַּשָּׁמַיִם וּבָאָרֶץ.

אַרְבַּע מִי יוֹדֵעַ? אַרְבַּע אֲנִי יוֹדֵעַ. אַרְבַּע אִמָּהוֹת, שְׁלֹשָׁה אָבוֹת, שְׁנֵי לֻחוֹת הַבְּרִית, אֶחָד אֱלֹהֵינוּ שֶׁבַּשָּׁמַיִם וּבָאָרֶץ.

חֲמִשָּׁה מִי יוֹדֵעַ? חֲמִשָּׁה אֲנִי יוֹדֵעַ. חֲמִשָּׁה חֻמְשֵׁי תוֹרָה, אַרְבַּע אִמָּהוֹת, שְׁלֹשָׁה אָבוֹת, שְׁנֵי לֻחוֹת הַבְּרִית, אֶחָד אֱלֹהֵינוּ שֶׁבַּשָּׁמַיִם וּבָאָרֶץ.

שִׁשָּׁה מִי יוֹדֵעַ? שִׁשָּׁה אֲנִי יוֹדֵעַ. שִׁשָּׁה סִדְרֵי מִשְׁנָה, חֲמִשָּׁה חֻמְשֵׁי תוֹרָה, אַרְבַּע אִמָּהוֹת, שְׁלֹשָׁה אָבוֹת, שְׁנֵי לֻחוֹת הַבְּרִית, אֶחָד אֱלֹהֵינוּ שֶׁבַּשָּׁמַיִם וּבָאָרֶץ.

---

real will be understood to be imaginary.

All the worlds which we experience do exist — but in terms of *our* senses and our own existence. With regard to the ultimately true existence, in terms of the Creator, they do not exist. For there is no existence like His existence.

We say, "Hear O Israel our God, HASHEM is one." There is no other and there is no existence beyond His existence; that is the truth in absolute terms. Yet, at the same time we say, "Blessed is the name of the glory of His majesty" (בָּרוּךְ שֵׁם כְּבוֹד מַלְכוּתוֹ) — in all the worlds — "forever and ever" (לְעוֹלָם וָעֶד).

שְׁלֹשָׁה אָבוֹת
Three are the Patriarchs

R' Yerucham of Mir   *Chazal* say that the Patriarchs are the *chariot* (*Bereishis Rabbah* 47); they carried the Divine on their backs. They brought It down to earth and they have borne It until our times.

Who knows three? I know three: three are the Patriarchs; two are the Tablets of the Covenant; One is our God, in heaven and on earth.

Who knows four? I know four: four are the Matriarchs; three are the Patriarchs; two are the Tablets of the Covenant; One is our God, in heaven and on earth.

Who knows five? I know five: five are the Books of Torah; four are the Matriarchs; three are the Patriarchs; two are the Tablets of the Covenant; One is our God, in heaven and on earth.

Who knows six? I know six: six are the Orders of the Mishnah; five are the Books of the Torah; four are the Matriarchs; three are the Patriarchs; two are the Tablets of the Covenant; One is our God, in heaven and on earth.

Rashi in his work *HaPardes* points out that the *Shemoneh Esrei* prayer requires a minimum attitude of thoughtful purpose (כַּוָּנָה) which must be sustained through the first blessing, *avos* — which centers about the Patriarchs. This is so, he says, because the deeds of our forefathers are great and the greatness of Hashem is highlighted in their blessing; the entire prayer is built on the single foundation of the God of Avraham, Yitzchak and Yaakov!

We say *Elokei Avraham,* "the God of Avraham." Our entire conception of *Elokei,* of Divinity, stems from Avraham. That is the essential meaning of the verse which applies to Avraham: "And you will be a blessing" (*Bereishis* 12:2). We understand what a blessing is from Avraham.

It is told that R' Shimon ben Shetach purchased a donkey from an Arab. He found a precious stone hidden in the reins and returned it to the donkey's former master. The Arab said, "Blessed be the God of Shimon ben Shetach" (*Devarim Rabbah* 3). Had he not known of Shimon ben Shetach's act he would have no conception of R' Shimon's God. So, too, we are aware of Avraham's God from the "kindness to Avraham" (*Michah* 6:20); from Yitzchak we can understand the "Fear (God) of Yitzchak" (*Bereishis* 31:42); from the "truth to Yaakov" (*Michah* 6:20) we see the God of Yaakov. Our entire service to Hashem consists in emulating and becoming one with the service of the Patriarchs: "saying: When will my

שִׁבְעָה מִי יוֹדֵעַ? שִׁבְעָה אֲנִי יוֹדֵעַ. שִׁבְעָה יְמֵי
שַׁבַּתָּא, שִׁשָּׁה סִדְרֵי מִשְׁנָה, חֲמִשָּׁה חֻמְשֵׁי תוֹרָה,
אַרְבַּע אִמָּהוֹת, שְׁלֹשָׁה אָבוֹת, שְׁנֵי לֻחוֹת הַבְּרִית,
אֶחָד אֱלֹהֵינוּ שֶׁבַּשָּׁמַיִם וּבָאָרֶץ.

שְׁמוֹנָה מִי יוֹדֵעַ? שְׁמוֹנָה אֲנִי יוֹדֵעַ. שְׁמוֹנָה יְמֵי
מִילָה, שִׁבְעָה יְמֵי שַׁבַּתָּא, שִׁשָּׁה סִדְרֵי מִשְׁנָה,
חֲמִשָּׁה חֻמְשֵׁי תוֹרָה, אַרְבַּע אִמָּהוֹת, שְׁלֹשָׁה
אָבוֹת, שְׁנֵי לֻחוֹת הַבְּרִית, אֶחָד אֱלֹהֵינוּ שֶׁבַּשָּׁמַיִם
וּבָאָרֶץ.

תִּשְׁעָה מִי יוֹדֵעַ? תִּשְׁעָה אֲנִי יוֹדֵעַ. תִּשְׁעָה יַרְחֵי
לֵדָה, שְׁמוֹנָה יְמֵי מִילָה, שִׁבְעָה יְמֵי שַׁבַּתָּא, שִׁשָּׁה
סִדְרֵי מִשְׁנָה, חֲמִשָּׁה חֻמְשֵׁי תוֹרָה, אַרְבַּע אִמָּהוֹת,
שְׁלֹשָׁה אָבוֹת, שְׁנֵי לֻחוֹת הַבְּרִית, אֶחָד אֱלֹהֵינוּ
שֶׁבַּשָּׁמַיִם וּבָאָרֶץ.

עֲשָׂרָה מִי יוֹדֵעַ? עֲשָׂרָה אֲנִי יוֹדֵעַ. עֲשָׂרָה
דִּבְּרַיָּא, תִּשְׁעָה יַרְחֵי לֵדָה, שְׁמוֹנָה יְמֵי מִילָה,
שִׁבְעָה יְמֵי שַׁבַּתָּא, שִׁשָּׁה סִדְרֵי מִשְׁנָה, חֲמִשָּׁה
חֻמְשֵׁי תוֹרָה, אַרְבַּע אִמָּהוֹת, שְׁלֹשָׁה אָבוֹת, שְׁנֵי
לֻחוֹת הַבְּרִית, אֶחָד אֱלֹהֵינוּ שֶׁבַּשָּׁמַיִם וּבָאָרֶץ.

---

deeds reach those of my forefathers Avraham, Yitzchak and Yaakov?'' (*Tana D'Vei Eliahu Rabbah* 25).

שְׁמוֹנָה יְמֵי מִילָה, שִׁבְעָה יְמֵי שַׁבַּתָּא
Eight are the days of circumcision, seven are the days of the week

R' Eliahu Dessler	The Midrash presents *Shabbos* and circumcision as having a debate. Each claims to be the more im-

Who knows seven? I know seven: seven are the days of the week; six are the Orders of the Mishnah; five are the Books of the Torah; four are the Matriarchs; three are the Patriarchs; two are the Tablets of the Covenant; One is our God, in heaven and on earth.

Who knows eight? I know eight: eight are the days of circumcision; seven are the days of the week; six are the Orders of the Mishnah; five are the Books of the Torah; four are the Matriarchs; three are the Patriarchs; two are the Tablets of the Covenant; One is our God, in heaven and on earth.

Who knows nine? I know nine: nine are the months of pregnancy; eight are the days of circumcision; seven are the days of the week; six are the Orders of the Mishnah; five are the Books of the Torah; four are the Matriarchs; three are the Patriarchs; two are the Tablets of the Covenant; One is our God, in heaven and on earth.

Who knows ten? I know ten: ten are the Ten Commandments; nine are the months of pregnancy; eight are the days of circumcision; seven are the days of the week; six are the Orders of the Mishnah; five are the Books of the Torah; four are the Matriarchs; three are the Patriarchs; two are the Tablets of the Covenant; One is our God, in heaven and on earth.

---

portant. Circumcision takes place on the eighth day, even if that day is *Shabbos*. It supersedes the prohibition against desecrating *Shabbos*. Circumcision, then, is proven to be the more important (*Yalkut Shimoni, Yirmeyahu* 321).

The debate is symbolic. The seven days of the week represent the physical world and *Shabbos* introduces a dimension of the holy into this round of the physical. But circumcision takes place on the eighth day, beyond the circumference of this circle. And it consists of the removal of a physical

אַחַד עָשָׂר מִי יוֹדֵעַ? אַחַד עָשָׂר אֲנִי יוֹדֵעַ. אַחַד עָשָׂר כּוֹכְבַיָּא, עֲשָׂרָה דִבְּרַיָּא, תִּשְׁעָה יַרְחֵי לֵדָה, שְׁמוֹנָה יְמֵי מִילָה, שִׁבְעָה יְמֵי שַׁבַּתָּא, שִׁשָּׁה סִדְרֵי מִשְׁנָה, חֲמִשָּׁה חֻמְשֵׁי תוֹרָה, אַרְבַּע אִמָּהוֹת, שְׁלֹשָׁה אָבוֹת, שְׁנֵי לֻחוֹת הַבְּרִית, אֶחָד אֱלֹהֵינוּ שֶׁבַּשָּׁמַיִם וּבָאָרֶץ.

שְׁנֵים עָשָׂר מִי יוֹדֵעַ? שְׁנֵים עָשָׂר אֲנִי יוֹדֵעַ. שְׁנֵים עָשָׂר שִׁבְטַיָּא, אַחַד עָשָׂר כּוֹכְבַיָּא, עֲשָׂרָה דִבְּרַיָּא, תִּשְׁעָה יַרְחֵי לֵדָה, שְׁמוֹנָה יְמֵי מִילָה, שִׁבְעָה יְמֵי שַׁבַּתָּא, שִׁשָּׁה סִדְרֵי מִשְׁנָה, חֲמִשָּׁה חֻמְשֵׁי תוֹרָה, אַרְבַּע אִמָּהוֹת, שְׁלֹשָׁה אָבוֹת, שְׁנֵי לֻחוֹת הַבְּרִית, אֶחָד אֱלֹהֵינוּ שֶׁבַּשָּׁמַיִם וּבָאָרֶץ.

שְׁלֹשָׁה עָשָׂר מִי יוֹדֵעַ? שְׁלֹשָׁה עָשָׂר אֲנִי יוֹדֵעַ. שְׁלֹשָׁה עָשָׂר מִדַּיָּא, שְׁנֵים עָשָׂר שִׁבְטַיָּא, אַחַד עָשָׂר כּוֹכְבַיָּא, עֲשָׂרָה דִבְּרַיָּא, תִּשְׁעָה יַרְחֵי לֵדָה, שְׁמוֹנָה יְמֵי מִילָה, שִׁבְעָה יְמֵי שַׁבַּתָּא, שִׁשָּׁה סִדְרֵי

foreskin and symbolizes a departure from the physical. Certainly, both *Shabbos* and circumcision are necessary; the question is which of the two stands higher than its fellow.

Many *mitzvos* involve sanctifying the physical: blessings pronounced over food; separating the tithes (*ma'aser*) from the produce; giving charity; enjoyment of the *Shabbos* (עֹנֶג שַׁבָּת). But such *mitzvos* are a potential danger. A man may bend to his will and become addicted to satisfying his desires under the pretense and guise of fulfilling a *mitzvah*. As R' Yisrael of Salant put it: One gulps down (and disposes) the *Shabbos* along with his *cholent*.

The only way to counter this inclination is to remove the striving for the physical by breaking the pull of desire. This is what the Midrash meant when it said that circumcision is more important than *Shabbos*.

Who knows eleven? I know eleven: eleven are the stars (in Yosef's dream); ten are the Ten Commandments; nine are the months of pregnancy; eight are the days of circumcision; seven are the days of the week; six are the Orders of the Mishnah; five are the Books of the Torah; four are the Matriarchs; three are the Patriarchs; two are the Tablets of the Covenant; One is our God, in heaven and on earth.

Who knows twelve? I know twelve: twelve are the tribes; eleven are the stars (in Yosef's dream); ten are the Ten Commandments; nine are the months of pregnancy; eight are the days of circumcision; seven are the days of the week; six are the Orders of the Mishnah; five are the Books of the Torah; four are the Matriarchs; three are the Patriarchs; two are the Tablets of the Covenant; One is our God, in heaven and on earth.

Who knows thirteen? I know thirteen: thirteen are the attributes of God; twelve are the tribes; eleven are the stars (in Yosef's dream); ten are the Ten Commandments; nine are the months of pregnancy; eight are the days of circumcision; seven are the days of the week; six are the Orders of the

---

שְׁנֵים עָשָׂר שִׁבְטַיָּא / Twelve are the tribes

R' Yerucham of Mir — Our forefather Yaakov blessed his sons "each according to his blessing" — "the blessing which each was to receive in the future" (*Bereishis* 49:28 and *Rashi* there).

The blessing could not affect or change their nature; it only indicated and made a point of an existent nature. It worked like Elisha's miracle of the oil-flask which poured oil without pause, but could only pour if there had originally been some oil in it (*II Melachim* ch. 4). Thus it was that Yaakov crossed his arms to bless Menashe and Efraim. He did not alter the text of his blessings; he could not. He could only grant them blessings which applied to them right from the start.

The qualities of the tribes were, then, established before the blessings.

מִשְׁנָה, חֲמִשָּׁה חֻמְשֵׁי תוֹרָה, אַרְבַּע אִמָּהוֹת,
שְׁלֹשָׁה אָבוֹת, שְׁנֵי לֻחוֹת הַבְּרִית, אֶחָד אֱלֹהֵינוּ
שֶׁבַּשָּׁמַיִם וּבָאָרֶץ.

חַד גַּדְיָא, חַד גַּדְיָא, דְּזַבִּין אַבָּא בִּתְרֵי זוּזֵי,
חַד גַּדְיָא חַד גַּדְיָא.

וְאָתָא **שׁוּנְרָא** וְאָכְלָה לְגַדְיָא, דְּזַבִּין אַבָּא בִּתְרֵי
זוּזֵי, חַד גַּדְיָא חַד גַּדְיָא.

וְאָתָא **כַלְבָּא** וְנָשַׁךְ לְשׁוּנְרָא, דְּאָכְלָא לְגַדְיָא,
דְּזַבִּין אַבָּא בִּתְרֵי זוּזֵי, חַד גַּדְיָא חַד גַּדְיָא.

וְאָתָא **חוּטְרָא** וְהִכָּה לְכַלְבָּא, דְּנָשַׁךְ לְשׁוּנְרָא,
דְּאָכְלָה לְגַדְיָא, דְּזַבִּין אַבָּא בִּתְרֵי זוּזֵי, חַד גַּדְיָא
חַד גַּדְיָא.

וְאָתָא **נוּרָא** וְשָׂרַף לְחוּטְרָא, דְּהִכָּה לְכַלְבָּא,
דְּנָשַׁךְ לְשׁוּנְרָא, דְּאָכְלָה לְגַדְיָא, דְּזַבִּין אַבָּא בִּתְרֵי
זוּזֵי, חַד גַּדְיָא חַד גַּדְיָא.

וְאָתָא **מַיָּא** וְכָבָה לְנוּרָא, דְּשָׂרַף לְחוּטְרָא,
דְּהִכָּה לְכַלְבָּא, דְּנָשַׁךְ לְשׁוּנְרָא, דְּאָכְלָה לְגַדְיָא,
דְּזַבִּין אַבָּא בִּתְרֵי זוּזֵי, חַד גַּדְיָא חַד גַּדְיָא.

Yosef was chaste, as the incident with Potifar's wife proves, and this quality
was highlighted in his blessing (*Onkelos, Bereishis* 49:26). Yehudah
confessed his part in the affair of Tamar and was crowned thereby, by his
brothers, as king. That, too, is pointed out in his blessing (*Targum Yonasan,
Bereishis* 49:5).

Mishnah; five are the Books of the Torah; four are the Matriarchs; three are the Patriarchs; two are the Tablets of the Covenant; One is our God, in heaven and on earth.

A kid, a kid, that father bought for two zuzim, a kid, a kid.

A cat then came and devoured the kid, that father bought for two zuzim, a kid, a kid.

A dog then came and bit the cat, that devoured the kid, that father bought for two zuzim, a kid, a kid.

A stick then came and beat the dog, that bit the cat, that devoured the kid, that father bought for two zuzim, a kid, a kid.

A fire then came and burnt the stick, that beat the dog, that bit the cat, that devoured the kid, that father bought for two zuzim, a kid, a kid.

Water then came and quenched the fire, that burnt the stick, that beat the dog, that bit the cat, that devoured the kid, that father bought for two zuzim, a kid, a kid.

The blessing expressed only the existing virtue. But it was given to ensure that the tribe would develop and display, in fact, the potential of that quality, just as they had done previously. Yosef had repulsed Potifar's wife and shown his chastity and Yehudah had had the strength to admit his fault with his "She was more righteous than I" (*Bereishis* 38:26).

This should teach each of us that we are only tested with respect to our private potential and the test serves as a means to rise. The *Alter* of Kelm explained the following statement of *Chazal* in this light: The righteous turn the quality of strict justice (מִדַּת הַדִּין) — of Hashem — into that of mercy (מִדַּת הָרַחֲמִים). They use all the good temperaments hidden within themselves to turn all the aspects of their personalities towards the good. And the wicked do the reverse (*Bereishis Rabbah* 33) — their bad qualities have the upper hand, so that they corrupt whatever good traits they have.

וְאָתָא **תוֹרָא** וְשָׁתָה לְמַיָּא, דְּכָבָה לְנוּרָא, דְּשָׂרַף לְחוּטְרָא, דְּהִכָּה לְכַלְבָּא, דְּנָשַׁךְ לְשׁוּנְרָא, דְּאָכְלָה לְגַדְיָא, דְּזַבִּין אַבָּא בִּתְרֵי זוּזֵי, חַד גַּדְיָא חַד גַּדְיָא.

וְאָתָא **הַשּׁוֹחֵט** וְשָׁחַט לְתוֹרָא, דְּשָׁתָא לְמַיָּא, דְּכָבָה לְנוּרָא, דְּשָׂרַף לְחוּטְרָא, דְּהִכָּה לְכַלְבָּא, דְּנָשַׁךְ לְשׁוּנְרָא, דְּאָכְלָה לְגַדְיָא, דְּזַבִּין אַבָּא בִּתְרֵי זוּזֵי, חַד גַּדְיָא חַד גַּדְיָא.

וְאָתָא **מַלְאַךְ הַמָּוֶת** וְשָׁחַט לְשׁוֹחֵט, דְּשָׁחַט לְתוֹרָא, דְּשָׁתָה לְמַיָּא, דְּכָבָה לְנוּרָא, דְּשָׂרַף לְחוּטְרָא, דְּהִכָּה לְכַלְבָּא, דְּנָשַׁךְ לְשׁוּנְרָא, דְּאָכְלָה לְגַדְיָא, דְּזַבִּין אַבָּא בִּתְרֵי זוּזֵי, חַד גַּדְיָא חַד גַּדְיָא.

וְאָתָא **הַקָּדוֹשׁ בָּרוּךְ הוּא** וְשָׁחַט לְמַלְאַךְ הַמָּוֶת, דְּשָׁחַט לְשׁוֹחֵט, דְּשָׁחַט לְתוֹרָא, דְּשָׁתָה לְמַיָּא, דְּכָבָה לְנוּרָא, דְּשָׂרַף לְחוּטְרָא, דְּהִכָּה לְכַלְבָּא, דְּנָשַׁךְ לְשׁוּנְרָא, דְּאָכְלָה לְגַדְיָא, דְּזַבִּין אַבָּא בִּתְרֵי זוּזֵי, חַד גַּדְיָא חַד גַּדְיָא.

Although the Haggadah formally ends at this point, one should continue to occupy himself with the story of the Exodus, and the laws of Pesach, until sleep overtakes him.

An ox then came and drank the water, that quenched the fire, that burnt the stick, that beat the dog, that bit the cat, that devoured the kid, that father bought for two zuzim, a kid, a kid.

A slaughterer then came and slaughtered the ox, that drank the water, that quenched the fire, that burnt the stick, that beat the dog, that bit the cat, that devoured the kid, that father bought for two zuzim, a kid, a kid.

The angel of death then came and killed the slaughterer, who slaughtered the ox, that drank the water, that quenched the fire, that burnt the stick, that beat the dog, that bit the cat, that devoured the kid, that father bought for two zuzim, a kid, a kid.

The Holy One, Blessed is He, then came and slew the angel of death, who killed the slaughterer, who slaughtered the ox, that drank the water, that quenched the fire, that burnt the stick, that beat the dog, that bit the cat, that devoured the kid, that father bought for two zuzim, a kid, a kid.

Although the Haggadah formally ends at this point, one should continue to occupy himself with the story of the Exodus, and the laws of Pesach, until sleep overtakes him.

Many recite שִׁיר הַשִּׁירִים, Song of Songs, after the Haggadah.

שיר השירים

א

א **שִׁיר הַשִּׁירִים** אֲשֶׁר לִשְׁלֹמֹה. ב יִשָּׁקֵנִי מִנְּשִׁיקוֹת
פִּיהוּ, כִּי טוֹבִים דֹּדֶיךָ מִיָּיִן. ג לְרֵיחַ
שְׁמָנֶיךָ טוֹבִים, שֶׁמֶן תּוּרַק שְׁמֶךָ, עַל כֵּן עֲלָמוֹת אֲהֵבוּךָ.
ד מָשְׁכֵנִי אַחֲרֶיךָ נָּרוּצָה, הֱבִיאַנִי הַמֶּלֶךְ חֲדָרָיו, נָגִילָה
וְנִשְׂמְחָה בָּךְ. נַזְכִּירָה דֹדֶיךָ מִיַּיִן, מֵישָׁרִים אֲהֵבוּךָ. ה שְׁחוֹרָה
אֲנִי וְנָאוָה, בְּנוֹת יְרוּשָׁלָיִם, כְּאָהֳלֵי קֵדָר, כִּירִיעוֹת שְׁלֹמֹה.
ו אַל תִּרְאוּנִי שֶׁאֲנִי שְׁחַרְחֹרֶת, שֶׁשְּׁזָפַתְנִי הַשָּׁמֶשׁ, בְּנֵי אִמִּי
נִחֲרוּ בִי, שָׂמֻנִי נֹטֵרָה אֶת הַכְּרָמִים, כַּרְמִי שֶׁלִּי לֹא נָטָרְתִּי.
ז הַגִּידָה לִּי, שֶׁאָהֲבָה נַפְשִׁי, אֵיכָה תִרְעֶה, אֵיכָה תַּרְבִּיץ
בַּצָּהֳרָיִם, שַׁלָּמָה אֶהְיֶה כְּעֹטְיָה עַל עֶדְרֵי חֲבֵרֶיךָ. ח אִם לֹא
תֵדְעִי לָךְ, הַיָּפָה בַּנָּשִׁים, צְאִי לָךְ בְּעִקְבֵי הַצֹּאן, וּרְעִי אֶת
גְּדִיֹּתַיִךְ עַל מִשְׁכְּנוֹת הָרֹעִים. ט לְסֻסָתִי בְּרִכְבֵי פַרְעֹה
דִּמִּיתִיךְ, רַעְיָתִי. י נָאווּ לְחָיַיִךְ בַּתֹּרִים, צַוָּארֵךְ בַּחֲרוּזִים.
יא תּוֹרֵי זָהָב נַעֲשֶׂה לָּךְ, עִם נְקֻדּוֹת הַכָּסֶף. יב עַד שֶׁהַמֶּלֶךְ
בִּמְסִבּוֹ, נִרְדִּי נָתַן רֵיחוֹ. יג צְרוֹר הַמֹּר דּוֹדִי לִי, בֵּין שָׁדַי
יָלִין. יד אֶשְׁכֹּל הַכֹּפֶר דּוֹדִי לִי, בְּכַרְמֵי עֵין גֶּדִי. טו הִנָּךְ יָפָה,
רַעְיָתִי, הִנָּךְ יָפָה, עֵינַיִךְ יוֹנִים. טז הִנְּךָ יָפֶה, דוֹדִי, אַף נָעִים,
אַף עַרְשֵׂנוּ רַעֲנָנָה. יז קֹרוֹת בָּתֵּינוּ אֲרָזִים, רָהִיטֵנוּ בְּרוֹתִים.

ב

א אֲנִי חֲבַצֶּלֶת הַשָּׁרוֹן, שׁוֹשַׁנַּת הָעֲמָקִים. ב כְּשׁוֹשַׁנָּה בֵּין
הַחוֹחִים, כֵּן רַעְיָתִי בֵּין הַבָּנוֹת. ג כְּתַפּוּחַ בַּעֲצֵי הַיַּעַר, כֵּן
דּוֹדִי בֵּין הַבָּנִים, בְּצִלּוֹ חִמַּדְתִּי וְיָשַׁבְתִּי, וּפִרְיוֹ מָתוֹק
לְחִכִּי. ד הֱבִיאַנִי אֶל בֵּית הַיָּיִן, וְדִגְלוֹ עָלַי אַהֲבָה. ה סַמְּכוּנִי
בָּאֲשִׁישׁוֹת, רַפְּדוּנִי בַּתַּפּוּחִים, כִּי חוֹלַת אַהֲבָה אָנִי.
ו שְׂמֹאלוֹ תַּחַת לְרֹאשִׁי, וִימִינוֹ תְּחַבְּקֵנִי. ז הִשְׁבַּעְתִּי אֶתְכֶם,

בְּנוֹת יְרוּשָׁלַיִם, בִּצְבָאוֹת אוֹ בְּאַיְלוֹת הַשָּׂדֶה, אִם תָּעִירוּ
וְאִם תְּעוֹרְרוּ אֶת הָאַהֲבָה עַד שֶׁתֶּחְפָּץ. ח קוֹל דּוֹדִי הִנֵּה זֶה
בָּא, מְדַלֵּג עַל הֶהָרִים, מְקַפֵּץ עַל הַגְּבָעוֹת. ט דּוֹמֶה דוֹדִי
לִצְבִי, אוֹ לְעֹפֶר הָאַיָּלִים, הִנֵּה זֶה עוֹמֵד אַחַר כָּתְלֵנוּ,
מַשְׁגִּיחַ מִן הַחַלֹּנוֹת, מֵצִיץ מִן הַחֲרַכִּים. י עָנָה דוֹדִי וְאָמַר
לִי, קוּמִי לָךְ, רַעְיָתִי, יָפָתִי, וּלְכִי לָךְ. יא כִּי הִנֵּה הַסְּתָו
עָבָר, הַגֶּשֶׁם חָלַף הָלַךְ לוֹ. יב הַנִּצָּנִים נִרְאוּ בָאָרֶץ, עֵת
הַזָּמִיר הִגִּיעַ, וְקוֹל הַתּוֹר נִשְׁמַע בְּאַרְצֵנוּ. יג הַתְּאֵנָה חָנְטָה
פַגֶּיהָ, וְהַגְּפָנִים סְמָדַר נָתְנוּ רֵיחַ, קוּמִי לָךְ, רַעְיָתִי, יָפָתִי,
וּלְכִי לָךְ. יד יוֹנָתִי, בְּחַגְוֵי הַסֶּלַע, בְּסֵתֶר הַמַּדְרֵגָה, הַרְאִינִי
אֶת מַרְאַיִךְ, הַשְׁמִיעִנִי אֶת קוֹלֵךְ, כִּי קוֹלֵךְ עָרֵב, וּמַרְאֵיךְ
נָאוֶה. טו אֶחֱזוּ לָנוּ שׁוּעָלִים, שֻׁעָלִים קְטַנִּים, מְחַבְּלִים
כְּרָמִים, וּכְרָמֵינוּ סְמָדַר. טז דּוֹדִי לִי, וַאֲנִי לוֹ, הָרֹעֶה
בַּשּׁוֹשַׁנִּים. יז עַד שֶׁיָּפוּחַ הַיּוֹם, וְנָסוּ הַצְּלָלִים, סֹב דְּמֵה לְךָ,
דוֹדִי, לִצְבִי אוֹ לְעֹפֶר הָאַיָּלִים, עַל הָרֵי בָתֶר.

ג

א עַל מִשְׁכָּבִי בַּלֵּילוֹת בִּקַּשְׁתִּי אֵת שֶׁאָהֲבָה נַפְשִׁי, בִּקַּשְׁתִּיו
וְלֹא מְצָאתִיו. ב אָקוּמָה נָּא וַאֲסוֹבְבָה בָעִיר, בַּשְּׁוָקִים
וּבָרְחֹבוֹת, אֲבַקְשָׁה אֵת שֶׁאָהֲבָה נַפְשִׁי, בִּקַּשְׁתִּיו וְלֹא
מְצָאתִיו. ג מְצָאוּנִי הַשֹּׁמְרִים הַסֹּבְבִים בָּעִיר, אֵת שֶׁאָהֲבָה
נַפְשִׁי רְאִיתֶם. ד כִּמְעַט שֶׁעָבַרְתִּי מֵהֶם, עַד שֶׁמָּצָאתִי אֵת
שֶׁאָהֲבָה נַפְשִׁי, אֲחַזְתִּיו וְלֹא אַרְפֶּנּוּ, עַד שֶׁהֲבֵיאתִיו אֶל
בֵּית אִמִּי, וְאֶל חֶדֶר הוֹרָתִי. ה הִשְׁבַּעְתִּי אֶתְכֶם, בְּנוֹת
יְרוּשָׁלַיִם, בִּצְבָאוֹת אוֹ בְּאַיְלוֹת הַשָּׂדֶה, אִם תָּעִירוּ וְאִם
תְּעוֹרְרוּ אֶת הָאַהֲבָה עַד שֶׁתֶּחְפָּץ. ו מִי זֹאת עֹלָה מִן
הַמִּדְבָּר, כְּתִימְרוֹת עָשָׁן, מְקֻטֶּרֶת מֹר וּלְבוֹנָה, מִכֹּל אַבְקַת
רוֹכֵל. ז הִנֵּה מִטָּתוֹ שֶׁלִּשְׁלֹמֹה, שִׁשִּׁים גִּבֹּרִים סָבִיב לָהּ,
מִגִּבֹּרֵי יִשְׂרָאֵל. ח כֻּלָּם אֲחֻזֵי חֶרֶב, מְלֻמְּדֵי מִלְחָמָה, אִישׁ

חַרְבּוֹ עַל יְרֵכוֹ, מִפַּחַד בַּלֵּילוֹת. ט אַפִּרְיוֹן עָשָׂה לוֹ הַמֶּלֶךְ
שְׁלֹמֹה מֵעֲצֵי הַלְּבָנוֹן. י עַמּוּדָיו עָשָׂה כֶסֶף, רְפִידָתוֹ זָהָב,
מֶרְכָּבוֹ אַרְגָּמָן, תּוֹכוֹ רָצוּף אַהֲבָה מִבְּנוֹת יְרוּשָׁלָיִם.
יא צְאֶינָה וּרְאֶינָה, בְּנוֹת צִיּוֹן, בַּמֶּלֶךְ שְׁלֹמֹה, בַּעֲטָרָה
שֶׁעִטְּרָה לּוֹ אִמּוֹ, בְּיוֹם חֲתֻנָּתוֹ, וּבְיוֹם שִׂמְחַת לִבּוֹ.

ד

א הִנָּךְ יָפָה, רַעְיָתִי, הִנָּךְ יָפָה, עֵינַיִךְ יוֹנִים, מִבַּעַד לְצַמָּתֵךְ,
שַׂעְרֵךְ כְּעֵדֶר הָעִזִּים, שֶׁגָּלְשׁוּ מֵהַר גִּלְעָד. ב שִׁנַּיִךְ כְּעֵדֶר
הַקְּצוּבוֹת שֶׁעָלוּ מִן הָרַחְצָה, שֶׁכֻּלָּם מַתְאִימוֹת, וְשַׁכֻּלָה
אֵין בָּהֶם. ג כְּחוּט הַשָּׁנִי שִׂפְתוֹתַיִךְ, וּמִדְבָּרֵךְ נָאוֶה, כְּפֶלַח
הָרִמּוֹן רַקָּתֵךְ, מִבַּעַד לְצַמָּתֵךְ. ד כְּמִגְדַּל דָּוִיד צַוָּארֵךְ, בָּנוּי
לְתַלְפִּיּוֹת, אֶלֶף הַמָּגֵן תָּלוּי עָלָיו, כֹּל שִׁלְטֵי הַגִּבּוֹרִים.
ה שְׁנֵי שָׁדַיִךְ כִּשְׁנֵי עֳפָרִים, תְּאוֹמֵי צְבִיָּה, הָרוֹעִים בַּשּׁוֹשַׁנִּים.
ו עַד שֶׁיָּפוּחַ הַיּוֹם, וְנָסוּ הַצְּלָלִים, אֵלֶךְ לִי אֶל הַר הַמּוֹר,
וְאֶל גִּבְעַת הַלְּבוֹנָה. ז כֻּלָּךְ יָפָה, רַעְיָתִי, וּמוּם אֵין בָּךְ.
ח אִתִּי מִלְּבָנוֹן, כַּלָּה, אִתִּי מִלְּבָנוֹן תָּבוֹאִי, תָּשׁוּרִי מֵרֹאשׁ
אֲמָנָה, מֵרֹאשׁ שְׂנִיר וְחֶרְמוֹן, מִמְּעֹנוֹת אֲרָיוֹת, מֵהַרְרֵי
נְמֵרִים. ט לִבַּבְתִּנִי, אֲחֹתִי כַלָּה, לִבַּבְתִּנִי בְּאַחַת מֵעֵינַיִךְ,
בְּאַחַד עֲנָק מִצַּוְּרֹנָיִךְ. י מַה יָּפוּ דֹדַיִךְ, אֲחֹתִי כַלָּה, מַה
טֹּבוּ דֹדַיִךְ מִיַּיִן, וְרֵיחַ שְׁמָנַיִךְ מִכָּל בְּשָׂמִים. יא נֹפֶת
תִּטֹּפְנָה שִׂפְתוֹתַיִךְ, כַּלָּה, דְּבַשׁ וְחָלָב תַּחַת לְשׁוֹנֵךְ, וְרֵיחַ
שַׂלְמֹתַיִךְ כְּרֵיחַ לְבָנוֹן. יב גַּן נָעוּל אֲחֹתִי כַלָּה, גַּל נָעוּל,
מַעְיָן חָתוּם. יג שְׁלָחַיִךְ פַּרְדֵּס רִמּוֹנִים, עִם פְּרִי מְגָדִים,
כְּפָרִים עִם נְרָדִים. יד נֵרְדְּ וְכַרְכֹּם, קָנֶה וְקִנָּמוֹן, עִם כָּל עֲצֵי
לְבוֹנָה, מֹר וַאֲהָלוֹת, עִם כָּל רָאשֵׁי בְשָׂמִים. טו מַעְיַן גַּנִּים,
בְּאֵר מַיִם חַיִּים, וְנֹזְלִים מִן לְבָנוֹן. טז עוּרִי צָפוֹן, וּבוֹאִי
תֵימָן, הָפִיחִי גַנִּי, יִזְּלוּ בְשָׂמָיו, יָבֹא דוֹדִי לְגַנּוֹ, וְיֹאכַל פְּרִי
מְגָדָיו.

ה

א בָּאתִי לְגַנִּי, אֲחֹתִי כַלָּה, אָרִיתִי מוֹרִי עִם בְּשָׂמִי, אָכַלְתִּי
יַעְרִי עִם דִּבְשִׁי, שָׁתִיתִי יֵינִי עִם חֲלָבִי, אִכְלוּ רֵעִים, שְׁתוּ
וְשִׁכְרוּ דּוֹדִים. ב אֲנִי יְשֵׁנָה וְלִבִּי עֵר, קוֹל דּוֹדִי דוֹפֵק,
פִּתְחִי לִי, אֲחֹתִי, רַעְיָתִי, יוֹנָתִי, תַמָּתִי, שֶׁרֹּאשִׁי נִמְלָא
טָל, קְוֻצּוֹתַי רְסִיסֵי לָיְלָה. ג פָּשַׁטְתִּי אֶת כֻּתָּנְתִּי, אֵיכָכָה
אֶלְבָּשֶׁנָּה, רָחַצְתִּי אֶת רַגְלַי, אֵיכָכָה אֲטַנְּפֵם. ד דּוֹדִי שָׁלַח
יָדוֹ מִן הַחוֹר, וּמֵעַי הָמוּ עָלָיו. ה קַמְתִּי אֲנִי לִפְתֹּחַ לְדוֹדִי,
וְיָדַי נָטְפוּ מוֹר, וְאֶצְבְּעֹתַי מוֹר עֹבֵר, עַל כַּפּוֹת הַמַּנְעוּל.
ו פָּתַחְתִּי אֲנִי לְדוֹדִי, וְדוֹדִי חָמַק עָבָר, נַפְשִׁי יָצְאָה בְדַבְּרוֹ,
בִּקַּשְׁתִּיהוּ וְלֹא מְצָאתִיהוּ, קְרָאתִיו וְלֹא עָנָנִי. ז מְצָאֻנִי
הַשֹּׁמְרִים הַסֹּבְבִים בָּעִיר, הִכּוּנִי פְצָעוּנִי, נָשְׂאוּ אֶת רְדִידִי
מֵעָלַי שֹׁמְרֵי הַחֹמוֹת. ח הִשְׁבַּעְתִּי אֶתְכֶם, בְּנוֹת יְרוּשָׁלָיִם,
אִם תִּמְצְאוּ אֶת דּוֹדִי, מַה תַּגִּידוּ לוֹ שֶׁחוֹלַת אַהֲבָה אָנִי.
ט מַה דּוֹדֵךְ מִדּוֹד, הַיָּפָה בַּנָּשִׁים, מַה דּוֹדֵךְ מִדּוֹד, שֶׁכָּכָה
הִשְׁבַּעְתָּנוּ. י דּוֹדִי צַח וְאָדוֹם, דָּגוּל מֵרְבָבָה. יא רֹאשׁוֹ כֶּתֶם
פָּז, קְוֻצּוֹתָיו תַּלְתַּלִּים, שְׁחֹרוֹת כָּעוֹרֵב. יב עֵינָיו כְּיוֹנִים עַל
אֲפִיקֵי מָיִם, רֹחֲצוֹת בֶּחָלָב, יֹשְׁבוֹת עַל מִלֵּאת. יג לְחָיָו
כַּעֲרוּגַת הַבֹּשֶׂם, מִגְדְּלוֹת מֶרְקָחִים, שִׂפְתוֹתָיו שׁוֹשַׁנִּים,
נֹטְפוֹת מוֹר עֹבֵר. יד יָדָיו גְּלִילֵי זָהָב, מְמֻלָּאִים בַּתַּרְשִׁישׁ,
מֵעָיו עֶשֶׁת שֵׁן, מְעֻלֶּפֶת סַפִּירִים. טו שׁוֹקָיו עַמּוּדֵי שֵׁשׁ,
מְיֻסָּדִים עַל אַדְנֵי פָז, מַרְאֵהוּ כַּלְּבָנוֹן, בָּחוּר כָּאֲרָזִים.
טז חִכּוֹ מַמְתַקִּים, וְכֻלּוֹ מַחֲמַדִּים, זֶה דוֹדִי וְזֶה רֵעִי, בְּנוֹת
יְרוּשָׁלָיִם.

ו

א אָנָה הָלַךְ דּוֹדֵךְ, הַיָּפָה בַּנָּשִׁים, אָנָה פָּנָה דוֹדֵךְ, וּנְבַקְשֶׁנּוּ
עִמָּךְ. ב דּוֹדִי יָרַד לְגַנּוֹ, לַעֲרֻגוֹת הַבֹּשֶׂם, לִרְעוֹת בַּגַּנִּים

וְלִלְקֹט שׁוֹשַׁנִּים. ‏ג‏ אֲנִי לְדוֹדִי, וְדוֹדִי לִי, הָרוֹעֶה בַּשּׁוֹשַׁנִּים.

‏ד‏ יָפָה אַתְּ רַעְיָתִי כְּתִרְצָה, נָאוָה כִּירוּשָׁלָיִם, אֲיֻמָּה כַּנִּדְגָּלוֹת. ‏ה‏ הָסֵבִּי עֵינַיִךְ מִנֶּגְדִּי, שֶׁהֵם הִרְהִיבֻנִי, שַׂעְרֵךְ כְּעֵדֶר הָעִזִּים, שֶׁגָּלְשׁוּ מִן הַגִּלְעָד. ‏ו‏ שִׁנַּיִךְ כְּעֵדֶר הָרְחֵלִים, שֶׁעָלוּ מִן הָרַחְצָה, שֶׁכֻּלָּם מַתְאִימוֹת, וְשַׁכֻּלָה אֵין בָּהֶם. ‏ז‏ כְּפֶלַח הָרִמּוֹן רַקָּתֵךְ, מִבַּעַד לְצַמָּתֵךְ. ‏ח‏ שִׁשִּׁים הֵמָּה מְלָכוֹת, וּשְׁמֹנִים פִּילַגְשִׁים, וַעֲלָמוֹת אֵין מִסְפָּר. ‏ט‏ אַחַת הִיא יוֹנָתִי תַמָּתִי, אַחַת הִיא לְאִמָּהּ, בָּרָה הִיא לְיוֹלַדְתָּהּ, רָאוּהָ בָנוֹת וַיְאַשְּׁרוּהָ, מְלָכוֹת וּפִילַגְשִׁים, וַיְהַלְלוּהָ. ‏י‏ מִי זֹאת הַנִּשְׁקָפָה כְּמוֹ שָׁחַר, יָפָה כַלְּבָנָה, בָּרָה כַּחַמָּה, אֲיֻמָּה כַּנִּדְגָּלוֹת. ‏יא‏ אֶל גִּנַּת אֱגוֹז יָרַדְתִּי לִרְאוֹת בְּאִבֵּי הַנָּחַל, לִרְאוֹת הֲפָרְחָה הַגֶּפֶן, הֵנֵצוּ הָרִמֹּנִים. ‏יב‏ לֹא יָדַעְתִּי, נַפְשִׁי שָׂמַתְנִי, מַרְכְּבוֹת עַמִּי נָדִיב.

<h2 style="text-align:center">ז</h2>

‏א‏ שׁוּבִי שׁוּבִי, הַשּׁוּלַמִּית, שׁוּבִי שׁוּבִי וְנֶחֱזֶה בָּךְ, מַה תֶּחֱזוּ בַּשּׁוּלַמִּית, כִּמְחֹלַת הַמַּחֲנָיִם. ‏ב‏ מַה יָּפוּ פְעָמַיִךְ בַּנְּעָלִים, בַּת נָדִיב, חַמּוּקֵי יְרֵכַיִךְ כְּמוֹ חֲלָאִים, מַעֲשֵׂה יְדֵי אָמָּן. ‏ג‏ שָׁרְרֵךְ אַגַּן הַסַּהַר, אַל יֶחְסַר הַמָּזֶג, בִּטְנֵךְ עֲרֵמַת חִטִּים, סוּגָה בַּשּׁוֹשַׁנִּים. ‏ד‏ שְׁנֵי שָׁדַיִךְ כִּשְׁנֵי עֳפָרִים, תָּאֳמֵי צְבִיָּה. ‏ה‏ צַוָּארֵךְ כְּמִגְדַּל הַשֵּׁן, עֵינַיִךְ בְּרֵכוֹת בְּחֶשְׁבּוֹן, עַל שַׁעַר בַּת רַבִּים, אַפֵּךְ כְּמִגְדַּל הַלְּבָנוֹן, צוֹפֶה פְּנֵי דַמָּשֶׂק. ‏ו‏ רֹאשֵׁךְ עָלַיִךְ כַּכַּרְמֶל, וְדַלַּת רֹאשֵׁךְ כָּאַרְגָּמָן, מֶלֶךְ אָסוּר בָּרְהָטִים. ‏ז‏ מַה יָּפִית וּמַה נָּעַמְתְּ, אַהֲבָה בַּתַּעֲנוּגִים. ‏ח‏ זֹאת קוֹמָתֵךְ דָּמְתָה לְתָמָר, וְשָׁדַיִךְ לְאַשְׁכֹּלוֹת. ‏ט‏ אָמַרְתִּי, אֶעֱלֶה בְתָמָר, אֹחֲזָה בְּסַנְסִנָּיו, וְיִהְיוּ נָא שָׁדַיִךְ כְּאֶשְׁכְּלוֹת הַגֶּפֶן, וְרֵיחַ אַפֵּךְ כַּתַּפּוּחִים. ‏י‏ וְחִכֵּךְ כְּיֵין הַטּוֹב, הוֹלֵךְ לְדוֹדִי לְמֵישָׁרִים, דּוֹבֵב שִׂפְתֵי יְשֵׁנִים. ‏יא‏ אֲנִי לְדוֹדִי, וְעָלַי תְּשׁוּקָתוֹ. ‏יב‏ לְכָה דוֹדִי, נֵצֵא הַשָּׂדֶה, נָלִינָה בַּכְּפָרִים. ‏יג‏ נַשְׁכִּימָה לַכְּרָמִים, נִרְאֶה אִם

פָּרְחָה הַגֶּפֶן, פִּתַּח הַסְּמָדַר, הֵנֵצוּ הָרִמּוֹנִים, שָׁם אֶתֵּן אֶת
דֹּדַי לָךְ. יד הַדּוּדָאִים נָתְנוּ רֵיחַ, וְעַל פְּתָחֵינוּ כָּל מְגָדִים,
חֲדָשִׁים גַּם יְשָׁנִים, דּוֹדִי, צָפַנְתִּי לָךְ.

ח

א מִי יִתֶּנְךָ כְּאָח לִי, יוֹנֵק שְׁדֵי אִמִּי, אֶמְצָאֲךָ בַחוּץ אֶשָּׁקְךָ,
גַּם לֹא יָבֻזוּ לִי. ב אֶנְהָגְךָ, אֲבִיאֲךָ אֶל בֵּית אִמִּי, תְּלַמְּדֵנִי,
אַשְׁקְךָ מִיַּיִן הָרֶקַח, מֵעֲסִיס רִמֹּנִי. ג שְׂמֹאלוֹ תַּחַת רֹאשִׁי,
וִימִינוֹ תְּחַבְּקֵנִי. ד הִשְׁבַּעְתִּי אֶתְכֶם, בְּנוֹת יְרוּשָׁלָיִם, מַה
תָּעִירוּ וּמַה תְּעֹרְרוּ אֶת הָאַהֲבָה עַד שֶׁתֶּחְפָּץ. ה מִי זֹאת
עֹלָה מִן הַמִּדְבָּר, מִתְרַפֶּקֶת עַל דּוֹדָהּ, תַּחַת הַתַּפּוּחַ
עוֹרַרְתִּיךָ, שָׁמָּה חִבְּלַתְךָ אִמֶּךָ, שָׁמָּה חִבְּלָה יְלָדַתְךָ.
ו שִׂימֵנִי כַחוֹתָם עַל לִבֶּךָ, כַּחוֹתָם עַל זְרוֹעֶךָ, כִּי עַזָּה כַמָּוֶת
אַהֲבָה, קָשָׁה כִשְׁאוֹל קִנְאָה, רְשָׁפֶיהָ רִשְׁפֵּי אֵשׁ,
שַׁלְהֶבֶתְיָה. ז מַיִם רַבִּים לֹא יוּכְלוּ לְכַבּוֹת אֶת הָאַהֲבָה,
וּנְהָרוֹת לֹא יִשְׁטְפוּהָ, אִם יִתֵּן אִישׁ אֶת כָּל הוֹן בֵּיתוֹ
בָּאַהֲבָה, בּוֹז יָבוּזוּ לוֹ. ח אָחוֹת לָנוּ קְטַנָּה, וְשָׁדַיִם אֵין לָהּ,
מַה נַּעֲשֶׂה לַאֲחוֹתֵנוּ בַּיּוֹם שֶׁיְּדֻבַּר בָּהּ. ט אִם חוֹמָה הִיא,
נִבְנֶה עָלֶיהָ טִירַת כָּסֶף, וְאִם דֶּלֶת הִיא, נָצוּר עָלֶיהָ לוּחַ
אָרֶז. י אֲנִי חוֹמָה, וְשָׁדַי כַּמִּגְדָּלוֹת, אָז הָיִיתִי בְעֵינָיו
כְּמוֹצְאֵת שָׁלוֹם. יא כֶּרֶם הָיָה לִשְׁלֹמֹה בְּבַעַל הָמוֹן, נָתַן אֶת
הַכֶּרֶם לַנֹּטְרִים, אִישׁ יָבִא בְּפִרְיוֹ אֶלֶף כָּסֶף. יב כַּרְמִי שֶׁלִּי
לְפָנָי, הָאֶלֶף לְךָ שְׁלֹמֹה, וּמָאתַיִם לְנֹטְרִים אֶת פִּרְיוֹ.
יג הַיּוֹשֶׁבֶת בַּגַּנִּים, חֲבֵרִים מַקְשִׁיבִים לְקוֹלֵךְ, הַשְׁמִיעִנִי.
יד בְּרַח דּוֹדִי, וּדְמֵה לְךָ לִצְבִי, אוֹ לְעֹפֶר הָאַיָּלִים, עַל הָרֵי
בְשָׂמִים.

❧ Appendix

❧ Biographical Sketches

Appendix:
The Mussar Movement

Shmuel, the *amora*, once exclaimed, "All the paths of the heavenly bodies are clear to me; all but the path of a comet" (*Berachos* 58). One can readily apply the image of the comet to R' Yisrael of Salant, the founder of the *mussar* movement (which was basically concerned with ethical behavior). The path of his life, like that of the comet, cannot be understood — from Salant to Vilna, to Kovna, to Warsaw, Berlin, Paris, Memel and Koenigsberg. We cannot determine the guiding principle behind his travels — we will touch upon it later — but we certainly stand agape at the brilliance of this human comet and the illuminated train which followed in his wake — his students who cultivated and developed the *mussar* movement.

❦ ❦ ❦

R' Yisrael, the son of the rabbi of Zamger, Lithuania, was born in 1810. At the early age of ten, he already gave highly complicated and incisive discourses to audiences. While yet a young man, he was known as an outstanding scholar of world renown (גְּדוֹל הַדּוֹר) and was offered a position as a main teacher (רֹאשׁ יְשִׁיבָה) in one of the celebrated *yeshivos* of Vilna. However, as soon as R' Yisrael sensed that the elderly head of the *yeshivah* felt a slight when the students streamed en masse to his *shiurim* (Torah lectures), he immediately left the prestigious post.

The exceptional care he took to avoid hurting another, which this story demonstrates, was to become an ingredient of the future *mussar* movement. *Mitzvos* involving man's obligation to his fellow man (בֵּין אָדָם לַחֲבֵרוֹ) were to be observed no less scrupulously then obligations towards Hashem (בֵּין אָדָם לַמָּקוֹם).

On many an occasion, R' Yisrael, the giant of a scholar, could be found in public, hammer and nails in hand, repairing a faulty shutter — of a stranger — lest the clatter it caused when blown about by the wind would rob the sleep of nearby neighbors — who were, also, strangers to him.

When R' Yisrael lived in the trade center, Memel, he made it his business to see that a fire was kept burning at night in the heating-stove

of the *beis knesses*. He felt that the wagon-drivers needed a warm resting spot. And when the local communal hostel was in such a state of dilapidation that it posed a threat to the poor who used it, he complained with all his might. His complaints fell on deaf ears and R' Yisrael moved into the hostel and slept on its floor, until the repairs were made.

If, after participating at the wedding of a student, R' Yisrael found that the hour was late, he would sleep in the hall rather than go home and risk waking the neighbors by knocking at his own door. His students once asked him before *Pesach* what *halachic* safeguards they should take while baking *matzos*. He instructed them to take care not to rush the widow who kneaded the dough. "Although speed in the kneading is important," he said, "it should not come at the expense of pressing a widow."

Many are the stories of R' Yisrael's exceptional sensitivity in dealing with people. Perhaps the most moving of them is that told of his last moments on earth. This giant of a man was about to return his soul to his Maker and give an accounting before Him. His entire life had been one of unremitting testing of self and constant striving to self-perfection. Most surely, he had much to ponder on how to prepare himself properly for the final moment. *Chazal* (the Sages) say: "For this, let each man pray to You when he comes upon the time" (*Tehillim* 32:6) — that time is the day of death (*Berachos* 8). And yet, R' Yisrael spent his last moments calming the man who attended him at his bedside. He explained, in restful tones, that the man need not fear to remain alone with the body of a man who has died. The dead cannot cause any harm whatsoever and the common fear which a body arouses is meaningless and without basis.

❧ ❧ ❧

The stories are, indeed, instructive, yet they reveal but a single aspect of R' Yisrael's *mussar* movement. The constant unbiased examination of each act and thought and keeping one's purpose and goal constantly in mind were features which lay at the very heart of R' Yisrael's philosophy. He would say, "Man must climb as stubbornly and diligently as the mountain climber. He must strive to reach the peak and be aware that the abyss lies below!" One can come to this through the study of *mussar*.

The Torah contains passages of *mussar* — the admonitions (אַזְהָרוֹת) and rebuke (תּוֹכָחוֹת); Prophets (נְבִיאִים) has long sections of admonishment and Sacred Writings (כְּתוּבִים) has full books of *mussar* such as *Mishlei* and *Koheles*. The *Mishnah* includes a *mussar* work — *Avos*; and

mussar discourses are part and parcel of the Talmud. Many of our teacher/scholars have written works of *mussar* and devotion. These are the materials to be studied.

R' Yisrael strongly suggested that one allocate the time concentrated on *mussar*, variously. One part should be spent accumulating knowledge of the material, another on making it an integral part of himself. He should review a single discourse, again and again, with enthusiasm — "with burning lips and tear-filled eyes" — until his heart would open up to it.

The head of the *yeshivah* of Slonim and R' Yisrael once found themselves sharing a room in an inn. They "spoke in learning" until the hour grew late and R' Yisrael suggested to the *rosh yeshivah* that he retire. He put out the light and, when he thought that the *rosh yeshivah* had fallen asleep, he removed his shoes and, pacing back and forth in his stockinged feet, for the remainder of the night, he repeated the final verse of *Koheles* with exceptional feeling, in a whispering voice: "In the end all is heard, fear God (אֱלֹקִים); observe His *mitzvos*. For that is the entire man."

❀   ❀   ❀

We perhaps may feel that the study of *mussar* is meant to help us avoid transgressions and add to our store of *mitzvos*. But that was hardly the goal of R' Yisrael and his disciples. For what transgressions did he commit? He was heard to confess, tearfully, for fifteen years, that he once forgot to look through his pockets before *Shabbos*, as *Chazal* (the Sages) recommend. He could be wrapped in concern, for hours on end, because he failed to pronounce a *berachah* without its full measure of thoughtful purpose (כַּוָּנָה). And once, *once* in his life, when he was fighting the cholera epidemic in Vilna, he became angry.

No! His study of *mussar* was not meant to encourage an examination of his deeds, but of his intentions. To him, it was not sufficient that man should only perform *mitzvos* and avoid transgressions; he must labor to change his nature and temperament and he must hold control over all his thoughts. "It is easier to go through the entire Talmud," he would say, "than to change a single trait." *Mussar* penetrates to the secret places of a man's personality and reveals all its twists and turns; it casts a cold light of examination on the world. "*Mussar*," said R' Yisrael, "shows that the heretics are far, far, from happy in this world and the pious very removed from the happiness of the next . . ." The man who studies *mussar* and governs his will and his thoughts shall inherit both worlds. He it is who is the *mishnaic* hero, conquering his will; the man of

wealth, happy with his lot and the wise man who foresees the future.

❀ ❀ ❀

The railroads came into widespread use in R' Yisrael's time. The train and its conduct provided him with three facts which served to exemplify lessons for life: He who comes late, by even a moment, misses the train; if the locomotive jumps the rail, even slightly, the entire train of cars may be overturned; a passenger without a ticket is subject to punishment.

Let us turn our attention to the last of these, "the passenger without a ticket," and see how it influenced R' Yisrael. He taught that nothing is free of charge; we pay for everything in this world. One receives Hashem's favors and repays His benevolence by proclaiming the glory of Heaven and magnifying the name of the Creator. Should he not do so, as R' Yisrael put it, "he runs the risk of consuming his entire afterlife reward in a dish of turnips."

"The world," he would say, "is an expensive hotel and one is required to pay in cash. There is one way to avoid payment. Join the staff; members of the hotel staff enjoy the food without paying . . ."

This attitude gives us an insight into understanding his unceasing labors in the service, and for the benefit, of the Jewish world at large. He battled to introduce the study of *mussar* into Lithuania; he took himself into a self-imposed exile in relatively loosely observant communities — Berlin, Paris, Memel, Koenigsberg — far from family and disciples, far from the deep-seated Jewish surroundings with which he was familiar. This explains why he organized circles for the study of Judaism, among university students; why he strove to have the Talmud translated into German to give assimilated families an easier road by which they might return to their roots. He would relate how he once slipped and fell on the streets of Paris. "But," he said, "I had no fear on falling. I had no personal reason for my stay in Paris. I was a soldier in the service of Hashem. I felt that He would keep me from harm." Everything for the sake of the Creator, as a member of His staff.

❀ ❀ ❀

R' Yisrael of Salant — the soldier in the service of his Creator — passed away in 1883, in Koenigsberg, far from home.

His last words, repeated by his bedside attendant, were, "Our Sages say that envy, desire and (the pursuit of) honor remove *the* man from the world. Do you know why the word *man* appears with the definite article, *the*, before it? Because even *the* man, that is the loftiest of men, is liable to fall into the trap of envy, desire and honor."

R' Yisrael left no legacy of material goods behind, other than a pair of *tefillin*. But his spiritual estate was a bursting treasure-house of thoughts and a coterie of disciples, towering giants of the Torah, who had drawn from his well. Among them were *R' Yitzchak Blazer*, the rabbi of Russia's capital, Peterburg, *R' Naftali Amsterdam*, who served as rabbi in Moscow and Helsingfors, and others. His disciples were living examples of modesty and piety, strove constantly to rise to greater heights and subjected themselves to vigorous examination of self. But they were, when all is said and done, individuals; they did not constitute a movement. Even the *mussar* centers which R' Yisrael had labored mightily to establish and develop in many a city attracted only a scattering.

It was the foremost of his disciples, *R' Simchah Zissel* (1824-1898), who gave the study of *mussar* an expanded base and formed the *mussar* movement.

The Alter of Kelm (הַסַּבָּא מִקֶעלְם), as he became known, poured his energy into educating and shaping the personalities who were to stand at the fore during the flood tide of the movement in the generation that followed. They were to put their imprint on the *yeshivos* of Lithuania in the period which preceded the Holocaust.

❈ ❈ ❈

The *Alter* of Kelm, however, spent even more energy in shaping his own character then he did in developing his disciples. He was weakly, so much so, that he chose a small *esrog*, that it not weigh down his hand during the *Hallel* service. Yet, he did not allow himself more than an hour of sleep a day. And, even so, he would rebuke himself before retiring for dropping off to sleep like a horse. When the hour came to its end he would leap up in a rush, so as not to sink into idleness. After his many fasts, he would have exceptionally bony fish to slow down the act of eating. When he suffered from pains in his feet he examined his deeds and discovered his "sin" — he had hurried *once* more quickly than was proper to enter the *succah*.

His son and son-in-law, who followed in his footsteps, were once asked to describe R' Simchah Zissel. *R' Nachum Ze'ev Ziev* answered that his father's behavior could be likened to that of a man with a sharp sword thrust into his throat. Any careless move could cost him his life. *R' Zvi Hirsch Broide* said that his father-in-law might be compared to an animal trainer in a cage with a fierce leopard; he can never allow his attention to wander. Just so did the *Alter* of Kelm keep control over his will and thoughts by his constant attention. He could recall in the

evening all that had passed through his mind during the day and examine it critically.

❧ ❧ ❧

R' Simchah Zissel established and conducted a *yeshivah* for the select — *Beis HaTalmud* — in Kelm. Although its student body never rose above thirty in number, it became world famous. The emphasis was on quality. A man's personality and behavior went through a process of refining and polishing. The *Alter* was highly critical and demanded perfection of his students. He once saw one glance up and look out during the period of study; he gave up any hope for the student's future, because he could not overcome his curiosity. And when another hopped over a low barrier, he was shaken. For if a barrier could not hold him back, he might throw off *all* restraints.

Kelm was the seat of the workshop where his thoughts bubbled over. His concentration and depth of mind, coupled to a rare brilliance and deeply emotional feel for morality, produced thousands of penetrating ideas, each with a world of meaning in itself, expressing an approach which profoundly affected the future leaders of the *mussar* movement, most of whom were his disciples; his thoughts in turn gave birth to theirs.

R' Simchah Zissel often said that the remarks of *Chazal* (the Sages) were stars and the ethical perspective a telescope which magnified them. That telescope in his hands did, indeed, reveal hidden worlds.

❧ ❧ ❧

Kelm — the symbol of unceasing, penetrating demand on the soul! Unceasing — not in terms of time, but constantly driving deeper and deeper into the chambers within chambers, the secret hiding places of a man's inner self.

Kelm — where thoughts were drawn from, and anchored in, the Torah: "Let us lift our hearts with outstretched palms" (נִשָּׂא לְבָבֵנוּ אֶל כַּפָּיִם — *Eichah* 3:41); this points to the possibility that we can lay bare all that lies hidden in our hearts. "Man is born a wild ass" (וְעַיִר פֶּרֶא אָדָם יִוָּלֵד — *Iyov* 11:12); from that "ass" one must create a man. "And Avraham lifted up his eyes" (וַיִּשָּׂא אַבְרָהָם אֶת עֵינָיו — *Bereishis* 22:4); even the uplifting of the eyelids must be the product of deliberate thought.

R' Simchah Zissel died as he had lived. Before he passed away, he laundered all of his clothes and distributed the cleaned and ironed clothes to the poor. After doing so, weak and dying though he was, he

leapt out of bed, wishing to see if, perhaps, his weakness stemmed from sloth. In his last moments, someone fanned him and just before he expired, he called on his last reserves of strength and folded the fan. It was not his and he did not want it to be damaged.

❀ ❀ ❀

Mussar was still the possession and concern of the few select lofty souls; it had not as yet come to be a movement. But the students of the Alter of Kelm stormed the yeshivos and conquered them. They started a revolution. They introduced a new world view and poured the yeshivos into a new mold. A daily period for the study of mussar was introduced into the yeshivah curriculum. They saw to the appointment of a mashgiach (מַשְׁגִּיחַ), a figure who would be among those at the helm of the yeshivah and would direct a program of ethical thought and would oversee the development of personality and behavior of the members of the student body. He would take it upon himself to deliver a weekly mussar discourse to a general assembly and would see to the formation of groups devoted to the study of mussar (וַעֲדִים). These innovations were accepted only after a long, hard struggle.

Today they are no longer innovations. They have been adopted by all yeshivos and have become part of a tradition. Before World War II and the Holocaust, a dual hierarchy could be found in each yeshivah. The rosh yeshivah, often as not a disciple of R' Chaim of Brisk, directed the general Torah studies and, at his side, could be found the mashgiach, most often a member of the Kelm circle. Not infrequently — and most especially in the large and important institutions — the rosh yeshivah stood in the shadow of the mashgiach and it was the mashgiach, and not the rosh yeshivah, who put his stamp on the students.

❀ ❀ ❀

Though there were variations on the theme, the central school of thought in mussar was, and remained, that of Kelm. The most outstanding of R' Simchah Zissel's disciples was one of his later proteges, R' Yerucham HaLevi Levovitz (1876-1936), the mashgiach of Mir. He developed his teacher's views in both breadth and depth and planned to write an enlarged edition of, plus commentary to, R' Simchah Zissel's works. His thought embraced all fields and the esteem in which he was held in Mir defies description. R' Eliahu Dessler called him "the profoundest thinker of our generation."

R' Yosef Leib Bloch (1860-1930), the rosh yeshivah of Telshe, was a product of the school of Kelm. He, himself, introduced mussar into his

yeshivah. His discourses were called, as befits a *rosh yeshivah, shiurim* (שִׁיעוּרֵי דַּת) and dealt with topics such as Creation, God's conduct of the universe, the parallelism of the mundane and celestial worlds. Not rarely, he touched upon the threshold of *kabbalah*.

R' Eliahu Dessler (1891-1954) could point to a long family association with *mussar*. His grandfather was a companion to the *Alter* of Kelm, his father a disciple of the *Alter* and he, himself, was a son-in-law of R' Simchah Zissel's son. In 1927 he accepted an invitation to serve as a rabbi in London and there, he was very instrumental in developing groups for the study of Torah and in establishing the Torah center in Gateshead. London was far from the thriving centers of *mussar*. But that very distance and his awareness of the problems which were the concern of the London intelligentsia moved him to develop an original all-embracing mode of thought. Principles of *chasidus* (חֲסִידוּת) were introduced into the warp and woof of *mussar*. *Kabbalistic* ideas were explained in terms of moral improvement. He used the language of science, psychology and education in formulating the reflections of *Chazal* (the Sages). The series of his work *Michtav Me'Eliahu* (מִכְתָּב מֵאֵלִיָּהוּ) is a mine of original conceptions, profound and currently relevant, built on the foundations of *mussar* and the words of *Chazal*. In the last years of his life, he served as *mashgiach* of the *yeshivah* of Ponoviez in Bnei Brak.

Many others of those who studied in Kelm served as *mashgichim* in the *yeshivos*. *R' Yehudah Leib Chasman* (1869-1935) arrived in Volozhin to learn at the feet of the *Netziv* (R' Naftali Zvi Yehudah Berlin) and R' Chaim of Brisk after having been in Kelm. He established a *yeshivah* in Shtuzin and, in 1926, he went up to *Eretz Yisrael* to become the *mashgiach* of the Chevron Yeshivah. His approach is totally that of the Kelm school — a fierce demand and a scrupulous constant watch, lest one fall from the tightrope stretched across the abyss.

R' Yosef Leib Nenedik was the *mashgiach* of the *yeshivah* of Kletzk until the Holocaust. *R' Eliahu Dushnitzer* (1876-1949) served as *mashgiach* of the *yeshivos* of Radin and Lomza. In 1926 he went up to Eretz Yisrael at the head of a group of students and founded a branch of the Lomza Yeshivah in Petach Tikvah. *R' Shlomo Harkavy* (1890-1941) was the *mashgiach* of the Grodno Yeshivah until its destruction in the Holocaust. *R' Abba Grossbard* (1896-1946) was the *mashgiach* of the Ponoviez Yeshivah in Lithuania and, after the Holocaust, he served as the first *mashgiach* of the re-established Ponoviez Yeshivah in Bnei Brak.*

**R' Moshe Rosenstein of Lomza* (1880-1941) was also a product of Kelm. But in his self-mortification he leans to the Novharodok school of thought.

Finally, let us mention two long-lived figures, the last of the giants, who were to portray the Golden Age of the *mussar* movement to a later generation. *R' Eliahu Lopian* (1872-1970) can be numbered among the last of the disciples of the *Alter* of Kelm. He was a friend to R' Yerucham of Mir and served as *mashgiach* of the *Yeshivah Ketanah* of Kelm. In 1950, he went up to *Eretz Yisrael* and became *mashgiach* of the *yeshivah* in K'far Chasidim, a post which he filled until his death. *R' Yechezkel Levenstein* (1884-1974) served as *mashgiach* of the *yeshivah* of Mir until World War II and went with the *yeshivah,* as a whole, to Japanese-occupied Shanghai, and then to the United States. After the passing away, in 1954, of R' Eliahu Dessler, he was invited to become *mashgiach* of the Ponoviez Yeshivah in Bnei Brak. Those who heard his talks still remember them with trembling. They expressed an overpowering sense of the fear of punishment (יִרְאַת הָעוֹנֶשׁ) and were an appeal to contemplate and see a proof for faith in everything.

All, all, belong to Kelm.

Kelm, in all its variations, was the essential center of the building of *mussar*; *Slobodka* and *Novharodok* were the adjoining, opposing wings which grew off and out of it. *Kelm* put man under a microscope; *Slobodka* placed him on a pedestal; *Novharodok* reduced him to naught.

The *Alter of Slobodka, R' Nasan Tzvi Finkel* (1849-1927), was among the most eminent disciples and aides of the *Alter* of Kelm. He was an esteemed figure and a gifted educator. In 1882 he established the Slobodka Yeshivah which became one of the greatest and most famous of the Lithuanian *yeshivos.* And from its halls he sent forth groups of select students to build and strengthen many *yeshivos* in the length and breadth of Lithuania and Russia. In 1926 he went up to *Eretz Yisrael* to establish the *yeshivah* in Chevron which later moved to Jerusalem. And there, in the Holy City, he passed away.

He viewed man as a lofty creature, the apex of Creation, destined for *Gan Eden* (Paradise). Through his sin, he was banished from there. But should he improve his ways, he can recreate a *Gan Eden* of his own making and return to it. Our forefathers, Avraham, Yitzchak and Yaakov recreated it within their tents; Israel did likewise in the desert wilderness; the *yeshivah* is an earthly *Gan Eden*! We cannot overestimate the latent powers of man.

The wise say that we can recognize the intelligent child. When given a rock, he casts it away; when handed a nut, he retains it. True judgment lies in understanding that a tasty kernel lies beneath the hard exterior.

The view of man's greatness did not pass away with the *Alter*. It is reflected in the probing work *Toras Avraham* of R' Avraham Grodzinski who became the *mashgiach* of Slobodka. And the *Alter's* son-in-law, R' Yitzchak Isaac Sher, the *rosh yeshivah* of Slobodka, would in every talk speak of man's potential greatness and note that the latent loftiness makes it possible to subject him to great demands.

The present *mashgiach* of Slobodka, R' Avraham Pollack, recalls: On the day of remembrance (*Yahrzeit*) of the *gaon* R' Isaac Sher, I visited the *mashgiach* of Ponoviez, the *gaon* R' Yechezkel Levenstein. He asked what had been said in the talk that had been held in Slobodka in memory of R' Isaac. I replied that they had quoted R' Isaac's statement: The first commandment given to Adam had been to create a *Gan Eden* — "And He placed him in the garden to work it and guard it." The *mashgiach* of Ponoviez broke out in laughter and said that he, a product of Kelm, exhorts students to constantly fear *Gehinnom* — but in Slobodka they run up the flag of *Gan Eden*.

❧ ❧ ❧

Novharodok was the other, opposite pole. R' Yosef Yoizel Horowitz, the *Alter of Novharodok,* (1848-1920), was oblivious of man. In Slobodka they dressed like the nobility; in Novharodok they wore cast-off tatters. When a student was sent to establish one of the many tens of its branches that were founded by the *yeshivah,* he would be provided with an outfit. The public mussar discourses in Novharodok were sharp and uncompromising, and in their zeal to improve themselves, the students insisted on frank criticism from their peers.

The extreme was central to the makeup of the *Alter of Novharodok* — extremism and unbounded trust in Hashem. When he decided to closet himself, he did so with a vengeance. He pierced the wall of his hut with two apertures and, on the outer wall, labeled one "meat," the other "dairy" and retired within, locking the door behind him. Some unrecorded soul took it upon himself to pass meals through the openings. When he ended his period of self-imposed solitary confinement, he broke the lock, emerged and, wandering into the dark forest, prayed to Hashem for a light. Of a sudden, a man approached, passed him a light — and disappeared into the forest. When the *Alter* later established his *yeshivah* in Novharodok, he placed that light on the east wall — a witness to faith that bore fruit.

He brought up generations of students to have such unshakeable faith and founded a many-branched network of tens of *yeshivos* in a period of danger and revolution — and without funds.

"I never asked myself," he would say, "if I could do anything or not. All that concerned me was if it was necessary to do so." And when it was necessary to act, he did and succeeded.

Once, on the day before the *seder* night, there was not a penny to be found in the house and the larder was empty — no wine, no *matzos*, nothing at all. His wife, the *rebbetzin*, began to cry but the *Alter* could not understand her tears. "Why all the commotion?" he asked. "We'll get the minimum measure of *matzah* (כְּזַיִת מַצָּה) to fulfill the *mitzvah*. And as far as wine for the four cups, the *halachah* states that one should go ask from door to door to obtain the money for it. I'll do just that." As he was speaking, the door opened and in walked the mailman, bearing a letter containing a sum of money sufficient for celebrating the festival with joy.

His outlook on life carried itself over to his disciples. *R' Yitzchak Elchanan Waldshein,* one of his great disciples, commented: When Israel was about to leave Egypt, they were commanded to slaughter the *Pesach* sacrifice (קָרְבַּן פֶּסַח) and smear of its blood on the lintel and the two doorposts. *Rashi* says that this (the lintel plus the doorposts) represents the three forefathers, Avraham, Yitzchak and Yaakov. Here we have the very essence of Novharodok — to aspire to the extreme! Israel is just emerging from utter corruption (מ"ט שַׁעֲרֵי טוּמְאָה); this is but their first *mitzvah*. And with it they are already told to stretch up to the lintel; they are given an allusion that they are to reach the level of the forefathers! A demand for the extreme without any intervening stages.

Biographical Sketches

R' Yisrael of Salant
(1810 — 1883)
[work: *Or Yisrael*]

R' Yisrael was born in 5570 in Zager, Lithuania. At the age of ten he already delivered involved public discourses of depth. And even as a young married man, he was widely known as one of the leading lights of his generation. He invested his vast knowledge, powers of analysis and energy in the study of *mussar* (ethics) and its propagation in the "houses of *mussar*" and study centers which he founded. He himself attained the highest possible level for a human being. It is of him that the *Alter* of Novharodok said, "I have seen one man blessed and content." He passed away on the 25th of Shevat 5643.

R' Simchah Zissel of Kelm — the Alter of Kelm
(1824 — 1898)
[works: *Chochmah U'Mussar; Kisvei HaGaon RaShaz* in ms.]

The *Alter* of Kelm was born in 5584 in Kelm, Lithuania. At his *bar mitzvah*, he gave a discourse on the completion of all of the order of *Nezikin*. In his youth he studied with his father, the *dayan* of Kelm and, after his marriage, he was a closely attached disciple of his master, R' Yisrael of Salant, who spoke of him as the wise one among his students. He combined meditative solitude and intense study — he slept all of two and a half hours a day — with devoted efforts to educate others, at first in Zager and afterwards in Kelm. It was in Kelm that he founded the "Talmud Torah" for select students. It was to become the preparatory school for most of the masters of *mussar*. He passed away on the 8th of Menachem Av 5658.

R' Yitzchak Blazer of Peterburg
(1837 — 1907)
[work: *Kochvei Or*]

R' Yitzchak Blazer, also known as R' Itzele Peterburger, was born in 5597 in Shnipishok, an outlying neighborhood of Vilna. His father published the

discourse which he held on the completion of the tractate *Bava Kamma* at the age of fourteen in which he gave fourteen solutions (tallying with his age) to a particular problem. After his marriage, he moved to Kovno where he became numbered among the closest disciples of R' Yisrael of Salant. Following his master's injunction, he accepted the rabbinate of the capital city of czarist Russia, Peterburg, at present Leningrad. There he published his work in *halachah, P'ri Yitzchak*. In his desire for a more spiritual life, he left his rabbinical post to lead a *kollel* (study group) of young married men in Kovno. He was among those who laid the foundations of the *yeshivah* of Slobodka and together with the *Alter* of Novharodok, R' Yosef Yoizel Horowitz, he established many *kollelim*; he can also be counted among the founders of the *yeshivah* of Slutzk. After the passing of his friend of R' Simchah Zissel he headed the Talmud Torah in Kelm. In 5664 he went up to *Eretz Yisrael* where he led the *kollel* of Vilna and Zamut in *Yerushalayim*. He passed away in the Holy City on the 11th of Menachem Av 5667.

R' Yosef Yoizel Horowitz — the Alter of Novharodok
(1848 — 1920)
[work: *Madregas Ha'Adam*]

R' Yosef Yoizel was born in 5608 in Plongian, Lithuania; his father was the town *dayan*. He was gifted with supreme intellectual ability and a fearless spirit, but upon the death of his father-in-law, he put his efforts into making a livelihood in trade. After a meeting and an incisive talk with R' Yisrael of Salant, in Memel, he left business and became a member of R' Yisrael's *kollel* in Kovna. For long periods of time, he lived in self-imposed solitude from which he emerged through the influence of the *Alter* of Kelm. He then threw himself with great vigor into the founding of *kollelim* throughout Lithuania. Afterwards he established his *yeshivah* in Novharodok which became the center for a network of *yeshivos* throughout Russia. While war raged and revolution clamored, he battled in deep-seated trust to maintain his Torah activities without compromise. He passed away in Kiev on the 17th of Kislev 5680.

R' Nasan Tzvi Finkel — the Alter of Slobodka
(1849 — 1927)
[work: *Or HaTzafun*]

R' Nasan Tzvi was born in 5609 in Rasein, Lithuania. At the age of fifteen he was already famed as an outstanding Torah scholar. R' Simchah Zissel took him under his wing and nurtured him. He was the right-hand man of the *Alter* of Kelm in directing a Talmud Torah which R' Simchah Zissel had founded in Grobin. R' Nasan Tzvi afterwards established a *kollel* in Slobodka

and in 5642 he founded the *yeshivah* there. It was then that he became known as the *Alter* of Slobodka. From his *yeshivah* he sent out groups of students to establish and strengthen *yeshivos* in the length and breadth of Lithuania and Russia. In 5685 he went up to *Eretz Yisrael* and founded the *yeshivah* in Chevron which later moved to *Yerushalayim*. It was there that he passed away on the 29th of Shevat 5687.

R' Yosef Leib Bloch of Telshe
(1860 — 1929)
[work: *Shiurei Da'as*]

R' Yosef Leib was born on the twenty-first of Shevat 5620 in Rasein, Lithuania. At the age of fourteen he went to Kelm to study with R' Eliezer Gordon of Telshe, who later took him as his son-in-law. He served as rabbi of Burna and Shtuba and, with the passing of his father-in-law, he became the rabbi of Telshe and the head of its *yeshivah*. His words on Jewish thought are ordered on the model of *halachic* writings and he gave them the name *Shiurei Da'as* (analogous to *Shiurei Torah* or *halachah*). He passed away in Telshe on the ninth of Marcheshvan 5690.

R' Yehudah Leib Chasman
(1869 — 1935)
[work: *Or Yahel*]

R' Yehudah Leib Chasman was born in 5629 in the town Irya in the Vilna area. He studied with R' Nasan Tzvi Finkel and R' Yitzchak Blazer in Slobodka. In 5648 he traveled to Kelm and became one of the most prominent disciples of R' Simchah Zissel, the *Alter* of Kelm. From Kelm he went to Volozhin to study under R' Naftali Tzvi Yehudah Berlin (the Netziv) and R' Chaim Soloveitchik of Brisk. From there he returned to Kelm. He subsequently became *mashgiach* of the *yeshivah* of Telshe and later served as rabbi first in Lodvinova and then in Shtutzin where he founded a *yeshivah*. In 5686 he went up to *Eretz Yisrael* and served as the *mashgiach* of the Chevron-Slobodka *yeshivah* until he passed away on the 11th of Marcheshvan 5696.

R' Yitzchak Isaac Sher of Slobodka
(1875 — 1952)
[work: *Leket Sichos Mussar*]

R' Yitzchak Isaac was born in 5635 in Halosk, Russia. In his youth he studied under R' Baruch Ber Leibovitz and in the *yeshivah* of Volozhin. Subsequently, he became attached to R' Nasan Tzvi Finkel, the *Alter* of

Slobodka, whose daughter he married. He continued his studies first in Kelm and later in Mir. He was appointed as a *rosh yeshivah* in Slobodka to teach and give *mussar*. In 5685 when his father-in-law, the head of the Slobodka *yeshivah*, went up to *Eretz Yisrael* to found the *yeshivah* in Chevron, he became the sole *rosh yeshivah* of the Slobodka *yeshivah*. After the Holocaust, he reestablished the *yeshivah* of Slobodka in Bnei Brak and it was there that he passed away on the 10th of Shevat 5712.

R' Yerucham HaLevi Levovitz of Mir
(1876 — 1936)
[works: *Da'as Chochmah U'Mussar; Da'as Torah*]

R' Yerucham was born in 5636 in Luban near Slutzk. In his youth he studied under R' Nasan Tzvi Finkel in Slobodka. From there, he journeyed to Kelm and had the good fortune to study for a year with the *Alter* of Kelm, who put his formative stamp on him. He also learned at the feet of R' Zvi Broide and R' Nachum Ze'ev of Kelm. He served as *mashgiach*, spiritual supervisor, in the *yeshivah* of Radin and was then invited to occupy the post of *mashgiach* of Mir. He edited the works of his master, the *Alter* of Kelm. His own talks, given in his style and at his behest, are collected in the volumes of *Da'as Chochmah U'Mussar* and *Da'as Torah*. He passed away in Mir on the 18th of Sivan 5696.

R' Yosef Leib Nenedik of Kletzk
[work: *Rachashei Ilan* in ms.]

R' Yosef Leib studied in Telshe and afterwards in Kelm under R' Simchah Zissel. He and his friends, R' Yerucham (of Mir) and R' Eliahu Lopian, directed the preparatory *yeshivah* in Kelm. He later became *mashgiach* in the *yeshivos* of Lomza, Radin and Grodno. He served as *mashgiach* in the *yeshivah* of Kletzk until it, and its students, fell in the Holocaust.

R' Eliahu Lopian of Kelm and K'far Chasidim
(1872 — 1970)
[work: *Lev Eliahu*]

R' Eliahu was born in Greiva, Poland in 5632. When he was some ten years of age, his parents migrated to the United States. He, however, remained behind to study in Lomza and later in Kelm under the tutelage of the *Alter* of Kelm. He, together with R' Yerucham (of Mir) and R' Yosef Leib Nenedik, established the preparatory *yeshivah* in Kelm and he headed it for

many years. In 5688 he was invited to teach in the *yeshivah* Etz Chaim of London and in 5710 he went up to *Eretz Yisrael*. At first he established himself in *Yerushalayim* and afterwards he became *mashgiach* of the *yeshivah* K'nesses Chizkiyahu which moved from Zichron Yaakov to K'far Chasidim. He served in that capacity until he passed away on the 20th of Elul 5730.

R' Moshe Rosenstein of Lomza
(1880 — 1941)
[works: *Yesodei HaDa'as; Ahavas Achim*]

R' Moshe was born in 5640 in Oizvinet, Lithuania. He studied in the *yeshivah* of Telshe. Through the influence of R' Yerucham Levovitz he was drawn to the study of *mussar* and went to study in Kelm. He became *mashgiach* of the *yeshivah* in Shtuba and afterwards in Lomza until the outbreak of World War I. He went with the *yeshivah* in its wanderings to Vilna and Plongian. There he passed away on the 13th of Nissan 5701.

R' Avraham Joffen of Novharodok
(? — 1970)
[work: *G'vilei Esh*]

R' Avraham was known in his youth as the *ilui* (genius) of Pinsk. After having studied in the *yeshivah* of R' Sender Shapira in Krinik, he reached Novharodok and became one of its prized students. In 5673 he married a daughter of the *Alter* of Novharodok and became the *rosh yeshivah,* in which position he was responsible for the network of the *yeshivos* of Novharodok. After R' Yosef Yoizel passed away, he became the head of the movement of Novharodok, first in Russia, then Poland, and after World War II in the United States and *Eretz Yisrael*. He passed away on *Erev Pesach* 5730 and is buried beside his great father-in-law in *Har HaMenuchot, Yerushalayim.*

R' Avraham Grodzinski of Slobodka
(1883 — 1944)
[work: *Toras Avraham*]

R' Avraham was born in 5643 in Warsaw. At the age of seventeen he arrived in Slobodka and rose in Torah and piety. He was sent as one of a group to strengthen the *yeshivah* of Telshe; there he gave both *halachic* discourses and *mussar* talks. When he returned to Slobodka, he was appointed to repeat the talks of R' Nasan Tzvi Finkel and he was the moving spirit in the *kollel*. After the *Alter* of Slobodka went up to *Eretz Yisrael* to

establish the *yeshivah* of Chevron, he was chosen to be the *mashgiach* of Slobodka. During World War II, he became ill in the ghetto of Kovno and was hospitalized. The cursed Nazis set fire to the hospital and burned it down over the heads of the patients on the 22nd of Tammuz 5704.

R' Yechezkel HaLevi Levenstein of Mir and Ponoviez
(1884 — 1974)
[works: *Or Yechezkel; Kovetz Inyanim; Likutim* in ms.]

R' Yechezkel was born in Warsaw in 5644. Both his father and mother traced their lineage to the Tosafos Yom Tov. After his *bar mitzvah*, he traveled to Radin to study in the *yeshivah* of the Chafetz Chaim. There he became closely attached to R' Yerucham Levovitz who sent him on to Kelm. After his marriage, he taught in the preparatory *yeshivah* in Kelm directed by R' Eliahu Lopian. Later he was called to serve in Mir by R' Yerucham. For a short while he was in the *yeshivos* of Kletzk, Poland, and Lomza, *Eretz Yisrael*. After the passing away of R' Yerucham, he served as *mashgiach* of Mir. With the outbreak of World War II, he went with the *yeshivah* when it was uprooted and made its way to Shanghai and from there, after the war, to the United States. He went up to *Eretz Yisrael* and *Yerushalayim* in 5714 and was invited to become *mashgiach* of the Ponoviez *yeshivah* in Bnei Brak. He served in that post until he passed away on the 18th of Iyar 5734.

R' Shlomo Harkavy of Grodno
(c. 1890 — c. 1945)
[work: *Me'imrei Shlomo*]

R' Shlomo was born in Grodno about 5650. He studied in Radin and became closely attached to R' Yerucham Levovitz, and when R' Yerucham left for Mir he went along with him. He grew in piety and learning and showed great devotion in prayer, in particular. Following R' Yerucham's advice, he went to Kelm to complete his development. Afterwards he returned to Mir and in 5682, on the recommendation of his master R' Yerucham, he was appointed *mashgiach* of the *yeshivah* of Grodno, in which capacity he served for more than eighteen years until the *yeshivah* was destroyed by the Nazis.

R' Eliahu Eliezer Dessler
(1891 — 1954)
[work: *Michtav Me'Eliahu*]

R' Eliahu Eliezer was born in 5651 in Homel, Russia. His father, R' Reuven Dov, was among the first of the students of Kelm. He himself arrived in Kelm

at the age of twelve. There, he acquired learning and grew in piety. He married the daughter of R' Nachum Ze'ev, son of the *Alter* of Kelm. In 5687 he accepted a position as rabbi in London and set up a network of study groups. In 5701 he established a *kollel* in Gateshead, which developed into an amalgamation of Torah institutions. On the invitation of the Rav of Ponoviez, he became *mashgiach* of the Ponoviez *yeshivah* in Bnei Brak in 5708. It was there he passed away on the 24th of Teves 5714.

R' Yitzchak Elchanan Waldshein of Ostrowze
(1894 — c. 1941)
[work: *Toras Yitzchak*]

R' Yitzchak was born in Sharshov, Russia in 5654. In his youth he studied in the *yeshivah* of R' Zalman Sender and afterwards in Novharodok where he became one of its important student members. He drafted the *Madregas Ha'Adam* of R' Yosef Yoizel. He worked strenuously in establishing the network of Novharodok *yeshivos* and was *mashgiach* in Bialystok, Rameiles, Pinsk and Ostrowze. At times he was invited to serve in that capacity in Baranowicz and he perished in the destruction of that *yeshivah* during the Holocaust.

R' Abba Grossbard of Ponoviez
(1896 — 1946)
[work: *Sichos* in ms.]

R' Abba was born in 5656 in the town of Twerig, Lithuania. He studied in Mir and was the disciple of R' Yerucham Levovitz, who sent him to Kelm to complete his development. There he became attached to R' Reuven Mowshowitz. He was invited to become the *mashgiach* of the *yeshivah* of Ponoviez and later served as *mashgiach* of the *yeshivah* in Riga. In 5699 he went up to *Eretz Yisrael* on the invitation of the *yeshivah* in Petach Tikvah and served as *mashgiach* there. In 5704 he met R' Yosef Kahaneman, who asked him to accept the post of *mashgiach* in the reestablished *yeshivah* of Ponoviez in Bnei Brak. He did so and remained there until his final day, the 27th of Menachem Av 5706.

This volume is part of
THE ARTSCROLL SERIES®
an ongoing project of
translations, commentaries and expositions
on Scripture, Mishnah, liturgy,
the classic Rabbinic Writings and thought.

For a brochure of currect publications
visit your local Hebrew bookseller
or contact the publisher:
Mesorah Publications, Ltd.
4401 Second Avenue
Brooklyn, New York 11232
(718) 921-9000

W9-CTZ-400